The Humanitarian Movement
in Eighteenth-Century France

SHELBY T. McCLOY

The Humanitarian Movement in Eighteenth-Century France

UNIVERSITY OF KENTUCKY PRESS

Publication of this book
is possible partly because of a grant
from the Margaret Voorhies Haggin Trust Fund
established in memory of her husband
James Ben Ali Haggin

To Joe, Cliff, and Matt

PREFACE

THIS ACCOUNT of the thought, discussion, and resulting legislation in France of the 1700's to create better living conditions considers the ideology of the times as presented in pamphlets, speeches, essays, journals, and laws. This humanitarian movement was led, on the one hand, by men who set out to mold public opinion and, on the other, by legislators who sought to give it legal expression.

My direct labors toward the project date from 1945, though indirectly I was at work on it much earlier. I acknowledge with appreciation a grant-in-aid from the Social Science Research Council which made possible six months' research in the Library of Congress in 1946, and sabbatical leave from the University of Kentucky during the academic year 1951-1952 for work in the Bibliothèque Nationale, and two summers free from teaching duties for further research and writing. In addition, I am under obligation to the Research Committee of the University of Kentucky for some travel aid and for assistance toward the purchase of books. The officials of the University of Kentucky Library, Duke University Library, the Library of Congress, and the Bibliothèque Nationale, where my research was done, rendered me every kindness. Several other libraries favored me with the use of their books through interlibrary loan.

Among individuals, I am indebted for suggestions to my colleague Professor Amry Vandenbosch and Professor Edward D. Seeber of Indiana University. To Mrs. Neva Armstrong and more especially to my wife I am indebted for assistance in the typing of my manuscript.

Finally, I acknowledge the kindness of Professor James H. Nichols in permitting me to reproduce here, with some modifications, two articles on French Protestantism that were published in the September and December, 1951, issues of *Church History*, sponsored by the University of Chicago.

CONTENTS

Introduction

THE HUMANITARIAN movement was to a large extent coextensive in development with enlightened despotism. Popular desire for reform was vastly more widespread in France, however, than in any other European country, largely because France dominated the Continent culturally. This culture, from 1748 (the publication date of the *Esprit des lois*) onward—if not indeed from the publication of the *Lettres persanes* in 1727—had been molded in thought by the *philosophes,* who made the betterment of human conditions their objective. In an age when French was the cultural language of Europe every invigorating book by a Frenchman was quickly placed in the drawing rooms of all Europe, and it was modish to sample the contents; the enlightened despots, therefore, for the most part became devotees of the *philosophes,* and even other rulers came in general to espouse their policies. These with some modifications included hostility to war, relaxation in censorship of the press, religious toleration, abolition of torture, judicial and legal reform, amelioration of serfdom, prison reform, increase of educational opportunity, promotion of science and technology, increase of hospitals, and improvement in public health. All were designed to better the social conditions, but some were less direct than others in promoting humanitarian welfare.

The word *humanité* was one of the most frequently used terms in the French language in the last three decades of the eighteenth century. Often employed for it as a synonym was the term *bienfaisance* (beneficence).[1] The older term *bénéficence* had no eighteenth-century popularity, and on the other hand the word *humanitarisme* was not coined until the 1830's.[2]

Humanité connoted a deeply felt concern over the welfare of one's fellow beings. It might even include an interest in animal welfare and consideration. It carried the idea of wishing to render service in some form to others in distress. It might take the form of philanthropies or generous actions in which money was not involved. A legislator might display it in efforts to remove discrimination against an oppressed class; a writer might exhibit it in espousing the cause of unfortunates; even a reader might manifest it by weeping as he read. "Your Humanity" was a complimentary term employed by Voltaire in a letter to Frederick the Great from The Hague on July 20, 1740, and on other occasions. Mercier in his utopian picture of Europe in 2440 declared that kings and their toadies would have passed away and been forgotten, but that the friends of humanity would be honored. Lafayette writing in the 1790's from his underground prison cell at Magdeburg to the editor of a Hamburg newspaper expressed a joy in his sufferings, since he considered that he was serving humanity.[3] Illustrations like these could be given ad infinitum.

Display of humanitarian sentiment became not only popular but an essential criterion of action. Turgot in his edict of 1776 abolishing the guilds claimed that his deed was motivated by humanitarian interests. Antoine Louis Séguier, one of Turgot's opponents in the royal council, on the other hand urged the king not to approve this measure and others, calling them "bizarre, tyrannical, [and] contrary to humanity and good manners." Prost de Royer, lieutenant of police at Lyons, urged Joseph II of Austria on the occasion of his visit to that city in 1777 to drive the Turks back to the Euphrates, declaring that it "would merit well both of Europe and of humanity."[4]

[1] Its first appearance in print, so far as we know, was in the dictionary of the French Academy in 1762, according to J. Drouet, *L'Abbé de Saint-Pierre, l'homme et l'oeuvre* (Paris, 1912), 212 n3.

[2] Edward D. Seeber, "Humanisme, Humanitisme, and Humanitarisme," *Humanisme*, XLIX (1934), 521-23; R. R. Palmer, *A History of the Modern World* (New York, 1950), 441. Professor Seeber points out that in 1765 and 1766 the Abbé Beaudeau had employed the terms *humanisme* and *humanitisme* in the same sense as the later *humanitarisme*, but that they were little used.

[3] *Posthumous Works of Frederic II, King of Prussia*, tr. by Thomas Holcroft (London, 1789), VII, 124; *L'an deux mille quatre cent quarante. Rêve s'il en fût jamais* (London, 1771), iv; letter quoted by Henry Dwight Sedgwick, *Lafayette* (Indianapolis, 1928), 324-25.

[4] *Oeuvres de Turgot*, ed. by Eugène Daire (Paris, 1844), II, 306-307, 337; J. P. Brissot, *Mémoires (1754-1793)*, ed. by C. Perroud (Paris, 1911), I, 261.

More and more as the century went on, the friends and followers of the *philosophes* came to arrogate the term *humanité*
as applicable only to that group. J. S. Schapiro, biographer of
Condorcet, speaks of the eighteenth-century *philosophes* as "these
humanity-intoxicated writers." The late Harold Laski states that
"the philosophes and the romantics gradually built up what may
fairly be termed a religion of service to one's fellow-man," and
he designates its features. Condorcet wrote that Voltaire's letters
revealed him as "impassioned for the progress and interests of
humanity." The *philosophes* as a group, he said, "had as their
war-cry: reason, tolerance, humanity." Raynal's *Histoire . . . des
européens dans les deux Indes,* according to Professor Daniel
Mornet, was "above all a history of crime and fanaticism and
superstition, an apology of tolerance and humanity," and the
Encyclopédie of Diderot and D'Alembert was permeated with
humanitarian sentiment. Jean Baptiste Mailhe, deputy for Haute-
Gironde to the Legislative Assembly and the Convention, went
so far as to write on December 30, 1794, that no royalist could
be a friend of humanity. Following the Reign of Terror the
Thermidorians massacred several hundred Jacobins, notably in
southern France, "in the name of humanity and justice."[5]

The idea that no royalist or enemy of the *philosophes* could be
a friend of humanity was of course ridiculous. Most of the *philosophes* themselves were royalists, only Rousseau and Mably perhaps being nonroyalist. Certain of the greatest humanitarians of
the century, as Chamousset, Montyon, and the Duc de la Rochefoucauld-Liancourt, were neither friends of the *philosophes* nor
enemies of the king. The physician Guillotin, inventor of a more
humane instrument of death than those in existence, and the
chemist Lavoisier, one of the greatest humanitarian dreamers of
the day, were both persecuted as royalists in the Reign of Terror.
One of the most generous tributes to humanitarian sentiment

[5] Schapiro, *Condorcet and the Rise of Liberalism* (New York, 1934), 215; Laski,
The Social and Political Ideas of Some Great Thinkers of the Age of Reason (New
York, 1930), 32-33; *Oeuvres de Condorcet,* ed. by A. Condorcet O'Connor and
M. F. Arago (Paris, 1847), IV, 304; A. Esmein, *Histoire de la procédure criminelle
en France* (Paris, 1882), 357-58 (cf. *Posthumous Works of Frederic II,* VI, 3,
where Voltaire speaks of being dominated by "love of the human race"); Mornet,
Les origines intellectuelles de la Révolution française (4th ed., Paris, 1947), 79,
218, 235; *Réimpression de l'ancien Moniteur,* ed. by A. Ray (Paris, 1858-1863),
XXIII, 91; Thibeaudeau's *Mémoires,* quoted by Earl Leroy Higgins, *The French
Revolution as Told by Contemporaries* (Cambridge, Mass., 1938), 386.

by an eighteenth-century writer may be found in a book by the proslave, moderate conservative Hilliard d'Auberteuil.[6]

At no time during the century was the term *humanité* more used than during the Revolution. Few words were more bandied about in the parliamentary speeches recorded in the *Moniteur universel.* It was a touchstone not only of the Revolutionists but even of their opponents. Whatever they found to condemn in their enemies, at home or abroad, was contrary to the interests of humanity; on the other hand, any objective they themselves sought to gain was consonant with this virtue. While the Revolutionists considered that they were acting for the best interests of their country, their opponents considered them as narrow, class-conscious, and fanatical, acting without due consideration for the harm their legislation might work in certain quarters. A twentieth-century reader can only stand amazed at the popularity once enjoyed by this word. As Professor Mornet has said regarding its synonym *bienfaisance,* it came to be the criterion of action for all persons, and almost a substitute for morality and religious sentiment.[7]

It is remarkable how many of those who espoused the humanitarian causes here treated were not themselves sufferers of the evils they wished to change. A few Protestants indeed pleaded for their own cause, two or three Jews, a single Negro slave, and until the Reign of Terror perchance a half-dozen prisoners; but these were all. It is startling furthermore to observe how few pleaders came from the masses or those limited in education. The overwhelming majority were of the middle class. Not a few were of the nobility. Indeed, the majority of the proponents for criminal law reform were of the nobility of the robe. There was perhaps no single issue that did not have the open support of one or more nobles. The nobility, however, was less inclined to write than was the middle class, and it would seem that the percentage of those who espoused reform in writing was less than that which voted for it in the Revolutionary assemblies. It is shocking that the clergy had so negligible a part in advocacy of reform. They represented a religion and a church that stood for brotherly love,

---

[6] *Considérations sur l'état présent de la colonie française de Saint-Dominque* (Paris, 1776-1777), I, 19-20.

[7] *Les origines intellectuelles,* 261-62.

but they were largely indifferent to the injustices of the age. Here and there indeed a priest stood forth and dared to speak, like Fénelon, the Abbé de Saint-Pierre, and the Abbé Grégoire, but they were relatively few. Happily it can be said that there were many priests humane at heart and that in the National Assembly many voted for the cause of reform.

As already observed, the basal proponents of most of the causes for reform here treated were the *philosophes*. They employed three words to set forth their cause and used them over and over again: *reason, humanity, justice*. In history, drama, philosophical treatise, essay, and fiction they pleaded their cause. In their hands the pen became mightier than the sword, and unfortunately it paved the way for the sword. For between 1770 and 1790 pugnacity and determination to accomplish the end at whatever cost came to replace the mild spirit of intellectual questioning. In the *avertissement* to the *Almanac des prisons* (1794) the charge was made that while the Revolutionists employed the words "vertu, bienfaisance et humanité . . . without ceasing, . . . the unfortunate victims [were] plunged in irons." Indeed in the name of humanity tragedies were enacted. The most bitter problem was that of the race question, which was solved not as its sober advocates wished but with hastiness and bloodshed. The price paid was frightful, and one is justified in questioning if it was solved wisely.

These same reforms would almost certainly have come about in time without the Revolution. Some would have come earlier than others, but all were on their way. Louis XVI had already initiated a number of reforms, and enlightened monarchs throughout Europe were absorbed with the matter of reform. It was the vogue of the times. Nowhere so much as in England and France, however, did reformers agitate for their cause, and indeed the intellectual leadership of France on the Continent enabled the French reformers to gain the ear and eye of the rulers. Louis XVI was well meaning but slow. It has been interesting to observe with what esteem, almost veneration, he was referred to by those writing for the humanitarian cause. Even the most radical of the lot—Mercier, Brissot, and Linguet—praised Louis XVI as a humanitarian monarch, and there is no reason to consider them insincere.

The legal historian Esmein has commented on the fact that all the lawyers who before the Revolution wrote on behalf of reform, even to those who opposed reform, claimed to be humanitarians. This they could do perhaps without being false. In an earlier study on aid by the French government to its needy subjects during the 1700's, I was amazed to find no mention of the *philosophes* and their followers, save for administrators like Turgot and Necker. The range of government assistance by the French was surprisingly great, and the men who stood out as leaders of that movement were the controllers general of finance and the provincial intendants and their subdelegates. No literary agitators or pressure groups needed to "work up" their cause to prevail on the government to aid the victims of flood, fire, famine, plague, or epizootic. The government had a pension system for aged and retired faithful servants, be they military, naval, political, or menial, that was surprisingly broad and liberal. It was a limited but very commendable social security program that cared for indigents and, unfortunates of every type. With the whole of that program the *philosophes* had virtually nothing to do. Their efforts were devoted elsewhere. The question may indeed be asked, Who were the real humanitarians—those who wrote or those who administered? The picture was complex: both agitator and philanthropist were but facets in the intricate civilization of eighteenth-century France. Even the church, which showed up badly in agitation for reform, did very well indeed, almost nobly in fact, in its work with the needy. Did any group have the exclusive right to the term humanitarian?

CHAPTER ONE

Protestant Disabilities

IN 1685 Louis XIV revoked the vestiges of the Edict of Nantes, inaugurating for France a century of religious persecution and hatred, and bringing only partial success for his scheme to Catholicize the nation in the course of a generation. At first the revocation threw consternation among the Protestants, who in their despair feared that Protestantism in France was doomed. Hence their desire to escape the country, or at least to get out their children, which resulted in heavy emigration continuing in spite of severe reprisals into the first decade of the eighteenth century. As time passed, however, they came to the realization that they could continue to exist in France, though as a stigmatized, persecuted group devoid of religious and civil rights. At no time did public worship cease, although it appears that most of the Reformed clergy left France in the years immediately after the revocation. Of those pastors who remained, more than a hundred were executed for conducting services, and countless laymen were sent to prison or the galleys for attending assemblies.

Gradually French Protestants gained the courage to reorganize their work, led by Antoine Court (1695-1760), a man of remarkable ability. Court reestablished the synod of France in a truly underground system. He insisted that the illegal open-air assemblies (known as "Churches of the Desert"), necessitated by confiscation or destruction of church buildings, continue and that pastors for these churches be trained from young Frenchmen at a theological seminary that he founded at Lausanne. Funds for this project were collected from the Protestant states of Britain, the Netherlands, Germany, and Scandinavia through Benjamin du Plan, a layman who traveled widely in its behalf; and professors in the Academy (or University) of Lausanne provided most of the teaching, for little or no pay. The result was that Lausanne after 1730 became the seedbed that furnished all the clergy of the Reformed faith in France.[1]

Many French Protestants did not agree with Court, considering him a fanatic. In 1719 Jacques Basnage, the distinguished exiled pastor at Rotterdam, wrote *Instruction pastorale aux Réformés de France* condemning Court's work and asking French Protestants not to oppose the king. The government realized the propaganda value of this pastoral letter and distributed copies gratis over France. In the north of France, save for parts of Lower Normandy, assemblies were rarely held; there Protestant difficulties with the government were much less than where defiance was expressed through the assemblies.

In the opinion, however, of Emile G. Léonard, probably the leading modern scholar on the history of French Protestantism, these "assemblies of the Desert" saved Protestantism in France.[2] In defiance of the government, fanatics would journey for miles to attend religious services in the hills or woods of southeastern France, sitting on the hard ground and singing with gusto the Psalms of David to the musical notes of Marot.

In the north of France it was possible for Protestants to make occasional trips to Paris to attend services in the chapels of the Dutch, British, and Swedish embassies. The Dutch in particular catered to this clientele, having always a chaplain who spoke French well and arranging for two Sunday morning services so as to provide seating for all who wished to attend.[3]

The Protestant clergy in France went by assumed names, avoided residence in towns as much as possible, slept during the day,

[1] Henry M. Baird, *The Huguenots and the Revocation of the Edict of Nantes* (New York, 1895), II, 462-63, 500.

[2] "Les Assemblées du Désert: charactères, adversaires et conséquences," *Bulletin for the Société de l'Histoire du Protestantisme Français* (hereafter *BSHPF*), LXXXVII (1938), 482.

[3] An interesting account of her visit to the Dutch chapel in 1773 has been left by a Madame Le Clerc, in a letter to her brother Louis du Ry at Cassel: "Paris en 1773 d'après une descendant de huguenots refugiés à Cassel," *BSHPF*, LI (1902), 555. See also, "Une dénonciation contre Marc Guitton, chapelain de l'ambassade de Hollande (1725)," *BSHPF*, LXV (1916), 305-12.

and engaged in pastoral visitation at night. The Protestants were intensely loyal to their clergy and very deferential. They used every method to protect them. When an assembly was surprised, they tried to enable the pastor to escape. They commonly placed outposts to give the alarm if hostile parties approached. Not infrequently they fought for their pastor and for other arrested members. When the pastor Désubas (or Deshubas) was arrested in his room at Vernoux in 1745, the Protestants of that region made repeated attempts for several days to deliver him from custody of the troops. On the first day of the encounters twenty-eight Protestants were killed and several wounded; on another day three of the attacking force of sixty were killed and others wounded. For a whole week tension continued, and rumors flew that the Protestants planned to attack in sufficient numbers to effect the rescue. The arrival of a hundred soldiers in reinforcement prevented this, but even then the government deemed it wise to transfer the prisoner to Beauregard for safekeeping.[4] It was always necessary that troops be present at executions, to prevent rescues. Here we see a body of people ready to defy their government in defense of what they considered their rights, nor was this spirit entirely confined to the Protestants, as French history of the period affords instances of citizens attacking the police or the military to rescue prisoners whom they considered unjustly arrested.

The Duc de Mirapoix, commandant of Languedoc, attempted to drive a bargain with the Protestants in 1756 when he offered to release two laymen arrested at an assembly just outside Nîmes on condition that the pastor, Paul Rabaut, already a leader in French Protestantism, consent to leave France. The offer was made to the three parties concerned, and all declined. One of the prisoners refusing was Jean Fabre, who had been permitted by the sergeant in charge to take the place of his seventy-eight-year-old father. Fabre, who acquired a European reputation as "L'Honnête Criminel," served six years in the galleys. The story no doubt had a tremendous influence in working for toleration. Abroad it was dramatized on the stage, and even at Versailles, but not in Paris, where the government tried to discredit the

[4] "Relation sur la prise du ministre Deshubas (11-12 décembre 1745)," *BSHPF*, LXXI (1922), 244-46.

story. When the Revolution came, however, it became a leading play on the Paris stage.[5]

Saint-Priest, intendant of Languedoc, tried another mode of stifling the Protestant assemblies in 1751. When a pastor and six attendants were captured at an assembly near Caila, he placed fines upon all the Protestants of the parishes in which the arrested men lived. The intendant's action, however, had no perceptible effect on the holding of assemblies.[6]

Persons of both sexes and of all ages and conditions of life risked the severe penalties for attendance at assemblies. Thus, out of nine persons sent to the galleys for attending a meeting near Mazamet, Languedoc, in 1745 were two nobles who had served in the army and been decorated with the Order of Saint Louis, one of the highest distinctions a Frenchman could win. In another group of eleven persons captured at a meeting at Dions in 1755, nearly all were children or young people, and all but six obtained freedom by denying that they had come to attend a religious service. Four of the convicted were young men, who oddly enough were not sent to the galleys but were put in the army on a six-year sentence. Since it was on the eve of the Seven Years' War (and the French and Indian War in America had already begun), it is possible that the government considered them more needed in the army than in the galleys. Two older men confessed that they attended this meeting for religious motives, and were sent to the galleys. One of them, the father of twelve children, spent ten years in the galleys before obtaining release. On a third occasion four girls taken at an assembly in 1702 were ordered whipped on the street of their home town of Beauvoisin. The intendant issuing this order was Bâville, who acquired a reputation for cruelty.[7]

[5] Athanase Cocquerel *fils*, *Les forçats pour la foi. Etude historique (1684-1775)* (Paris, 1866), 105-35; Armand Lods, "Paul Rabaut et le Duc de Mirapoix: à propos de la condemnation aux galères de Jean Fabre et d'Honoré Turge, d'après un document inédit," *BSHPF*, LXXIII (1924), 210-14; Baird, *The Huguenots and the Revocation*, II, 493-95; Armand Lods, "Les dernières victimes de l'intolérance," *BSHPF*, LI (1902), 509-10.

[6] Emile G. Léonard, "La vie des Protestants au XVIIIe siécle dans le marquisat d'Aubais," *BSHPF*, LXXII (1923), 216-17; Joseph Dedieu, *Histoire politique des Protestants français (1715-94)* (Paris, 1925), I, 83-85, 99, 241.

[7] *Histoire générale de Languedoc*, ed. by Claude de Vic and Jean Joseph Vaissete (Toulouse, 1872-1892), XIII, 1073; André Fabre, "Une Assemblée du Désert surprisé en 1755 à Dions," *BSHPF*, LXXXVII (1938), 140-42; Albert Atger, "Gaspard de Calvière. Sa Famille. Sa mort (1702)," *BSHPF*, LXXXVI (1937), 330.

There were other grounds, too, on which Protestants ran afoul of the law. At every turn, it seemed, they met difficulty in living as they wished. Marriage, for example, could legally be performed only by a Catholic priest, who was required by his church to demand the promise that children born of the marriage be reared as Catholics. Some Protestants took the Catholic vows and then repudiated them; the majority refused them. The children born of marriages performed by Protestant pastors were regarded as illegitimate, legally not entitled to inherit property; but government officials chose to close their eyes rather than meet the weltering confusion that otherwise would have faced them. A few lawsuits appear to have been brought by greedy Catholic next-of-kin. In general the marriages were recognized not only by their fellow Protestants but by the Catholics also. Rarely did the government interfere to disrupt one of these illicit marriages. In some cases the government sent the young husbands into the army after giving them the choice between military service and remarriage by a curé.[8]

Near the frontiers couples slipped across the border for marriage and then returned to France, despite the fact that this procedure was legally forbidden under penalty of confiscation of their property and sentence of the men to the galleys for life. Similarly it was forbidden for a French Protestant to marry a foreigner without royal consent, under like penalty; and it was equally forbidden for any tutor or custodian to arrange such a marriage.[9]

Mixed marriages between Catholics and Protestants were not uncommon, although they were discouraged by the clergy of both denominations. It was found, oddly enough, that the Protestants benefited from such marriages more than did the Catholics, since according to one contemporary report drawn up on the testimony of three priests, the Catholic wives in all cases adopted the faith

[8] Léonard, "La vie des Protestants," LXXII, 15-18, 116 n2; L. Greib, "Etat civil protestant; rapports des Reformés du pays messin et de la Champagne, avec les paroisses de Diedendorf et de Rauweiler (1698-1776)," BSHPF, LXXXI (1932), 170-74; "Le service militaire imposé aux Huguenots comme une châtiment (1767-1768)," BSHPF, L (1901), 251-56. The parlement of Grenoble in 1766 did order one Jean Antoine Delegue and "his pretended wife" to cohabit no longer, since their marriage was null and void, and it pronounced any children to be born of it illegitimate. BSHPF, LI (1902), 423.

[9] Greib, "Etat civil protestant," LXXXI, 170-71; Edme de la Poix de Freminville, Dictionnaire ou traité de la police (Paris, 1771), 312.

of their Protestant husbands, while the Catholic husbands were willing to let their daughters adopt the faith of their mothers and their sons to follow theirs. Of course the law required that all children be reared in the Catholic faith. An edict of November, 1680, forbade intermarriage in France between Protestants and Catholics; nevertheless in the 1700's it seems to have been commonly permitted when performed by priests. Not until 1774, however, do mixed marriages appear to have been legalized in Alsace. All children of such marriages were to be reared as Catholics.[10]

As already indicated, one of the chief points of conflict was the matter of rearing the Protestant children. A royal declaration of May 14, 1724 (by the Duc de Bourbon as regent), gave new vigor to the conflict by reasserting that all children of Protestant parents must be sent to school and taught the Catholic catechism until twelve years of age, and must attend Catholic services regularly until they were twenty. The Catholic clergy were directed to give particular pains to see that such children and youths were well instructed in the principles of Catholicism. Every month local officials were to require of curés, schoolmasters, and schoolmistresses a list of all children not attending school and the names of their parents; and every six months these local officials in turn were to submit a report on the matter to their national superiors. Parents failing to send their children to school were to be fined, while those sending them outside France for their education were liable to the heavy fine of six thousand livres per year that the children were abroad. This law required the baptism of all children born in France within twenty-four hours after birth, and it might be deferred beyond the twenty-four-hour period only on the permission of the bishop or archbishop.[11]

Only in rare instances did the Protestants, without further constraint, proceed to send their children to the Catholic schools. Some, however, sent their children to the schools and then set

10 Léonard, "La vie des Protestants," LXXII, 86; Jean Albert, "Un projet d'édit de tolérance (1776)," BSHPF, LXXXXVI (1937), 630; Rod. Reuss, "Un chapitre de l'histoire des persécutions religieuses: le clergé catholique et les enfants illégitimes protestants et israélites en Alsace, au XVIIIe siècle et au début de la Révolution," BSHPF, LII (1903), 26 n1; Archives parlementaires de 1787 à 1860, ed. by Jérôme Madival et al. (1st ser., Paris, 1862-1913) (hereafter to be cited as AP), XXI, 461.
11 Freminville, Dictionnaire, 305-307.

about in their homes to counteract the Catholic instruction. Finding that the law was not being met, curés and zealous neighbors reported many cases of negligence to the officials and obtained lettres de cachet for the Protestant children and youth to be removed from their homes to monasteries, convents, or Catholic homes, and subjected in their new environs to careful Catholic indoctrination. Literally hundreds of Protestant youths were uprooted from their families in this fashion in the 1700's.[12] The convents where they were kept were designated Maisons des Nouvelles Catholiques. The expenses of those incarcerated were defrayed from fines imposed on Protestants in the kingdom or from sales or revenues arising from confiscated Protestant property. Thus the émigrés involuntarily furnished a large part of the financial support of the Catholic missionary effort with Protestant youth in France.

Paradoxical as it may seem, some Protestant parents in poor circumstances asked to have their children confined in these homes, to avoid the burden of their upkeep; and a number of Protestant youths seized this opportunity to obtain an education at state expense. Many girls remained in the Maisons des Nouvelles Catholiques throughout their lives, even to the age of eighty or ninety.[13] The education given in the convents and hospitals (asylums) of the eighteenth century, however, was not of a high type.

In some cases parents petitioned the government for the return of their children, and their requests were granted on the solemn promise that they would in no way interfere with the indoctrination of their children by the local ecclesiastical authorities.[14]

One Protestant youth removed from his home for this indoctrination was placed with the Héberts, a Catholic family at Alençon. The later celebrated Revolutionist Jacques Réné Hébert

[12] Many Catholic youth were treated similarly in seventeenth-century Scotland. See Alphons Bellesheim, *History of the Catholic Church of Scotland* (Edinburgh and London, 1890), IV, 16-17, 34-35, 144-45. See also Shelby T. McCloy, *Government Assistance in Eighteenth-Century France* (Durham, 1946), ch. xv.

[13] McCloy, *Government Assistance*, 325-28; G. Dubois, "Les enlèvements d'enfants protestants et la communauté des Nouvelles Catholiques de Rouen au XVIIIe siècle," BSHPF, LXXXV (1936), 280-327.

[14] As an illustration, see L. Duval, "Hébert chez lui," *La Révolution française* (hereafter RF), XII (1887), 976-77.

was a son in this home, and it has been suggested that possibly this case had something to do with instilling into him his bitter hatred of king and priest.[15] For not only did this state of things antagonize the Protestant subjects of the Bourbons, it also antagonized great numbers of Catholics.

Not even the Protestant dead and dying were left unmolested. An edict of 1680 enjoined city officials to call on Protestants on their deathbed and insist on their conversion, and if they agreed, to call a priest. It was in fact common for priests to visit Protestants seriously ill and demand conversion. Those declining were subject to heavy penalty if they recovered, and if they died, their bodies were to be dragged through the streets on a hurdle. Moreover, they could not be buried in Catholic cemeteries, else these cemeteries would be regarded as polluted until the bodies were removed and the ground reconsecrated. In consequence of these regulations, it became common practice for the Protestants to bury their dead in fields at night and seldom with the attendance of a pastor, for such occasions provided traps for his capture. It is reported that even today throughout those regions of southern France inhabited by Protestants, from Auvergne to Poitou, the traveler may see hundreds of small burial plots surrounded by hedges in the fields, often with no more than one or two or three graves.[16]

Before anyone in France could be licensed as a physician, surgeon, lawyer, apothecary, bookdealer, or printer, it was necessary that he be a Roman Catholic in good standing and produce a statement from his curé or vicar to this effect. In fact, he could not study medicine in any of the French universities unless he fulfilled this condition, or serve in any capacity in a law court or in the administration of law in France, or hold any political office, even to being mayor or alderman. This was clearly set forth in a royal declaration of May 14, 1724, and it was not revoked or modified until 1789, when the National Assembly granted full civil rights to Protestants. Despite this legal situation, however, it was possible for certificates of Catholicity to be se-

15 *Ibid.*, 979-80.
16 Th. Maillard, "Les sépultures huguenotes en plein champ," *BSHPF*, LXXI (1922), 59; Léonard, "La vie des Protestants," LXXII, 22-24; Freminville, *Dictionnaire*, 116-17.

cured through bribery here and there, especially at Paris, and there were some few Protestants in these professions, notably in that of law.

In view of the nettling disabilities that faced them at every turn, it is not surprising that the Protestants of the mountains in southeast France, known as the Cevennes, rose in insurrection during the years 1702-1704, when France and her ally Spain were fighting most of the nations of Europe in the War of the Spanish Succession. It is only surprising that she did not experience a similar uprising in every great war from 1685 to the outbreak of her Revolution. The insurrection of 1702-1704, known as the War of the Camisards from the fact that the Protestant fighters wore *camisas* (peasant shirts) as a means of mutual recognition, particularly in their night attacks, was a brutal civil war of guerilla type, in which little or no quarter was shown by either side and burnings of churches and homes of the priests offset the burnings of Protestant villages.

The insurrection was provoked by the intense anti-Protestant crusade in southeast France, directed by both officials and priests, the most active of whom was the Abbé Chayla (name also written Cheyla and Cayla). One night in July, 1702, the Abbé was attacked and killed by a Protestant mob inflamed by the news that a number of Protestants fleeing to Switzerland had been arrested with their guide and confined in the same house with the Abbé. The mob released the prisoners. They then set fire to a chapel in the house. Chayla leaped from a window, hoping to escape, but was captured and offered the alternative of abjuring Catholicism or death. Refusing to abjure, he was dispatched with several bayonet thrusts. His valet was wounded and so, too, the schoolmaster. Then, according to report, the mob held an assembly and sang Psalms.[17] The incident aroused great indignation among officials and Catholics in general, and the government determined on severe punishment.

The chief Protestant leader was Cavalier, a young man in his twenties who possessed exceptional qualities of leadership. A leader of lesser ability but of more determined zeal was a romantic young man called Rolland (his real name, Pierre La-

---

[17] *Histoire générale de Languedoc*, XIV, 1567-74.

porte). The king's forces were led at first by Montrevel, and later by the Protestant apostate Julien. Both used brutal methods, even as did the Camisards.

Two years of terrorism followed, and members of the clergy on both sides were captured and executed, innocent members murdered, and churches and villages burned. On several occasions the Camisards made attacks clad in the uniform of government troops. They captured the Comte de Broglie, a leader of the government forces, cut off his head, and nailed it to the bridge of Anduze. Bâville, intendant of Languedoc, and Marshal Montrevel thought to win the war by devastating the country and incarcerating women, children, and old men.[18]

After two years of this savage contest, the government changed commanders, replacing Montrevel by Marshal Villars, a man of first-rate ability fresh from victories at Friedlingen and Keyl. Villars at once adopted a policy of moderation. He offered pardon to those Camisards who would lay down their arms and fight for the king against the enemies of France, although he did not offer in any way to modify the terms under which the Protestants in France lived. He threw a cordon of troops around the Camisard territory, cutting them off from outside supplies and reinforcements, but he refrained from attacking them, and ordered all executions, burnings, or other reprisals stopped. Cavalier was bribed with a pension of two thousand livres, and Rolland was surprised at a tryst with his fiancée and killed. This left the Camisards without an able leader, and in early January, 1705, Villars was able to report to the minister of war that the insurrection could be regarded as ended.[19]

It was the common charge of government authorities of the time—Bâville, Broglie, Villars, and others—that the Camisards were aided, encouraged, and even instigated in their uprising by parties or governments outside France. This the Protestant lead-

[18] *Ibid.*, 1581, 1583; Frank Puaux, "Le dépeuplement et incendie des Hautes-Cevennes (octobre-décembre 1703)," *BSHPF*, LXIV (1915), 64-67, 604-605; Frank Puaux, "Les mémoires de Cavalier sur la guerre des Cevennes," *BSHPF*, LXVII (1918), 11, 13.

[19] *Histoire générale de Languedoc*, XIV, 1884-85, 1989, 1990-99, 2008. Cavalier agreed to become advisor to the government on the Protestant question, on the understanding that concessions would be made them, but by Villars and many of the Protestants he was regarded as bribed. He shortly saw his error, fled to Britain, and there reached some posts of high distinction.

ers denied, but the government found proof of it through letters found on the body of a dead soldier and through the capture of two foreign officers serving with the Camisards.[20] This proof of foreign instigation and aid has been substantiated by a recent Catholic scholar, the Abbé Joseph Dedieu, in his book *Le rôle politique des Protestants français (1685-1715)*.

While the Camisards might have gotten some aid from foreign sources, it is clear that they received much more aid from sympathetic fellow Catholics. Bâville executed six persons at Nîmes in July, 1703, two by breaking at the wheel and four by hanging, for aiding the Camisards. Mialet was depopulated in 1704 for sheltering Camisard fugitives. Food, wine, and other assistance were given. In fact, if aid had not been rendered them and sympathy for them did not exist on the part of their Catholic neighbors, the Protestants could not have resisted the government. Not only would the Camisard insurrection have been brief, Protestantism itself would probably have been rapidly exterminated. That Protestantism survived at all in France in the eighteenth century appears to have been contingent upon the fact that a large element of the French people, more particularly the friends and neighbors of the Protestants, did not approve of the barbarous edicts and ignored them. No less a person than Lebret *père*, celebrated intendant of Provence in the early 1700's, shared these views. He advocated mildness in dealing with Protestants and permitted all to emigrate who so desired. Protestants and their Catholic neighbors were often on very friendly terms. It was not uncommon, in fact, for Protestants to have priests to meals, and vice versa.[21] In general, however, the curés were more zealous than their parishoners, and the Protestants laid most of their troubles at the door of priestly zeal. The Jesuits were regarded as more zealous in this respect than the other priests, and it is worth noting that after the Jesuit trouble with the government began in 1762, persecution of the Protestants was never again severe, although for this relaxation other factors, too, were present.

[20] *Ibid.*, 2006-2008, 2017, 2020, *et passim;* Frank Puaux, "Au camp des Camisards," *BSHPF*, LIX (1910), 425-36.
[21] Puaux, "Au camp des Camisards," LIX, 425-27, 432; Puaux, "Le dépeuplement et incendie," LXIV, 594-95; Léonard, "La vie des Protestants," LXXII, 29-30.

Following the War of the Camisards, persecution of the Protestants diminished somewhat. The drastic laws remained, to be sure, and the professional disabilities continued in effect, but there was often a tendency to wink at their enforcement, except at intervals. Some of the periods of intensified Protestant persecution coincided with the wars in which France was engaged; among them were the years 1714-1715, 1724, 1745-1746, 1748, 1752-1754, and 1762. By 1757, however, conditions had become lax enough in some regions for the Protestants to rebuild their temples, although subsequently demolished by dragoons, and assemblies were held openly and unmolested in some villages.[22] In fact, it appears that after the half-century mark Protestant pastors were seldom molested and often were allowed to move about freely. Certainly in the 1780's Paul Rabaut and his two sons worked undisturbed as pastors in certain cities of southeast France, highly regarded by their Catholic neighbors as well as their own flocks. One of the sons, Rabaut Saint-Etienne, was elected by the Third Estate of Nîmes as its deputy to the Estates General of 1789, where he played the leading role in obtaining civil rights for the Protestants.

This relaxation of the penal laws, however, came slowly, as indeed do most social changes. This was due above all to the revolt in men's minds against persecution. The calmness with which most of the executed went to their death made a profound impression on the spectators, as Villars in 1704 pointed out in a letter to the government. After he had put to death five of Rolland's bodyguard in this fashion before three thousand onlookers, he urged that a quicker mode of execution be used than breaking on the wheel because the executed won the sympathy of the crowd.

It was another trial and execution, however, that deeply stirred French public opinion. This was the case of Jean Calas, a Protestant wholesale importer living in Toulouse, who was arrested and brought to trial before the parlement of that city. Calas was charged with murdering his eldest son Marc Antoine, a supposed Catholic convert, in October, 1761. At length he was declared guilty by the court and executed by breaking on the wheel on

22 Léonard, "La vie des Protestants," LXXII, 13-14.

March 10, 1762. The case has become one of the most noted *causes célèbres* of history.

Calas was convicted on circumstantial evidence. A stern Calvinist, he had already revealed his dislike for the Catholic conversion of his second son, Louis, who wished to become a physician and found his religion barring the way. In 1760 Louis appealed to the intendant Saint-Priest to compel his father to grant him financial aid, which he said had been withheld from him for five years because of his conversion. Saint-Priest, after investigation, learned that the father was a well-to-do but very stubborn Huguenot and ordered that he should pay six hundred livres to meet the son's indebtedness for apprenticeship and to provide for his upkeep until he could earn his own way. Even then Calas haggled and had to be ordered again to make the payment. Only in September, 1761, was payment made.[23]

Hardly had this matter ended before the death of the oldest son, Marc Antoine, occurred on the night of October 13, 1761, in a shop on the ground floor of the Calas home. For supper that night the family had as guest a young man named Robert Lavaisse, son of a celebrated lawyer and a Protestant. As supper ended, Marc Antoine arose and left, departing through the kitchen. The rest of the family and their guest retired to the living room and chatted until 9:45 or 10:00 o'clock, when Lavaisse prepared to go. Pierre went with a torch to accompany Lavaisse to the street. As they descended the steps, they beheld the body of Marc Antoine suspended by a cord in the shop and cried out. The parents rushed down and tried to revive him with brandy. The young man's coat lay folded on a counter. Was it a case of murder or suicide? According to Madame Calas, her sons, and the servant, all present at supper had been upstairs throughout the evening.[24] Moreover, so far as known no one else had entered the home. The city aldermen and a surgeon at once were summoned by the family. The body was removed to the hôtel de ville and examined by a surgeon who gave sworn testimony,

---

[23] *Histoire générale de Languedoc*, XIV, 2234-36.

[24] The details are given in a letter by the Widow Calas written June 15, 1762, and in statements by the sons Donat and Pierre dated July 22 and 23, 1762, reprinted in *Oeuvres complètes de Voltaire* (new ed., Paris, 1877-1885), XXII, 365-69, 372, 388-89.

and the aldermen concluded that Jean Calas, possibly assisted by his wife, son, Lavaisse, or Jeannette, the servant (a Catholic), or even all, had strangled Marc Antoine, and ordered them to jail, where they spent the next five months.

The aldermen requested that all persons with information on the matter report it, and a crowd did so, with the result that the slain son was made to appear a Catholic martyr. It was averred that he was to have abjured Protestantism the next day and to have received his first communion as a Catholic. It was even reported that he was to have entered the order of the White Penitents the next day. Thereupon the aldermen ordered the dead youth buried in the Church of Saint-Etienne. There was a pompous ceremony, in which forty priests and all the White Penitents of the city took part. This was followed by requiem services for him. Marc Antoine, the dead Protestant, had suddenly become a Catholic martyr. On the other hand, Protestants having confidence in Jean Calas began trooping into the city, and the authorities feared that they planned to release him by force. Guards about the prison were doubled, and no one was permitted to see the prisoners.[25]

At a preliminary trial by the parlement of Toulouse on December 5 a tentative decision was reached that Calas was guilty of murder, but no verdict was passed. The definitive trial came March 9, 1762, when Calas was pronounced guilty of filicide and was condemned to be broken on the wheel and his body to be burned and the ashes scattered. In accordance with sentences of this type, his property was ordered confiscated.

Execution took place the next day. Calas went to his death with remarkable fortitude, bearing the pain silently and spurning all efforts to make him abjure Protestantism. So reported both the subdelegate Amblard and the diarist Pierre Barthès. Barthès described Calas as sixty-seven, tall and well proportioned, little given to sentiment, self-reliant and determined.[26]

[25] *Ibid.*, 389; *Histoire générale de Languedoc*, XIV, 2238-39.
[26] *Histoire générale de Languedoc*, XIV, 2239-47. Even today there is divergence of opinion on the question of Calas' guilt. Marc Chassaigne in a detailed study entitled *L'affaire Calas* (Paris, 1929) tries to convince his readers that Calas was guilty, while Alexandre Coutet, in his *Jean Calas, roué vif et innocent* (Mialet, 1933), insists on his innocence. Both authors examined the original court records of the case. Perhaps it will never be possible for all persons to reach the same decision on the case.

Few executions have had greater significance. To begin with, the question of Calas' guilt was far from certain. Madame Calas sought to rehabilitate his name, going to Paris in efforts to obtain a new trial. Her fellow Huguenots raised a fund to aid her in this fight. So, too, did the Protestants of Great Britain. Voltaire became interested in the case and invited to Ferney two of the Calas sons, who had fled to Geneva, to inform him on the details of the case. Convinced of the innocence of Calas, he threw his full efforts into the fight to get a new trial, and during the next three years wrote and edited many brochures to this end, the most famous being his *Traité sur la tolérance*. His propaganda brought the matter anew before the French public. The royal council on March 7, 1764, ordered a retrial, and on June 4 set aside the verdict of the parlement of Toulouse. In March, 1765, the case was at length tried anew before a special court of forty judges, masters of requests, in Paris, one of the number being Turgot. Unanimously these judges declared Calas an innocent man. At last his name was restored. The government proceeded to indemnify the Calas family by a gift of thirty-six thousand livres, half of it to the widow for gratification and for reimbursement of expenditures in connection with the trial, the remainder to be divided between the two daughters, the three sons, and the servant.[27] This sum, however, was not as ample as it might have been, since the costs to Madame Calas in her efforts to obtain a new trial had been very great.

The case, however, was not closed. With the outbreak of the Revolution, Calas became a martyr—a representative of oppressed France. Three separate dramas based on the Calas episode were presented in Parisian theaters in December, 1790, and January, 1791, following the extension of full civil rights to Protestants by the National Assembly.[28]

The condemnation and execution of Calas acted as a boom-

[27] *Histoire générale de Languedoc*, XIV, 2249; *Oeuvres de Turgot et documents de concernant*, ed. by Gustave Schelle (Paris, 1913-1923), II, 434-35. According to Du Pont de Nemours, Turgot took an active part in the retrial proceedings. The details are given in *Mercure historique et politique* (henceforth *MHP*) for May, 1765, CLVIII, 550-51.

[28] By the authors Marie Joseph Chénier, Lemière d'Argy, and J. L. Laye respectively. All three plays were published as well as performed on the stage. In 1791 a fourth play, by Pujoulx, entitled *La veuve Calas à Paris*, also was performed at Paris and published. *Oeuvres complètes de Voltaire*, XXII, 367n.; Lods, "Les dernières victimes d'intolérance," LI, 514.

erang. As nothing else during the century this affair convinced the French public of the gross unfairness with which the Protestants of their country were treated. A large portion of the French people had little desired the policy of persecution from the outset, and this body grew steadily during the eighteenth century. Their humanity cried out against ecclesiastical zeal.

Shortly after the Calas Case of 1762-1764 the more severe anti-Protestant laws fell into disuse. Raids on the open-air religious meetings ceased; no clergy were executed; no laity were sent to the galleys; and no property apparently was seized. The Protestant pastors became bolder and, in the 1780's, Paul Rabaut and his son Rabaut Saint-Etienne, the two foremost of them all, lived without molestation as they served their flock in the city of Nîmes. The pastor Frossard, the author later of an able antislavery pamphlet, worked without harm in Lyons, where in 1782 he was visited by Brissot. Court de Gebelin, son of the daring pastor Antoine Court and himself a clergyman without pastorate, lived openly in Paris from 1763 to 1784 without annoyance, became secretary of the celebrated Freemason's Lodge of the Nine Muses frequented by Voltaire and Franklin, and acquired some reputation as a writer and scholar. And when he died (in 1784) his funeral was unmolested, and Quesnay de Saint-Germain, a councilor of the parlement of Paris, and the pastor Rabaut Saint-Etienne addressed the assemblage. Even earlier, in 1748, Simon Louis de Ry, son of a Protestant refugee at Cassel, came to Paris and studied architecture. Either the government did not know or did not care who he was. Likewise his sister, married to a French Protestant refugee named Le Clerc, returned to Paris for a period of three months in 1773 without molestation. The Protestant physician Paul Bosc went to Paris in the 1750's and not only lived untroubled but even became a court physician and a member of the Académie Royale des Sciences, and was sent on a government mission to England. He died a noted scientist in 1784.[29] As a youth he had even been a Protestant pastor. What

[29] Brissot, *Mémoires*, I, 264-65; André Girodie, "Lafayette, Charles X et les Protestants français," *BSHPF*, LXXXVI (1937), 248; P. Fonbrune-Berbinau, "Court de Gebelin à Paris (1763-1784)," *BSHPF*, LIX (1910), 374-78; A. Atger, "Court de Gebelin franc-maçon," *BSHPF*, LI (1902), 601; J. Lindeboom, "Un journal de Paul Bosc (1753-1757), d'abord pasteur, puis physician," *BSHPF*, LXXXVIII (1938), 73-74.

did it matter? Paris did not care. Paris throughout the eighteenth century was perhaps the safest place for a Protestant in France.

French Protestants continued to be wary, even during the 1770's and 1780's, however, for they never knew when the storm might break again. The Protestants at Montpellier did not feel as secure as did those at Nîmes, and when in 1774 the Swiss clergyman Rudolph Schinz went to the former city with a note of introduction from Paul Rabaut to his son Rabaut Pommier, pastor of Protestants at Montpellier, he experienced great difficulty in finding his man and was able to do so only by secret channels. Schinz was surprised at the caution taken. Lafayette, when he called on Paul Rabaut and Rabaut Saint-Etienne in 1785 to learn more accurately the condition of the French Protestants, did so in secrecy, and in writing Washington of his plan to use his influence to aid the French Protestants, who he said were suffering under "an intolerable despotism," he took the caution to send the letter by John Adams in person and bade Washington not to allude to the subject in his letters, lest they be opened in the French post office.[30] The king himself might appoint Necker as director general of finances in his cabinet, but he drew back in timidity and let Necker go when the latter in 1781 demanded the title of controller general of finances. Had Necker been Catholic, the full title would almost certainly have been his all the time.

And yet the handicaps to the Protestants after 1784 were not insignificant. Scores of Protestant youth continued to be placed in institutions on lettres de cachet for Catholic indoctrination; Protestant marriages and funerals were still subject to the rigorous law of 1724, despite some relaxation; and Protestants still were barred from entering the professions. In short, they continued to be a subcaste of Frenchman, without the rights of citizens. Such was the situation down to the eve of the Revolution.

[30] *Mémoires, correspondance et manuscrits du Général Lafayette*, (Paris, 1837-1838), II, 121-22.

CHAPTER TWO

Protestant Toleration
and Civil Rights

IT IS SURPRISING that for several decades after the Revocation in 1685 there were so few to plead with the public the cause of the unfortunate Protestants, and especially so since it was an era in which humanitarian sentiment was rising. Unfortunates of other types received attention, such as the sick, the disabled, and even the American redskin whose soul needed saving, but the only pleader for toleration at home was the Protestant refugee Pierre Bayle residing at Rotterdam. In his great *Historical and Critical Dictionary* and other works he employed delicate satire to expose the folly of superstition and intolerance. At the time he appeared to be a lone voice crying in the wilderness, but actually he was sowing seed that was to bear fruit later.[1]

Within France itself few in the first half of the eighteenth century espoused the Protestant cause. Even the saintly Fénelon in his celebrated *Télémaque* (1699) criticized much in Louis XIV's government but made no plea for Protestant toleration. Neither did Vauban, who in his *Projet d'une dîme royale* (1706) found much else to criticize, nor Villars, who in his letters to the government from Languedoc (1704-1706) limited himself to pleas for treatment of Protestants as human beings.[2] In the twenties and thirties some faint appeals for toleration were made by Montesquieu and Voltaire. Their pleas, however, were for toleration in general, saying little of the Huguenots in particular.

Of the two, Montesquieu was the earlier advocate. Several times in his *Persian Letters* (1721) he had the Persians Usbek and Rica, traveling in Europe, write back to their friends at home depicting signs of intolerance here and there and making satirical comments.[3] The French Protestants were not mentioned, but Montesquieu must certainly have had them in mind at several places where he satirized religious intolerance. He ridiculed both the trial for heresy and the mode of execution. He suggested that it might not be harmful for a state to have more than one religion. All religions, he asserted, have "some precepts useful to society." Later, in his *Esprit des lois* (1748), he took a more cautious stand, asserting that minor sects plead for toleration until they get in control and then in turn become persecutors. For peace and sobriety, therefore, he would prefer that a state maintain a single church (or religion). Where others, however, are permitted, embroilments between them must not be permitted.

Voltaire was more outspoken, although his *Lettres sur les Anglais* (1734) with much on toleration in general contained little about toleration of the French Protestants in particular. At one point he referred to his own age as one "where all the world is fed up (*rassasié*) with disputes and sects." Of the Quakers, whom he discussed in the first four letters, he showed himself an admirer. He particularly liked the fact that they had no sacraments and no paid clergy, but permitted any member, male or female, to arise in a meeting to speak his mind. He eulogized George Fox and William Penn, the latter not only for his kindly treatment of the Indians and his setting up of a colony with religious liberty in America, but also for declining to join the other English Protestants in driving James II out of England. He spoke of England as "the land of many sects" and said that the Englishman was allowed to choose his own road to heaven. Happily, he observed, the multiplicity of sects operated to bring England religious liberty. If there were only two (the implication could not have been lost), they would be at each other's throat.

This pamphlet was but the beginning of a large number that came from his pen during the next four decades, entitling him to be considered perhaps the greatest single champion of Protestant toleration during the century. No wonder that the Protes-

---

[1] In recent decades Bayle has been the subject of a number of scholarly books, the best of which is that by Howard Robinson, entitled *Bayle the Sceptic* (1931).
[2] Villars' correspondence is in vol. XIV of the *Histoire générale de Languedoc*.
[3] Letters no. XXIX, XXXVI, and XLVI.

tants looked to him with respect and that their leaders, like Court de Gebelin and Rabaut Saint-Etienne, were often charged with holding *philosophic* ideas. Some of his treatises were merely anticlerical attacks that operated for toleration by indirection. The most influential, perhaps, were those that he wrote in connection with the Calas Case. Not until the Calas Case arose, however, did he become greatly interested in the religious question. Afterward he was a crusader for toleration.

Before this case developed, Protestant alleviation had received considerable attention in the 1750's. In fact it was with the 1750's that the Protestant question became a warm one. During the two great midcentury wars, as already pointed out, France had been too engrossed with the enemy abroad to give much attention to the Protestants at home, with the result that Protestant assemblies reportedly flourished, and some of the rasher Protestant leaders advocated the rebuilding of temples. The government replied with some spasmodic persecutions, which as previously had a limited effect. Some of the more zealous Catholics were scandalized at the licenses of the Protestants, and in 1751 and 1755 the bishops of Alais and Agen published pamphlets denouncing the scandals and calling for more rigorous law enforcement by the intendants. If they incited more persecution, they also provoked a series of anonymous pamphlets calling for Protestant toleration, their authors being identified as Antoine Court, Turgot, Ripert de Monclar, and the Abbé Quesnel.

Court was the author of two pamphlets at this time, the first in 1751 entitled *Le patriote français et impartial,* of which a second edition appeared in 1753, and the second, *Lettre d'un patriote sur la tolérance civile des Protestants de France* (1756). In the latter, which is evidently a condensed restatement of the first, Court pleaded for nothing less than revocation of all the laws against the Protestants and permission for them to enjoy the full exercise of their religion. In this way, he said, the commerce and welfare of the French people would be greatly bettered. The repeal of the oppressive laws would lead to a return of Protestant manufacturers to France from the other countries of Europe. French commerce would boom, while that of the other states would fall in like proportion. No additional Protestants would seek refuge abroad, and other European countries would be forced to repeal their laws prohibiting the entry of French goods. Great Britain he cited as a country where toleration persisted, and toleration, he asserted, was essential to commerce. The United Provinces, too, a commercial state, tolerated all. He assured his reader that nine-tenths of French Protestants abroad yearned to return home, and that a repeal of these laws would result in at least a million returning to France.[4] It is of interest that he emphasized the economic aspect of the matter, for the French were alarmed at their economic stagnation and shortly were to resort to various expedients to catch up with the British.

Possibly Court had read the pamphlet of 1754 attributed to Turgot, entitled *Le conciliateur, ou lettres d'un ecclésiastique à un magistrat sur les affaires présentes*,[5] in which the same request for full civil rights was made. The pamphlet consisted of two letters: the first, dated May 1, 1754, urging that the king separate church and state, permit full toleration and civil rights to all his subjects, and enable Protestants, Jansenists, bishops, and parlements to live together in peace; the second, dated May 8, 1754, longer and more outspoken, began by showing Jesus urging toleration to his disciples, and proceeded to cite a number of the early Church Fathers on toleration. He deplored the intolerant zeal of Ximenes and the Council of Trent, and also the mingling of state and ecclesiastical affairs. First and last the treatise is a criticism of the union of church and state. He repudiated the idea that a king should not tolerate all forms of religion. This idea, he said, has been the cause of many religious wars. The ancient pagans permitted all forms of religion. So, too, did the Chinese, the Prussians, and the Dutch of his own day. England and France, unhappily, stood for a single religion. They wished the blood of their citizens to flow. It is only the oppression of sectaries of a faith and denial of rights to them that makes them fanatical and dangerous. He would permit assemblies, marriages, and burials to Protestants, even as to Catholics; and these privileges he would also accord to the Jansenists. He would return to the conditions of the early church when the legitimacy of children and their rights as heirs were not dependent upon a sacrament. Existing conditions in France were indefensible; the

[4] See in particular pp. 34-40 and 119.
[5] *Oeuvres de Turgot et documents le concernant* (Paris, 1913-1923), I, 391-411.

only solution was toleration.[6] In his arguments and facts one recognizes much that Voltaire had used in his *Lettres sur les Anglais* and was later to use in his *Traité de la tolérance,* but this was an independent and able treatise. The stock of arguments and facts, indeed, were to be shared by all the advocates of toleration during the century. Turgot was at this time merely a master of request; he kept hidden his authorship, and there is no evidence that the pamphlet had the slightest influence, except possibly to fan discussion.

The other pamphlet that came forth at this time in reply to the bishops, the *Mémoire théologique et politique au sujet des mariages clandestins des Protestans de France* (1755), has been attributed to Ripert de Monclar, who reportedly was aided somewhat by the Abbé Quesnel. Ripert was procuror general to the parlement of Aix, a man of learning and tolerance. Subsequently he was the author of several books on economic matters. In this pamphlet Ripert pronounced the government's attempt to force the Protestants back into the Catholic fold a failure. He quoted the bishop of Alais as saying that not more than two Protestants out of two hundred married in the Catholic Church remained Catholics. Ripert declared that half or more of the French Protestants were married in the Catholic Church but that they continued as Protestants afterward. He called for a frank recognition of failure and a revised government policy toward leniency. He set forth the misfortunes for France that the Protestant emigration had brought. In particular he would validate Protestant marriages by setting up for them a civil form of marriage. Britain and the United Provinces permitted Catholic marriages if performed by a magistrate. France should reciprocate. However, he would go far beyond the validation of marriages; he would grant toleration in general.[7] He cited a long series of outstanding figures in history, pagan and Christian, whom he declared had opposed persecution, and asserted that persecution never converts people but only God's grace. Evidently Ripert had Jansenist sympathies. Replies were made to him the next year by Abbé Novi de Caveirac and Abbé Montégut; accordingly he aroused discussion.

Such was the state of things when in the early 1760's the Calas

[6] *Ibid.*   [7] Pp. 34-36, 107-12.

Case developed. Some public interest in the condition of the
Protestants had already been awakened. Very shortly, thanks to
Voltaire, the attention of the entire country was to be focused
on it. This he did in part by the publication of a series of tracts
informing the public of the facts of the case. He supplemented
them by one of his most eloquent writings, the *Traité de la
tolérance* (1763). The work began with a detailed account of
the Calas Case and proceeded from it to a discussion of tolerance
in general, among various nations and peoples, ancient, medieval
and modern. From first to last the author showed himself the
champion of freedom for religious expression. In England, Germany, and Holland, he said, differences of religion persisted but
no trouble arose therefrom as in France. Even in the Ottoman
Empire "the Grand Seigneur governs in peace twenty peoples of
different religions." "Go to India, Persia, Tartary, you will see
the same tolerance and the same tranquillity." In China likewise
tolerance existed, despite the fact that one emperor had expelled
the Jesuits after hearing of their quarrels with other Catholic
orders. The Japanese, too, were tolerant until the Jesuits came
and a civil war resulted. In Alsace, he added, Lutheranism existed peaceably with Catholicism. Why? Because there was no
persecution. He pleaded likewise for Jews and Jansenists. If our
religion is from God, he said, God will support it and man's intolerance is not needed. Tolerance should be shown toward men
of whatever race or creed. "What! My brother the Turk? The
Jew? The Siamese? Yes, without doubt; are not we all children
of the same Father and creatures of the same God?" He addressed a universal prayer to God, calling on him as the Father
of all mankind. The work ended as it began with a discussion
of the Calas Case in particular. The last pages were added in
1765, after the earlier decision had been reversed by the special
court in Paris. The new decision had been rendered on the third
anniversary of the day on which Calas had been broken on the
wheel, and Voltaire depicted the great rejoicing in Paris evoked
by the acquittal. It was a very popular decision, and Voltaire
praised the king not only for his part in calling for this retrial of
the case but also for his grant of thirty-six thousand livres by way
of indemnity for the Calas family.

The trial became a test of public opinion, and it will be recalled that coincidentally with it, from 1762 to 1764, the Jesuits, champions of orthodoxy, had been expelled from France. From 1759 to 1773 this wave of anti-Jesuit feeling ran through the Latin countries of Europe and ended with the Pope himself abolishing the order, in 1773. These circumstances no doubt created greater interest in the Calas Case. It is not without interest that the cause of Madame Calas was espoused by Elie de Beaumont, celebrated Parisian lawyer, who published in her behalf a memoir and a consultation, as did lawyers Loiseau de Mauléon and Mariette. While in her prison cell in Paris, Madame Calas was visited by many persons, some of high rank, offering consolation and aid. When on March 7, 1763, the council of state decided to demand a retrial of the case, "a prodigious crowd of persons of every rank sat in the gallery of the Château." And when the decision of the Court two years later was made known, there was, according to Voltaire, "universal joy"; "they trooped together in public places and in the promenades; they ran to see this family so unfortunate and so well justified; they clapped hands as the judges passed and heaped them with benedictions."[8] Of course, this was a sensational trial, and the enthusiasm evoked was primarily for rectification of injustice; it would be hard to say how far the crowd was favorable toward Protestant toleration.

Besides Voltaire, several of the *philosophes* openly espoused the cause of tolerance for French Calvinists, and probably the others did so at heart. Rousseau was timid on the matter, refusing on two occasions (1761 and 1764) to come out openly for the French Protestants when requested by Paul Rabaut to do so, giving as his excuse that he himself was a foreigner and a Protestant and that he should not abuse French hospitality. He did come out briefly for toleration on several occasions. In his letter to Voltaire of August 18, 1756, later published at Berlin in 1759 under the title of *Lettres sur l'état présent des sciences et des moeurs*, he came out strongly for religious freedom so long as it did not jeopardize stability in the state. Only if it should be seditious would he stamp out this freedom. In fact he would have the state to set forward a code of moral principles to be followed, and a set of intolerant maxims that were to be avoided. He denied to kings "the right to torment their subjects here below

---

[8] *Oeuvres complètes de Voltaire*, XXV, 24, 112, 117, 118.

in order to force them to go to paradise." Their prerogatives extended only to civil matters, and not in any respect to the religious. In his *Emile* and *Contrat social*, both published in 1762,
he likewise advocated toleration. The closing chapter of the
Contrat social in fact dealt with civic religion. Rousseau would
have his state insist on a state religion, which would be required
of all subjects.[9] Tolerance would be inculcated so far as sedition
did not occur; then he would persecute even with death. He thus
substituted a sort of civil intolerance for ecclesiastical intolerance.

Marmontel, another *philosophe*, without mentioning the cause
of the French Calvinists in particular, rendered a powerful challenge for religious toleration in his classic little dialogue *Bélisaire*
(1766). The theological faculty of the University of Paris attacked it in a pamphlet in 1768, to which Voltaire issued a reply.
In fact, Voltaire wrote four or five pamphlets on the matter, holding up the clerical opponents to ridicule. The section of *Bélisaire*
to which the Sorbonne and Christophe de Beaumont, archbishop
of Paris, took exception was Chapter XV, on tolerance.[10] This
book was a series of imagined dialogues between the outcast and
allegedly blinded Belisarius and his unknown conversationalist
Justinian, who in jealousy and fear had recently disgraced and
blinded him. In a series of conferences Justinian was the ques-
tioner, on problems of state, and Belisarius the philosophic sage—
a Socrates or Mentor. In Chapter XV Marmontel raised the
question of the state's attitude toward religious dissenters and
insisted on a policy of toleration, since God himself is good and
tolerant. Justinian, like a Louis XIV, insisted that "the tranquillity
of the state depends upon unity of sentiment," but to this Belisarius would not agree, asserting that the domination of one
faction in a state makes for bitterness in the other group and
that this is unwholesome for the state. When Justinian said that
this means desertion of the cause of God, Belisarius declared that
"the cause of God wants no enthusiasts to support it." Let it be
recalled that the Calas Case had only been reversed by the court

[9] *The Political Writings of Jean Jacques Rousseau*, ed. by C. E. Vaughan (Cambridge, 1915), I, 89-90; II, 163-65.
[10] *Nouvelle biographie générale* (hereafter *NBG*), s.v. "Marmontel, Jean François," XXXIII, 903-904, and "Bélisaire," V, 204; Quérard, *La France Littéraire*,
V, 548-49. Belisarius was not blinded; Marmontel has based his story on inac-
curate history. Nevertheless the book led to his being made royal historiographer
of France.

in Paris a few months before this booklet appeared from the press, and it can readily be seen that to French readers it would have powerful suggestions on the Protestant Question.

Marmontel's wife's uncle, the Abbé Morellet, likewise a *philosophe* and at one time secretary to the Académie Française, was the author of a pamphlet published at Toulouse in 1756 urging Protestant toleration. It was one of his earliest writings and was written partly out of his admiration of Paul Rabaut, at a time when persecution was rife. In his *Mémoires* he relates how this pamphlet with others obtained for him a certificate of civism before the commune of Paris during the Reign of Terror, and how it possibly helped save his life when he was charged with royalism. Not only in this pamphlet but elsewhere he pleaded the cause of tolerance. On a trip to Italy in the 1750's he found a copy of a fourteenth-century *Manuel des Inquisiteurs* issued by the grand inquisitor Nicolas Eymeric and in order to horrify French readers with its barbarity, he published a portion of it in 1762. In 1760, he edited Pope's *Universal Prayer*, with critical footnotes. And to the *Encyclopédie* of Diderot and D'Alembert he contributed several articles. One in particular, "Gomariste," called for civil toleration of religious opinions. Because of his broad tolerance the Abbé was a welcome member of the *philosophic* circle and a regular attendant of certain of the more famous salons of the day.[11]

That Diderot was keenly interested in the Calas Case is revealed in several of his letters to Mademoiselle Volland from 1762 to 1765. In his *Le Neveu de Rameau* he commented that he would like "to have rehabilitated the memory of Calas," adding that to have done so would have been a greater achievement than to have written the sublime play *Mahomet*. This was a delicate compliment to Voltaire. In various articles in the *Encyclopédie* he was the ardent advocate of toleration. He began his article on St. Bartholomew's Day by calling it "this day forever execrable," and denounced it with all his vigor. In another article, on "Intolerance," he asserted that in an intolerant state the ruler was only a hangman for the clergy, whereas a "prince is [or

---

[11] *Petit écrit sur une matière intéressante: la tolérance.* For the occasion of the writing, see *Mémoires inédits de l'Abbé Morellet* (Paris, 1821), I, 38-39; II, 62-99. Those of Madame Geoffrin, Madame Necker, and Madame D'Holbach.

ought to be] the common father of his subjects." He then proceeded to quote Christ, St. Paul, Tertullian, Origen, and several
other eminent Fathers of the early church as being opposed to
intolerance. In his article on "Persecution," he declared that "persecution is contrary to evangelical mildness and the laws of humanity, as well as to reason and sound statecraft." He depicted
Philip II as one whose fanatical zeal brought disaster to Spain,
and made the biting remark that "princes ought to imitate Di-
vinity if they wish to be its images on earth."[12] The *Encyclopédie*
was saturated with this spirit.

Condorcet, one of the later *philosophes,* was an outspoken advocate of Protestant toleration. In 1781 he published a group of
several essays and letters under the title *Recueil de pièces sur
l'état des Protestants en France.* His attitude was Voltairean,
straightforward, caustic, pleading. In his *Notes sur Voltaire*
(1787) he had more to say on the subject. He stated erroneously
that "under Louis XV the Protestants were treated with moderation," and that "tolerance is established in all Europe save Italy,
Spain and France." But he asserted correctly that "the laws
against them [the Protestants] were not altered," that "they were
not able to perform any religious act without incurring the penalty of the galleys," and that "they were excluded not only from
the honorable places, but from most of the trades." He hoped
that such fanatical legislation shortly would be removed, as it
ought if statesmanship should prevail. It was nothing less than
economic folly to maintain such laws when "America bids for
industry and offers liberty, toleration and fortune to every man
who wishes to quit his country." If the laws were not removed,
he could only foresee some further emigrations from France, sad-
der even than those of the previous century, and that France
would lose such advantages from trade that she might have hoped
to gain in assisting the Americans in their recent Revolution.[13]
This reference to the loss of citizens, industry, and trade as a result of Louis XIV's fatal policy was a recurrent theme with the
eighteenth-century champions of Protestant toleration. And to
appreciate the weight of this argument, one must be aware of

[12] *Oeuvres complètes de Diderot,* ed. by J. Assézat and Maurice Tourneux (Paris,
1875-1877), V, 426; XV, 235-40, 316; XVI, 253-56; XIX, 97, 141-43, 166, 168-69.
[13] *Oeuvres de Condorcet,* IV, 474-75; V, 395-573.

the great emphasis, by government-sponsored authors and others, which was placed upon increasing the population, increasing industry, and increasing trade, more particularly in the economic rivalry with Britain.[14]

In his *Eloge* of De Tressan before the Académie Royale des Sciences, Condorcet spoke of the Massacre of Saint Bartholomew's Day as "this horrible conspiracy of a king against his people," and praised the Protestant ancestor of De Tressan who mounted his horse in Paris that day and fought his way out—to his lands in Languedoc. He then discussed a king's responsibility toward his subjects. The *philosophes*, as these references demonstrate, were strong advocates of toleration, daring and poignant in their language.

Closely associated with the *philosophes* in thought, although not of their actual number, were other champions of Protestant toleration, such as Turgot, Mercier, and Malesherbes. Two of these were at one time or another members of the king's cabinet: Turgot, controller general of finances in the years 1774-1776, and Malesherbes, about the same time minister of the king's household. Earlier Turgot had been intendant of Limoges, and Malesherbes for several important years in the midcentury had been director of the book trade and printing, in which capacity he relaxed the censorship of the press and permitted the *philosophes* to flood the market with their books, the most notable of which was the *Encyclopédie*. The influence of this pair for toleration thus extended beyond their publications.

Turgot's earliest effort to aid the Protestants, *Le conciliateur* (1754), has already been described. In 1775, on the eve of the coronation of Louis XVI, Turgot urged the king to delete from the royal oath the promise "to exterminate the heretics" *(exterminer les hérétiques)*, which had been a part of the oath since the medieval days of Louis the Débonnaire, but which in modern times neither Henry IV, Louis XIII, nor Louis XIV had taken. Only Louis XV among modern kings had subscribed to it. Turgot, indeed, wanted to revise the royal oath even more and have

[14] On the economic rivalry of the two countries, see the article of John U. Neff, "The French Revolution Reconsidered," in *The Journal of Economic History* for May, 1943; and on France's desire for increased population, see Marcel Marion, *Histoire financière de la France depuis 1715* (Paris, 1914-1931), II, and Joseph J. Spengler, *France Faces Depopulation* (Durham, 1938) and *French Predecessors of Malthus* (Durham, 1942).

the king promise to make war "only for a just and indispensable cause," and to declare that he would rule without oppression. In this proposal Malesherbes and a friend were collaborators, but the last of the Bourbon kings before the Revolution did not follow their suggestion.

In the same year, shortly after he had sent the king his proposed revision of the oath, Turgot wrote the king a letter in regard to it, with some remarks that he had not dared to make earlier. This letter is designated by Schelle, Turgot's latest editor, *La tolérance religieuse: projet de mémoire au roi*. It is a magnificent appeal for religious toleration by a man of great intellectual capacity—broad, rational, courageous, and courteous.[15] He asked what religion is and defined it as man's fulfillment of his sense of obligation toward God and his fellow man. He argued that it was up to every man to carry out his religion in the eyes of God as he thought he ought, and that there was great variation in what men considered "the true religion." All the great religions are divided into a multitude of sects. Even rulers do not have the same religion. In fact, he asserted, only a portion of the human race was governed by Catholic rulers. Did subjects ever render to their rulers the right of controlling their religion? No. He reviewed the Social Contract theory, saying that to prevent anarchy, men appointed certain persons to rule over them, but not in religious matters. Louis XIV did attempt to rule in religious matters, and thereby blundered. (These were courageous words for a man like Turgot.) He himself acknowledged "that his education had been neglected," and yet he set about to rule on the religion of his subjects, taking away from his Protestant subjects the right of freedom of conscience. Turgot praised Louis XIV as a ruler who meant well but who made some tragic policies in regard to religion, being led into this error by certain priests at court who abused their influence over him. Not only did he blunder in regard to the Protestants but also in regard to the Molinists and Jansenists. No king should subordinate the civil to the ecclesiastical, but the two should be kept separate. Thus he revived the leading idea of his *Le conciliateur*.

Princes do not have the time for deep study of religious matters; Turgot said that he knew of only one king who had devoted

---

[15] *Oeuvres de Turgot et documents le concernant*, IV, 551-52, 557-67.

much study to it—James II of England—and he had turned out miserably. His advice to Louis XVI was therefore to desist from interference in the religion of his subjects. Let them follow their own religious practices as they would.

Interestingly enough, Louis XVI did very largely refrain from attempts to constrain his Protestant subjects, and moved gradually toward giving them a phase of legal toleration by his edict of November, 1787. To what degree was Turgot responsible for this? That is anyone's guess.

In several of his writings Louis Sebastien Mercier, dramatist and popular writer, made reference to French intolerance of the Protestants and put in his plea for them. The earliest was in his *L'an deux mille quatre cent quarante* (1771), where he referred to "the horrible night of St. Bartholomew" and "the hard revocation of the Edict of Nantes." In the year 2440 he pictured France on her knees doing penance for them. His play *Jean Hennuyer,* produced anonymously in the bicentenary year of St. Bartholomew's Day (1772), was both a satire and a sermon on tolerance. It praised the action of Jean Hennuyer, bishop of Lisieux, who purposely held up the order of massacre in Lisieux and thereby saved most of the Protestants there. In another play, *La destruction de la Ligue, ou la réduction de Paris* (1782), he struck several times at the intolerance both of the sixteenth century and of his own day. He thought that if Henry IV might have taken the throne on other terms and divorced France completely from Rome, all her subsequent history, not only in religion but also in commerce, would have been improved. In his *Tableau de Paris,* published also in the 1780's, he favored granting the Protestants of Paris the right to erect a temple and to enjoy civil status. He acknowledged, however, that tolerance in a very high degree already prevailed at Paris, saying that a man might live there thirty years in a parish without ever attending church or even knowing how his curé looked, and that unless he were poor and unknown, the curé would never call on him, even in sickness, unless invited; and if the curé should come uninvited, he could be shown the door.[16] Mercier was not significant enough in his

---

[16] *L'an deux mille quatre cent quarante,* 143-45; Léon Béclard, *Sebastien Mercier, sa vie, son oeuvre, son temps* (Paris, 1903), 298-307; *La destruction de la Ligue,* xxxiii-xxxv; *Tableau de Paris* (new ed., rev. and enl., Amsterdam, 1782-1788), III, 88-94.

day to be a friend of the *philosophes*, but he was one of a number of writers on the eve of the Revolution who shared their views.

Lamoignon de Malesherbes came from the high nobility. He had distinguished himself as a lawyer, a member of the parlement of Paris, director of the book trade and printing, and minister of the *maison du roi*. He enjoyed the intimacy of the king himself. More than a century had passed since great nobles had come to the support of Protestantism in France, but now it was different, for Malesherbes and other great nobles of the late eighteenth century who came to the aid of the Protestants were not themselves Protestants but Catholic. This is a fact that should not be lost sight of—that most of the champions of Protestant rights in eighteenth-century France, down to the Revolution and the granting of full civil rights in 1789, were at least nominally Catholic. Many, perhaps the majority, were deistical or Jansenist, but they had a Catholic background.

Save for his collaboration with Turgot in 1775 in the matter of the royal oath, Malesherbes was somewhat late in participation in this movement. It was not until 1785 and 1787 that he published two *Mémoires sur le mariage des Protestants*. The first appeared without mention of place or date of publication; the second on its title page indicated that it appeared in London in 1787. Both were fairly bulky pamphlets and displayed a considerable amount of research into documentary material of the 1600's and 1700's, which he said was chiefly in family papers handed down to him by his father, who had held a prominent legal position. While these treatises were published, indicating that they were designed to influence public opinion, their primary purpose was to influence the king, as Malesherbes himself stated.[17] He presented copies to the king, in fact.

Malesherbes in these pamphlets pleaded only for limited toleration—for the removal of the wretched laws pertaining to the marriage and burial of Protestants. He said nothing about giving them the right to public worship or to enter the professions and to receive honors for distinguished service. If his goal was low and his procedure timid, there is ground for belief that he did not think that he could attain everything at one blow. Male-

[17] *Mémoire sur le mariage des Protestans, en 1785*, 131-32; *Second mémoire sur le mariage des Protestans*, i.

sherbes was historically minded; the first of his two pamphlets was organized chronologically and both abounded in historical detail. They were well written and interesting, although there was a preponderance of legal matter. A modern reader is vexed at his repeated statement that Louis XIV never intended intolerance and persecution as it happened after the revocation of the Edict of Nantes.[18] It is possibly not too much to say that he convinced few readers of this point, but of course he was writing primarily for a Bourbon ruler to whom Louis XIV was a sort of ancestral demigod.

In tracing Protestant marriages from 1685 to his own day, he pointed out the great legal injustices which had evolved in inheritance—so great that for several decades the courts had been compelled to close their eyes to the obnoxious laws. He pleaded with the king to recognize openly a situation that already prevailed in fact. Indeed, he showed how ridiculous was a law of 1715 that asserted that legally there were no Protestant subjects, when there were as many Protestants at that moment as in 1685 when the Edict of Nantes was revoked. The government's coercion had been of no avail save to condemn to wholesale bastardy a million Protestant subjects, who held the religious laws in contempt and adhered proudly to the religion of their fathers. Conversion of the Protestant nobility had been achieved only through persecution and their desire for advancement. A fraction of the rank and file had been converted by the kindliness of certain of the Catholic clergy, but the multitudes that had been coerced into marriage in Catholic churches, before Catholic priests, and had declared their adherence to Catholicism in the earlier part of the century had only put on a farcical act. None were more willing to acknowledge this than the priests themselves. In fact, for some decades the clergy would only marry Protestant couples that had been under their observation for sufficient time to demonstrate their conversion.[19]

Although he felt that a large part of the public in 1785 was in

18 "Mais je vais plus loin, & je soutiens, contre l'opinion commune, que jamais Louis XIV n'a voulu prononcer contre les Familles Protestantes l'espèce de mort civile à laquelle elles sont réduites aujourd'hui." *Mémoire sur le mariage des Protestans,* 7.

19 See, e.g., *ibid.,* 4-6, 14-15, 19-20; *Second mémoire,* 1-3, 11.

favor of revoking all the anti-Protestant legislation enacted since 1685, Malesherbes himself did not wish to go that far. He advocated merely rectification of the shameful laws in regard to Protestant marriage and burial, removal of statutes in regard to Protestant inheritance, and permission for the Protestant clergy to work peaceably in France.

He suggested that the fees for Protestant marriages should go to the king, which could hardly have failed to impress Louis XVI, who at that moment (1787) was seeking new revenues. He also suggested that those Protestants already married should be given the opportunity to register their marriages upon payment of the fee.[20] Interestingly enough, these suggestions were actually adopted. The edict of November, 1787, issued by the king and his council, set forth almost precisely the recommendations of Malesherbes, the only feature omitted being the privilege of Protestant clergymen to labor in France. That the edict was due to Malesherbes alone would be too much to claim, for there were others of influence who had been working at this time to sway the king.

An influence that should be mentioned at this point was a treatise that had been drawn up in 1767 by Gilbert de Voisins, eminent lawyer, royal councilor, and Jansenist with sympathy for the Protestants. Subsequent to the Calas Case, Louis XV thought that the Protestant Question merited attention, and indirectly at his request Gilbert was asked to undertake this study and offer suggestions. This was in 1766. After consultation with various government officials and prominent churchmen, Gilbert in the summer of 1767 presented his manuscript report, but no action was taken on it because of ecclesiastical opposition. In 1787, when the matter again came to the forefront of public attention, his grandson published this treatise under the title *Mémoire sur les moyens de donner aux Protestans un état civil en France.* The author was a conservative and his sympathy for the Protestants, at least as expressed in his pamphlet, was very limited; nevertheless he recognized that from the legal point of view the Protestant marriages *au désert* had produced a scene of utmost confusion, and that something must be done. Accordingly he recommended that priests marry the Protestants in the church

[20] *Second mémoire,* 69, 123, 132, 136-37, 159-60, 166-69, 174.

but withhold from them the blessing (the sacrament), and require them to bring up their children as Catholics. He denounced the assemblies *au désert* and the neglect of Protestants to rear their children as Catholics. Even before priests should marry Protestants, they should make every effort to have them become Catholics.[21]

A much more generous and influential participant in the controversy in the 1780's was the Marquis de Lafayette. In the late 1770's and early 1780's he had been in America assisting Washington in the Revolution. There he had been impressed with the relatively harmonious manner in which the divergent religious sects lived together. On his return to France he gave consideration to what he could do for the unfortunate French Protestants, who, he wrote Washington in May, 1785, were "submitted to an intolerable despotism." Shortly afterward he visited the aged Paul Rabaut at Nîmes and other pastors in the Cevennes. The following year he invited Rabaut Saint-Etienne, son of Paul Rabaut, to Paris and there introduced him to the ministers at court interested in the Protestant cause. The next year, 1787, Lafayette attended the first Assembly of Notables and spoke twice to that body—once on the need of criminal law reform, and once on the need of giving civil status to the Protestants. In his plea on the Protestant Question he was supported by De Luzerne, bishop of Langres, whose brother had been ambassador to Philadelphia.[22] Nothing came of the efforts, but it was a chance to air the matter.

The bishop of Langres was one of the few priests in favor of toleration. With him were Brienne, archbishop of Toulouse, Cicé, archbishop of Bordeaux, and Henri Grégoire, curé of an Alsacian village. Most of the clergy, however, were bitterly opposed. During the century several priests had written books on the Protestant issue, certain of them cited and described by Malesherbes, virtually all taking a stand against toleration in any form. One 388-page book by the Abbé J. B. Bonnaud, ex-Jesuit, was published in 1787 opposing government concessions to the Protes-

[21] *Mémoire sur les moyens de donner aux Protestans un état civil en France*, 60-74, 137-42.

[22] *Mémoires, correspondance et manuscrits du Général Lafayette*, II, 178, 182; André Girodie, "La Fayette, Charles X et les Protestants français," *BSHPF*, LXXXVI (1937), 248-49.

tants. Two years later the king was to call for *cahiers de doléances* from the Three Estates, and the clergy in them were to protest against such liberties as the king gave the Protestants in 1787. I have examined the scores of cahiers sent from Languedoc, found printed in the *Histoire générale de Languedoc,* and observed the reactionary character of all the clerical cahiers on the Protestant Question. It is not without significance that those who championed the cause of toleration for the Protestants, even to the conservative Malesherbes, placed the blame for intolerance on the priesthood, as did the Protestants. There is an anticlerical vein in all the pleas for tolerance of the period, more bitter in the writings of the *philosophes* but discernible in them all. Turgot reveals it least.

One of the cabinet ministers to whom Lafayette introduced Rabaut Saint-Etienne was the baron de Breteuil, minister of the Maison du Roi. He engaged an understudy, De Ruhlière, to write a treatise on the Protestant issue. De Ruhlière was a prolix writer, and his work was a two-volume affair published at Paris in 1788 under the long title of *Eclaircissements historiques sur les causes de la Révocation de l'Edit de Nantes, et sur l'état des Protestants en France depuis le commencement du règne de Louis XIV jusqu'à nos jours, tirés des différens archives du gouvernement.* He began with a striking statement: "The beneficent and religious intentions which determined Louis XIV to revoke the Edict of Nantes have been cruelly deceived. There has not been a single day during the course of a century which has not demonstrated this truth. But did this prince, whose magnanimity equaled his power, order an odious and cruel persecution?" Thus he adopted the point of view of Malesherbes. Thenceforth he plodded along through two volumes, presenting much detailed matter, obtained at several designated government archives, on the unfortunate story of the Protestants since the 1680's. He ended his treatise by expressing the hope that the government would grant more liberty to the Protestants and "repair the evils that intolerance has caused."

Like Malesherbes, he said that the severe laws were no longer enforced. The government itself permitted the number of Protestant pastors to increase, as it wished to eradicate as much as possible the assemblies *au désert* and considered this the best way to do it. The bishops, he asserted, applauded this new state of things. Thus, "in the place of the legal tolerance that Louis XIV meditated establishing, a tolerance tacit, precarious, and insufficient has set itself up in all the kingdom."[23]

In the agitation for more liberties, the Protestants themselves had but a small part. Paul Rabaut in 1762 had published a brochure of twelve pages, entitled *La calomnié confondue,* defending both Calas and the Protestants against the dark charge of murder. Court de Gebelin, son of Antoine Court, like his father a clergyman and a teacher in the seminary at Lausanne, went to Paris in 1763 to serve as a self-appointed agent of the Protestants at the French court, his expenses being defrayed by the four Protestant consistories. Thenceforth for two decades he boldly sent protest after protest to the government in instances where he considered Protestants mistreated.[24] Rabaut Saint-Etienne likewise attempted to influence public opinion. His first attempt was through a historical novel, *Le vieux cévenol,* which played on the pathos of the reader by relating the misfortunes that overtook one Ambroise Borély, a Protestant Cévenol, during the course of his 103 years. The age was one deeply given to sentiment, as all familiar with the novels of Richardson and Rousseau are aware. The next year the work was republished at London, with a prefatory essay by Condorcet, and again on the Continent in the early 1780's.[25] His success with the novel led him to strike the same chord through an essay written and published in the 1780's under the title *Justice et necessité d'assurer en France un état légal aux Protestans.* His theme was the sufferings of France due to the persecutions of the Protestants. He showed how stupid it was and how incongruous with the *philosophic* and humanitarian spirit of the age. He denied the charge made by the curé of Saint-Sulpice and others that the French Protestants wished to subvert the monarchy and impose a republic. He pointed to monarchical governments of the Protestants in Europe, and for Switzerland he stated that democracy antedated the Reformation and was Catholic in origin. He assured the reader

23 *Eclaircissements historiques,* II, 209-10.
24 Baird, *The Huguenots and the Revocation,* II, 501-502.
25 Robert Mirabaud, *Un président de la Constituante et de la Convention: Rabaut-Saint-Etienne* (Paris, 1930), 29, 56-57, 63.

that French Protestants prayed for their king and country and were loyal.[26]

That Protestants ever obtained repeal of the harsh penal laws was due to the change of sentiment in the French public, and in this they had only a faint part. The great change was effected by those Catholic or at least born Catholic. Their champions had been primarily the *philosophes* and their friends, and secondarily the Jansenists and their sympathizers. Others, too, had their influence. There was Franklin, American ambassador to France who reportedly had much influence in obtaining the edict of 1787. Then there was Mirabeau, the scapegrace marquis from Provence. He shared sentiments with the *philosophes* but was not of their number. In his *Lettres de cachet et des prisons d'état* (1782) he found occasion to mention the great injustices done the Protestants and to beg for them the right of toleration. He would revoke all the harsh laws against them and give them full civil rights. Later in the early days of the Revolution he was their ardent advocate in his journal, the *Courrier de Provence*,[27] and on the floor of the assembly. The Abbé Prévost in a series of novels in the earlier half of the century had many references to French Protestants, both in France and abroad, and portrayed their sufferings in a sympathetic vein.

Of course not all the pleadings found their way into print. Malesherbes mentioned a number that were sent as letters or reports through government channels. One in the 1720's or 1730's, curiously enough, was by an old priest of Languedoc named Robert, who after forty years of work at trying to convert the Huguenots urged Cardinal Fleury to give up the policy on marriage and let them have a civil ceremony. Fleury was favorably inclined but knew that clerical opposition was too great. Joly de Fleury drew up a *mémoire* on the marriage question in 1752 and sent it to the government, and the Duc de Richelieu, military governor of Languedoc, likewise sent a report to Versailles advocating toleration. He succeeded in getting a temporary revocation of the order to hang the Protestant clergy for preaching and

---

[26] *Justice et necessité,* 4-5, 84, 74-76, 104-105.

[27] *Mémoires biographiques, littéraires et politiques de Mirabeau écrits par lui-même, par son père, son oncle et son fils adoptif* (Paris, 1834-1835), IV, 323n. See long quotation from the *Courrier de Provence* in *Réimpression de l'ancien Moniteur,* I, 376.

for marrying couples *au désert*. Cardinal Fleury, Joly de Fleury, and the chancellor D'Aguesseau were all sympathetically disposed toward the Protestants, and the last two were suspect of Jansenism for their laxity.[28]

As the century wore on toleration was by no means a factor in France alone, but, as already mentioned, something that affected all Europe. Toleration was in the air, as seen in actions of the enlightened despots of the period in Russia, Prussia, Austria, and elsewhere. Indeed, it is surprising that the Edict of Toleration granted by Louis XVI in November, 1787, did not go farther than it did. That verbose document which ran many pages and greatly excited the French did little more than enable the Protestants to have marriages, baptisms, and burials in France under faintly more favorable conditions. Even then the marriages and baptisms had to be administered by priests, and not the Protestant clergy, the promise to rear the children as Catholics alone being omitted. Burials presumably might be conducted by Protestant clergymen, but without singing and preaching. The police were to protect them against disturbance. Marriages that had been performed *au désert* in previous years might be legalized through registration with a fee. A scale of fees was integrated in the edict, and it has been estimated that an income of 300,000 or 400,000 livres resulted. Why did not Louis set the scale of fees higher when he needed the money so badly? And why did he not sell other privileges? Protestant clergymen were permitted to reside in France but they must not wear sacerdotal garb; they could not hold assemblies; and they could not erect temples. Their pastoral work, clearly enough, was limited to visitation and conversation. Protestants gained the privilege of entering the professions, but were expressly excluded from the magistracy and public teaching.[29]

Why there should have been great joy among the Protestants over such a slender grant of privileges is surprising, but there was. In all parts of France they rushed to the registry offices

[28] Malesherbes, *Mémoires sur le mariage des Protestans*, 87-88, 120; *Mercure de France*, April 19, 1791, pp. 69-70; Malesherbes, *Second mémoire*, iii, 64 and n.
[29] *La législation des cultes protestants, 1787-1887. Receuil complet des lois, ordonnances, decrets, arrêtés ministeriels et avis du Conseil d'Etat relatifs aux églises protestants de novembre 1787 à janvier 1887, annoté par Armand Lods* (Paris, 1887), xii, 1-15, and Article I; Louis Mazoyer, "L'application de l'Edit de 1787 dans le Midi de la France," *BSHPF*, LXXIV (1924), 157, 174-75.

and recorded their marriages. There seemed to be a feeling among them that it was but the prelude to something better.[30] There was deep resentment, on the other hand, among a large portion of the Catholics, more particularly the clergy.[31] In some areas the edict of 1787 was not put into operation, as wording of some of the cahiers of 1789 revealed. The parlement of Besançon had to be compelled by a lettre de cachet to publish the edict, and the parlement of Bordeaux waited fifteen or sixteen months before doing so. Bitter hostility to it was seen in large numbers of the cahiers of 1789, more particularly in those of the clergy. The demand for its repeal was widespread. Its advocates called for a single church in France, and that the Holy Apostolic Catholic Church.

The religious issue in 1789 was therefore a grave one. The Protestants wanted nothing less than full religious toleration and full civil rights, although few cahiers expressed this wish. The clergy, for the First Estate was the center of the opposition to it, were adamant in wishing to see no extension of privileges, and most of them wished to see even the edict of November, 1787, revoked. There was no lull before the Revolution on the matter. Not only in cahiers but also in pamphlets and the press was the matter discussed. Pierre Edouard Lemontey, a publicist and historian of Lyons, wrote a treatise urging that the Protestants be permitted to send delegates to the Estates General and that full civil rights be granted the Protestants by that body. Madame Necker wrote a pamphlet to the same effect, and the physician Jean Gabriel Gallot, of Protestant descent, published a memoir in their favor. Later he was a deputy to the Estates General from Poitou and made a speech on their behalf on August 22-23, 1789. Opponents of the Protestants tried, without success, to get the government to exclude the latter from voting in the election

[30] Mazoyer, "L'application de l'Edit de 1787," LXXIV, 151-54. This early joy is said to have been later replaced by regret at the slenderness of the grant.

[31] Mallet du Pan stated in his diary that the majority of Parisians were opposed to the edict, and that the clergy were bitterly opposed. Quoted by A. Sayous, *Memoirs and Correspondence of Mallet du Pan, Illustrative of the History of the French Revolution* (London, 1852), I, 137-38. Michelet on the other hand says that many Catholics were delighted with the edict and that some even attended worship in Protestant temples (were there any other than those of the foreign embassies in Paris?) to show their pleasure. *Historical View of the French Revolution, from its Earliest Indications to the Flight of the King in 1791* (London, 1908), 358.

of deputies, and from the privilege of becoming a deputy to the Estates General. The government, however, was tolerant, and the Protestants were permitted both to exercise the suffrage and to serve as deputies. In consequence, fifteen Protestants were among the six hundred deputies elected from the Third Estate, the most distinguished being Rabaut Saint-Etienne, representing the *sénéchaussée* of Nîmes.[32]

His previous experience and connections in Paris no doubt served him in good stead. Placed on the important committee of the constitution, he found himself in an admirable position for achieving the goal of his ambitions, which was nothing less than complete toleration and full civil status for his coreligionists. His first big step in that direction was his success, through the aid of powerful friends, in getting Article Ten written into the Declaration of the Rights of Man and the Citizen, in August, 1789. This article, calling for liberty of conscience, was expressed as follows: "No one is to be disquieted because of his opinions, even religious, provided their manifestation does not disturb the public order established by law." The statement was less positive than the plain provision for full freedom in religion that he wished. He introduced a motion that would have provided for the latter, but it was defeated. Then he persuaded Alexandre de Lameth and the Comte de Castellane to introduce motions to the same purport. That by Lameth, calling for full religious liberty, was defeated. The milder motion by the Comte de Castellane that followed attained success. Rabaut Saint-Etienne made a speech in its behalf.[33] Actually it did not go very far: the right to build temples or to engage in public worship was not stipu-

[32] Edme Champion, *La France après les cahiers de 1789* (5th ed., Paris, 1921), 216; A. Aulard, "La féodalité sous Louis XVI," *RF*, LXIV (1913), 110-11; Alfred Leroux, "Histoire externe de la communauté des religionnaires de Bordeaux de 1758 à 1789," *BSHPF*, LXVIII (1919), 60; Armand Lods, "L'attitude du clergé catholique à l'égard des Protestants en 1789," *RF*, XXXIII (1897), 132-37; Louis Mazoyer, "La question protestante dans les cahiers des Etats Generaux," *BSHPF*, LXXX (1931), 45-46, 53-56, 58, 59-60, 65-68; *Histoire générale de Languedoc,* XIV, 2523, 2535, 2538-39, 2557-58, 2599, 2609, 2625, 2785; *Les cahiers de doléances du bailliage de Cotentin,* ed. by Emile Bridrey (Paris, 1907-1912), III, 153, 448; *Cahiers de doléances du bailliage de Honfleur pour les Etats Généraux de 1789,* ed. by Albert Bloissier (Caen, 1913), 86, 102, 107; *Cahiers de doléances de la sénéchaussée de Nîmes pour les Etats Généraux de 1789,* ed. by E. Bligny-Bondurand (Nîmes, 1908-1909), II, 452-53.

[33] Dedieu, *Histoire politique des Protestants français,* II, 314-17; *Mercure de France,* Sept. 5, 1789, pp. 66-82.

lated, neither was it forbidden. When considered in its context with the other articles of the Declaration, however, its significance was enhanced. In actuality the clause, though negatively stated, was regarded as giving the Protestants full religious toleration, and they took advantage of it in that respect.

Their civil disabilities, however, were regarded as still existent, despite the wording of Articles One and Six stating the equality of men before the law. Accordingly in December, 1789, a motion was made on the floor of the assembly by Brunet de la Tuque that would give Protestants full civil equality, making them eligible for magisterial posts from which the edict of 1787 excluded them. The measure lay on the table three days while the assembly discussed other matters having priority, and then passed with little discussion on December 24.[34] One speaker declared that there was no need for this special legislation, since, according to him, Protestants already had been given equal rights. The vagueness, however, was now cleared up. Actually the broader term of "non-Catholics" was employed in the motion rather than that of "Protestants," but Jews were expressly excluded, with the statement that the assembly reserved the right to enact legislation in regard to them at a later date. The motion stipulated that henceforth non-Catholics who fulfilled the prescribed requirements for citizenship might be elected to all government offices and be eligible to all civil and military positions.

The significance of the decree for the Protestants was enormous. For the first time since the revocation of the Edict of Nantes in 1685 they were definitely placed on civil equality with other Frenchmen. Privileges that Louis XVI might have given them two years previously in the Edict of Toleration had been generously granted by their fellow citizens. And yet further legislation was needed on certain matters, particularly in regard to property confiscated from the Protestants since 1685. The Committee on Domains gave attention to the matter and on July 10, 1790, presented a bill to restore "the property of non-Catholics, which finds itself today in the custody of the administration for the goods of religionists [Protestants], . . . to the heirs, successors, or agents of the said fugitives," provided that they made proper application and met the requirements of the law. The

[34] *Réimpression de l'ancien Moniteur*, II, 439, 463-64.

bill, however, was little more than a resolution because of its brevity. The Committee on Domains soon found that legislation with details on procedure was needed in the matter, and accordingly on December 9, 1790, it presented a bill with twenty-two articles to deal with the mode of returning the property. This measure, also, was adopted almost without discussion. It ordered a list made of the property taken from Protestants since 1685. All petitions by Protestants for property likewise were to be recorded. Barère, who presented the measure, spoke well of the manner in which the government had managed the confiscated property. At the moment the annual revenue arising from it was around 110,000 livres. The decree moreover gave French citizenship to the descendants of the fugitive Protestants and stipulated that they might return to France and enjoy it.[35] This last provision was later embodied in the Constitution of 1791.

The last ineligibility was removed on September 26, 1791, when the Legislative Assembly opened to Protestants the military orders. The Ordre Militaire had been created in 1759 for the Swiss and other foreign Protestants serving in the French army, but French subjects were ineligible. Moreover, the Order of St. Louis had been open only to Catholics. The new extension of privilege, however, was short-lived, since the orders were abolished in 1792-1793.[36]

By a stroke of irony Protestants came to receive preferential treatment over Catholics in one particular. When in 1790 the National Assembly decided to secularize the property of the church and assume its expenses, it exempted from secularization the church property of the Lutherans and Calvinists of Alsace and four districts in Franche-Comté. The French kings, despite some encroachments, had adhered fairly faithfully to the promises made in the treaty of 1648 to the Protestants of Alsace, and the Alsatian Protestants had lived on an entirely different footing from the Protestants elsewhere in France. Elsewhere the Protestants had little or no ecclesiastical property to lose. The Protestant deputies appear to have supported the decisions from first to last in regard to the church, and this led to the charge that

[35] *Ibid.*, V, 93; VI, 597-98.
[36] Emile Léonard, "L'institution du mérite militaire," *BSHPF*, LXXXII (1933), 301-304, 316-18.

they were anti-Catholic. Grégoire in his *Mémoires* made the charge, and in our own day it has been repeated by Dedieu and Madelin.[37] The Protestants in general and Barnave in particular, according to Dedieu, were responsible for the adoption of the oath of the Civil Constitution of the Clergy, which proved so objectionable to Rome and was one of the chief causes of the dispute between church and state that resulted.

A certain faction of the Catholics had bitterly opposed concessions to the Protestants all along. With what appeared to them in 1790 as Protestant persecution of the Catholics the animosity reached the stage at Nîmes and other localities in southeast France that riots broke out and several hundred persons were killed.[38]

It was not long that the Protestants basked in the sunlight of privilege, for in 1793 they came to be engulfed in the quarrel between church and state which hitherto during the Revolution had concerned only the Catholics and which had become steadily more serious. Those who invoked the Terror saw little difference between the sects and banned all public worship, save the worship of the Supreme Being which the state came to sponsor. Thus for a period in 1794-1795 all Catholic churches, Calvinist and Lutheran temples, and Jewish synagogues were closed. Bitterness against religion reached such a point that many priests, pastors, and rabbis voluntarily unfrocked themselves before audiences that cheered. Several Protestant pastors were among this number. A deputy from Brittany even took the strange step of debaptizing himself in a letter to the Committee of Public Safety.[39] In this anticlerical wave the Protestants suffered greatly in loss of zeal and constancy, and even by the loss of many of their members at the guillotine, but they were never singled out for attack like the Catholics.

[37] Lods, *La législation des cultes protestants*, 20-21; *Réimpression de l'ancien Moniteur*, VI, 522-23; *Mémoires de Grégoire* (Paris, 1840), II, 70; Dedieu, *Histoire politique des Protestants français*, II, 321-23, 343-45; Louis Madelin, *Figures of the Revolution* (New York, 1929), 82, 88, 89.

[38] Letter in *RF*, XXXV (1898), 171-72; *Mercure de France*, March 5, 1791, p. 60.

[39] *Réimpression de l'ancien Moniteur*, XVIII, 369; Dedieu, *Histoire politique des Protestants français*, II, 358-60; Armand Lods, "Rabaut de Saint-Etienne, sa correspondance pendant la Révolution (1789-1793)," *RF*, XXXV (1898), 179 n2; A. Kuscinski, "Une débaptisation en 1793," *Revue historique* (henceforth *RH*), XXVIII (1895), 66-67.

As a body they were regarded as supporters of the Revolution. An occasional Protestant was royalist, but such were rare. More common among them was Girondism, and it was as Girondins that many of their leaders, such as Rabaut Saint-Etienne and Barnave, were executed. Ten Protestants sat as deputies in the National Convention, most of them Girondins. The majority wished to spare the king's life, although all had voted for his suspension from office. Certain of them, however, did vote for his death. Several of the Protestant deputies to the Revolutionary bodies were pastors, and some of them attained high distinction. Dedieu has charged that they became increasingly political, increasingly *philosophic* or rationalistic.[40]

In early 1795 the churches were permitted again to open their doors. The crisis between the state and the Catholic Church had lessened in intensity but did not terminate until 1801, when the concordat was agreed upon. Church and state had been separated in 1795, in like fashion as in America. Some in France had suggested that Protestantism should be adopted as the state religion, and it is said that Napoleon held this as a club over the Pope's head in the negotiations leading to the concordat.[41]

The decisions of the National Assembly in 1789 essentially determined the status that Protestantism in France has subsequently exercised. Thenceforth, save for the period of the Reign of Terror, it ceased to be discriminated against in any way. It still remained for the assembly to remove the features of discrimination against the Jews, but religious toleration had taken a giant stride and had set the pattern for the future, not only in France but in all countries where the influence of the Revolution was to permeate.

[40] F. A. Aulard, "La séparation de l'église et de l'état, 1794-1802," *La Revue de Paris* (Feb. 1897), 140; Léonard, "L'institution du mérite militaire," LXXXII, 455-56; Duval, "Hébert chez lui," XII (1887), 966 n1; C. Ballot, "Philippe de Girard et l'invention de la filature mécanique du lin," *Revue d'histoire économique et sociale*, VII (1914-1919), 142-44; Mirabaud, *Un president de la Constituante*, 229-30; Dedieu, *Histoire politique des Protestants*, II, 354-55, 368-70; Armand Lods, *Le pasteur Rabaut-Pommier, membre de la Convention Nationale (1744-1820)* (Paris, 1893), 8-9.

[41] Aulard, "La séparation de l'église et de l'état," 141.

CHAPTER THREE

The Jewish Question

PRIOR TO 1789, interest in the condition of the Jews was limited to a few vocal advocates. With the outbreak of the Revolution, however, the situation quickly changed, and it became a major movement. At the time there were about 40,000 Jews resident in France, of whom 20,000 or slightly more lived in Alsace, 4,000 in Lorraine, 2,500 in Avignon and the Comtat (Papal territory until 1791), 2,300 at Bordeaux, 1,200 at Bayonne, 500 at Paris, and smaller numbers in many other towns and cities. The precise numbers are not known, inasmuch as prior to 1800 there was no official French census. A private census of the Jews in Alsace, undertaken at government request, was made in 1784-1785 by the Jews themselves and revealed 19,707 Jews living in that province. While this figure has generally been accepted as accurate, even it, for reasons advantageous to the Jews, might have been an understatement. Probably the best basis for arriving at an accurate estimate is the census of 1808, which revealed a Jewish population in France of 46,290, scattered widely in forty-four departments. Allowing for the normal increase of a very fecund group and for an influx of several thousand immigrants, notably from Germany, consequent to the granting of Jewish civil rights in 1790-1791, the population in 1789 could not have been above 40,000 and might have been as low as 35,000.[1]

Contemporaries had a tendency to classify French Jews into three groups—those of Avignon, those from Portugal (resident in southwestern France), and the German Jews of Alsace and Lorraine. Those of Avignon, who also lived in small groups in other cities of southern France, were considered the oldest settled of the three. They were disliked largely on economic grounds, but this dislike was not bitter. The second group, consisting of those expelled from Portugal in the 1500's, were small in number, resident at Bordeaux and Bayonne, rich and cultured, and were accepted socially in those cities. Possibly this was due in part to the fact that they had gained the royal privilege for admission there on the ground that they were Christian converts, a pose they continued until the early eighteenth century, when they considered the intellectual atmosphere tolerant enough to discard their masks. Even then their action produced a shock, but they did not lose favor because of it. The third group, the German Jews, were living in Alsace and Lorraine when those provinces were annexed to France by Louis XIV and XV, in 1648 and 1768 respectively. The French kings recognized the regulations under which the Jews of those provinces were living at the time of annexation. They had been resident there from the Middle Ages, were in general poor and uncultured, were intensely disliked, and constituted a serious racial problem.[2] Besides these three groups, smaller units resided in Paris, Le Havre, and various other cities. They probably grew by infiltration from the three larger bodies, but they were seldom mentioned in the discussions of the period and were considered apart.

The Jews constituted a problem for France and as a result were forced to live under exasperating conditions. They made no effort to integrate themselves with the French population, and in turn they were regarded by the French as a foreign people resident on their soil and increasing more rapidly than themselves.

There was also the economic problem. The Jews took no part in agriculture but devoted their attention wholly to moneylend-

[1] See census figures of 1808 for France, by departments, as given by Eugène Coquebert de Montbret, *Notice sur l'état des Israélites en France, en réponse à des questions proposées par un savant étranger* (Paris, 1821), 1-3, and estimates by the following: Robert Anchel, *Les Juifs de France* (Paris, 1946), 235; Sigismond Lacroix, "Ce qu'on pensait des Juifs à Paris en 1790," *RF*, XXXV (1898), 99; M. Liber, "Les Juifs et la convocation des Etats Généraux (1789)," *Revue des Etudes juives* (henceforth *REJ*), LXIII (1912), 185; Edmond Seligman, *La justice en France pendant la Révolution (1789-1791)* (Paris, 1901), 160 n1; and Henri Grégoire, *Motion en faveur des Juifs* (Paris, 1789), 3-4.

[2] Coquebert de Montbret, *Notice sur l'état des Israélites en France*, 6-10, 16-23; Liber, "Les Juifs et la convocation des Etats Généraux," LXIII, 194-95, 200-201; Rod. Reuss, "Quelques documents nouveaux sur l'antisemitisme dans le Bas-Rhin de 1794 à 1799," *REJ*, LIX (1910), 248-49.

ing and commerce. For many centuries they had played the part of the middleman almost exclusively among whatever peoples they lived. A large portion of the French regarded them as parasitic and would be rid of them, but others, including French officialdom, considered that they contributed greatly to keep gold and silver in circulation. The Jews in Europe had a reputation of hoarding coin and of transporting it by clever device when expelled from a country, be the attempt to prevent it ever so carefully managed.

It is not surprising that under these circumstances the Jewish population of France was subjected to a rigorous legislation designed to curb its growth and activity and at the same time to see that its presence was profitable to France. They were required to pay not only the normal taxes demanded of the French but also certain additional ones. The tax most vexing was a contribution that the Jews of Alsace had to make in the form of an annual sum of twenty thousand livres to the Duc de Brancas and his family for their protection at the royal court. It was apportioned at the rate of forty livres per family each year. Granted to the Duc de Brancas and his sister the Comtesse de Fontête in 1715, it was continued until July, 1790, when abolished by the National Assembly. Another aggravating tax was that of the "forked foot" (*pied-fourchu*), commonly levied on animals of the cloven hoof, such as swine, sheep, and cattle. Its imposition on the Jews was a holdover from earlier times and of course was greatly resented by them. The chemist Lavoisier, an active humanitarian, is reported to have been instrumental in its abolition in the region of Clermont in 1786.[3] Proponents of the Jews claimed that their tax load kept at least those in Alsace and Lorraine on the border line of penury, while their opponents insisted that their tax load was light and their life one of luxury.

Besides the taxes, there were economic restrictions. Jews were forbidden to own land, although until 1784 they had been permitted to buy and sell a tract within the same year. This in itself would have prevented the Jews from engaging in agriculture,

[3] *Réimpression de l'ancien Moniteur,* IV, 186; Liber, "Les Juifs et la convocation des Etats Généraux," LXV, 100-101; Grégoire, *Motion en faveur des Juifs,* 4; F. Ferdinand-Dreyfus, *Misères sociales et études historiques* (Paris, 1901), 254; Louis Farges, "La question juive, il y a cent ans," *RF,* XI (1886), 209-10; W. R. Aykroyd, *Three Philosophers (Lavoisier, Priestley and Cavendish)* (London, 1935), 89.

had they been so minded, unless they rented the land. They were also forbidden to enter the guilds. They might not travel from one French city to another without permission, and license had to be granted them before they could display their goods at fairs in a city other than their own.[4] It was charged by their proponents that agriculture and industry were closed to them and that they were compelled to resort to moneylending, colportage, selling of secondhand goods, dealing in livestock, and stockjobbing. The Jews of Bordeaux and certain other Atlantic cities engaged in overseas shipping and in wholesale supply. Some of the leading shipowners in France were Jews. It is of interest that they were permitted to participate in overseas trade and to migrate to Santo Domingo (1776), which incidentally was closed to Protestants, but they were excluded from Martinique (1683) and Louisiana (1724).[5]

Their numbers were sharply limited. In Metz, for example, the government permitted only 480 Jewish families to live, and this number could not be exceeded. In Strasbourg none were permitted, by city ordinance, until the royal government in 1775 granted the privilege of residence to the family of a wealthy Jew, Cerf Berr (also written Cerf Beer), who had made his wealth and ingratiated himself with the government by supplying its armies with animals during the Seven Years' War. He and his family, however, were already residents of Paris and continued to live in that city. Cerf Berr, by his opulence and honors, became the leader of the Jews of Alsace and Lorraine and was destined for a major role in the battle for Jewish civil rights.[6]

[4] Liber, "Les Juifs et la convocation des Etats Généraux," LXV, 104-105; Léon Dutil, L'état économique du Languedoc à la fin de l'ancien régime (1750-1789) (Paris, 1911), 744-48. Dutil states that the parlement of Toulouse in 1787 registered letters patent permitting two Jews to acquire landed property in France, and that in the 1780's Jews were received without opposition in certain merchant guilds at Montpellier.

[5] Coquebert de Montbret, Notice sur l'état des Israélites en France, 53-54; Cahiers de doléances du bailliage du Havre (secondaire de Caudebec) pour les Etats Généraux de 1789, ed. by E. Le Parquier (Epinal, 1929), xvii.

[6] Mémoires de Grégoire, I, 324; Reuss, "Quelques documents nouveaux," LIX, 249; Coquebert be Montbret, Notice sur l'état des Israélites en France, 20; M. Ginsburger, "Les Juifs de Metz sous l'ancien régime, REJ, L (1905), 128. On the eve of the Revolution, Michel Berr, a nephew of Cerf Berr, was permitted to become a surgeon, doubtless because of his family's status. In 1793 he also became a physician. Liber, "Les Juifs et la convocation des Etats Généraux," LXV, 131-32.

Proponents of the Jewish cause stated that because of the severity in regulation of Jewish numbers in France only the eldest son was permitted to marry, and yet these same pamphleteers remarked that all the Jews married at an early age and had large families. Despite all government attemps at limitation, the Jewish population constantly increased. The Jews found a way in this matter as in others to get very much what they wanted, although they would have preferred to gain their ends differently. The Jewish census in Alsace in 1784-1785 was made by the government for the purpose of obtaining more accurate information on the Jewish population there. It is interesting that an enactment of 1784 affecting the Jews of that province specified that any rabbi who thenceforth should marry a couple without government permission would be subject to the heavy fine of three thousand livres, and for a second offense would be expelled from the country. Only if converted to Christianity could a Jew or Jewess marry a Christian, but so great was the social chasm between the two groups that there appears to have been no interest in intermarriage. Moreover it was provided that a child of illegitimate birth, whether one or both parents were Jews, was to be reared as a Catholic. Ordinarily such children were placed in convents.[7]

Not permitted to own real estate, the Jews were obliged to rent their residences which in Alsace and Lorraine at least were cramped and undesirable. The Jews of this region were charged with lack of personal cleanliness. They were required by law to wear a small but offensive badge on their garments indicating their race. Save for their rabbis, they had little education. Even Grégoire, who was to prove their champion in the Revolutionary assemblies, declared that they were steeped in ignorance. Apparently the sole Jew of eighteenth-century France to make a contribution to culture was Jacob Rodrigues Pereire, member of a wealthy Bordeaux family, who invented a method of instruc-

[7] Liber, "Les Juifs et la convocation des Etats Généraux," LXIII, 190; *Recueil général des anciennes lois françaises,* ed. by François André Isambert *et al.* (Paris, 1822-1833), XXVII, 438-44; Rodolphe Reuss, "Un chapitre de l'histoire des persécutions religieuses: le clergé catholique et les enfants illégitimes protestants et israélites," *BSHPF,* LII (1903), 28-30. Elaborate regulations concerning the Jews of Alsace, on what they might do and might not do, were set forth in the letters patent of April 26, 1784, reproduced by Isambert in the pages above cited.

tion for deaf-mutes and a calculating machine. None entered the professions of that time, which indeed were closed to them; none attended the universities, apparently for the same reason. The remarkable role that Jews have played in the cultural development of Europe has been largely subsequent to the French Revolution, when the barriers to their progress were removed and they themselves underwent a revolution in interests.[8]

In regard to marriage and religion the Jews had greater privileges than did the Protestants. For not only did their own rabbis perform their marriages, but in many places prior to the Revolution they had synagogues and were permitted to have public worship. Thus there were synagogues at Bordeaux, Bayonne, Sarreguemines, Lunéville, Metz, Nancy, Paris, and possibly elsewhere. There were some nettling restrictions but they were not grave.

The real troubles of the Jew had their basis in the economic sphere, and until late in the century it was the merchants who led in the attacks. In 1717-1718 in Alsace and Burgundy, in 1731-1732 in southeastern France, and in 1767 rather generally, the merchants made vigorous attacks, asking for the curb of Jewish activities and in some instances for their expulsion. Government officials were compelled to give attention to the demands, and the Jews experienced setbacks in consequence.[9] So severe were the attacks that the Jews engaged agents to defend them in propaganda, both in 1717 and 1767. French officials often took the part of the Jews as best they could. The intendant of Montpellier, Bernage de Saint-Maurice, in 1736 and 1737 granted permission to Jews of the Comtat to bring their livestock for trading into Languedoc for periods of six months each year, despite the fact that legally they were excluded from that province. In the midcentury the Controller General Orry protected them, and later the intendant of Bordeaux, Dupré de Saint-Maur,

[8] Henri Grégoire, *Essai sur la régéneration physique, morale et politique des Juifs* (Metz, 1789), 171, 173-74; *Instruction salutaire adressée aux communautés juives de l'Empire par le célèbre Harwic Weisly, Juif de Berlin; traduit en françois, en l'année 1782* (new ed., Paris, 1790), 61 *et passim*.

[9] Charles Muteau, *Les écoles et collèges en province depuis les temps les plus reculés jusqu'en 1789* (Dijon, 1882), 537; David Wolfson, "Le Bureau de Commerce et les réclamations contre les commerçants juifs (1726-1746)," *REJ*, LX (1910), 81-82; LXI (1911), 88-101; *MHP*, November, 1767, pp. 528-29; *Histoire générale de Languedoc*, XIII, 66; David Wolfson, "L'expulsion des Juifs de la principauté d'Orange en 1732," *REJ*, LIX (1909), 95-96.

recommended that they should be given the same status as citizens.[10]

Many of the French nobles also acted as their protectors in return for monetary or other advantages. The Brancas family was not alone in this respect. Jewish opponents at the period of the Revolution charged the nobility with being pro-Jewish and mercenary.[11]

During the first half of the eighteenth century little mention of the Jews was made in publications, but like other mistreated groups during the second half, increasing attention was given them. In that century of enlightenment it was inevitable that champions would espouse their cause. The great impulsion in this, as in other causes, was given by the *philosophes* and their followers, although they took divergent stands in the matter. Among the *philosophes*, for example, we find Montesquieu and Diderot sympathetic in attitude, Voltaire caustic; among their followers, we find Turgot, Mercier, Lacretelle, Brissot, Mirabeau, Talleyrand, Robespierre, Duport, and Clermont-Tonnère their advocates, while among their sharp critics were Malouet, Hell, and Rewbell.

From the standpoint of time Montesquieu was the leader. In his *Esprit des lois* he gave brief but sympathetic treatment of the Jews for the notable part they played in the commerce and finance of the Middle Ages and deplored the cruelties to which they were subjected.[12]

Diderot in the *Encyclopédie* also deplored their persecutions. His long article on the Jews dealt almost entirely with their ancient and medieval history and with their ideas of religion and philosophy, with only brief account of their persecutions. Of their treatment in France, he said: "In France the same [cruel] practices against the Jews have been employed; they are put in prison, pilloried, sold, accused of magic, of sacrificing children, of poisoning fountains; they are chased from the kingdom, they are allowed to re-enter for money; and at the same time that

[10] Dutil, *L'état économique de Languedoc*, 744; Wolfson, "Le Bureau de Commerce," LXI, 97-101; *Inventaire sommaire des archives départementales antérieures à 1790 . . . Gironde*, C 3662, II, 112.

[11] Wolfson, "Le Bureau de Commerce," LXI, 90; Liber, "Les Juifs et la convocation des Etats Généraux," LXIII, 190.

[12] *The Spirit of the Laws*, tr. by Thomas Nugent (6th ed., London, 1793), 275-77.

they are tolerated, they are distinguished from the other inhabitants by some infamous marks." Once the French burned those who refused to become Christian; later they banished them. It was at this period that the Jews resorted to the adoption of letters of exchange. "Since that time," he proceeded, "princes have opened their eyes to their own interests and have treated the Jews with more moderation." He deplored the way in which they were chased from Spain and persecuted in France. He was happy, however, that a new era had come and that they were better treated, in conformity with Christian principles.[13]

Voltaire, following in the footsteps of Bolingbroke and Bayle, was bitter toward the Jews, charging them with a hatred of all other nations and with showing exceeding cruelty toward them. He denounced Joshua's savage treatment of the Canaanites, the horrible sacrifice of Jephtha's daughter, the brutal slaughter of Eglon and Sisera, the unnecessary Benjamite war and the near extermination of the Benjamites. He condemned the attending story of sodomy and charged the Jews with cohabitation with goats. He sneered at the idea of their returning to Palestine and making it a prosperous country. He alluded to certain Jews of Strasbourg as coin clippers (*rongeurs*). He bade them to reflect that the Guèbres and Banians of India were older peoples than they and had suffered longer. Repeatedly a turbulent people, he charged the Jews with resorting on various occasions to human sacrifice. While several times he referred to them as "my friends" or in similar terms and professed sympathy for their sufferings, he pointed out bluntly that they had dealt about as much cruelty as they had received.[14]

Elsewhere, as in his *Essay on Tolerance,* he made it clear that he would grant them freedom to hold religious exercises and to practice their customs insofar as these brought no disturbance to other people. Toward no other group, except the Christian priesthood, was Voltaire so harsh.

An anonymous reply was published by the Abbé Guénée, under the title *Letters of Certain Jews to Monsieur Voltaire, Contain-*

[13] *Encyclopédie, ou dictionnaire raisonné des sciences, des arts et des métiers, par une société de gens de lettres* (3rd ed., Livourne, 1773), IX, 23.

[14] See the article "Juifs" in his *Dictionnaire philosophique,* the *Défense de mon oncle,* and the *Examen important de milord Bolingbroke ou le tombeau du fanatisme écrit sur la fin de 1736,* in *Oeuvres complètes de Voltaire,* XIX and XXVI.

ing An Apology For their Own People, and for the Old Testament (1769). Despite its anonymity, Voltaire discovered its author and covered him with ridicule in an article in the *Dictionnaire philosophique*.[15]

Among those influenced by Voltaire on the Jewish Question was Pierre Victor Malouet, former administrator in the colonies, who seemingly was asked by the government in 1776 for his opinion on the request of some Jews in southwest France to settle in Guiana. Malouet's experience in Santo Domingo and Guiana qualified him as an expert on matters colonial. He submitted a lengthy report, which though not published, possibly had weight in setting government policy and therefore was of some importance. Both in letters to De Sartine, minister of the marine, and in his report he opposed the settling of Jews in the colonies. They had shown themselves to be an unsocial race, refusing to mix with other peoples. Like Voltaire, he charged them with hatred of all other peoples, even though permitted to dwell among them. They used dissimulation, trickery, and fraud, and operated to the destruction of commerce and agriculture in a state. They despoiled a nation of its precious metals, and taught their children to regard themselves as the "dominators of nations." "For eighteen centuries," he said, "they have not furnished the human race a single laborer or artisan." He accused them of being a roving people that never settled permanently in any country. They had a tendency to siphon the coin of a country into their own hands. And one rich Jewish merchant, he remarked, prepared the way for twenty generations of successively richer Jews. They took advantage of a nation's indulgence toward them and became its financial masters.[16]

He differentiated between the Jew and the Protestant. The Protestant, too, differed from the rest of the French, but the Protestant had French blood and interests. His religious difference did not in the slightest prevent him from being a loyal and useful citizen. It was otherwise with the Jew, who never identified himself with a people. It was true that he obeyed the laws and police of a country, and was never involved in plots or espi-

[15] *Ibid.*, XIX, 166-67.
[16] V. P. Malouet, *Collection de mémoires et correspondances officielles sur l'administration des colonies, et notamment sur la Guiane française et hollandaise* (Paris, 1801/1802), I, 122-28.

onage, but his international connections and character always rendered him suspect in these matters. Since he refused to be melted into the national mass, he was to be rejected as a citizen.

Two years after this report a yet more caustic position was taken in a pamphlet published anonymously at Frankfort. It was the work of an administrative official in Alsace, François Joseph Antoine de Hell, who fiercely attacked the Jews, especially those of Alsace, as being cruel, avaricious, unscrupulous, and as having their greatest pleasure in humiliating Christians. His chief grievance was that they were usurers and by their unscrupulous practices bled some hundreds or thousands of simple Alsatian peasants.[17]

It was their practice when loaning money, he charged, to sign one contract in the presence of legal officials, and another secretly. In this second they predated the contract sometimes as much as two years. The peasant never received more than about half the sum indicated on the face of the contract. If he wanted to pay it off, the Jew made a show of indifference and urged him to wait and pay later. If the peasant invested his money and was unable to pay, the Jew at once beset him. The peasant was thus forced to borrow more and more. Often the Jew did not give receipts or the peasant lost them and had to pay a second time. The peasant in fact hardly ever knew just where he stood in regard to payments. The real crisis came when a hailstorm, flood, or other adversity hit the region. Then the Jew insisted on payment, and at such times made his biggest gains. If the peasant in desperation went to borrow of another Jew to pay off the first one, he ran into a trap of the same nature. He seldom if ever extricated himself from the clutches of his creditor. Paying several times the original value of the loan, he was nevertheless unable to pay it off because of the wiles and tricks of the Jew. Even if he took the matter to court, he did not gain. The Jew held the papers made in his favor, and if the decision went against him, he appealed it and for years kept the matter dangling in the courts.[18]

Hell accused the Jews moreover of declaring themselves insolvent in their business and thereby escaping with light adjust-

[17] *Observations d'un Alsacien sur l'affaire présenté des Juifs d'Alsace 1779* (Frankfort, 1779), 17, 32.
[18] *Ibid.*, 41-51, 60-61, 90.

ments. Sometimes they put their business in their wives' names. Hell expatiated not only on their trickery but also on their cruelty. Like Voltaire, he charged that they were cruel toward their fellow Jews even as toward other peoples. They had everywhere been made the victims of persecution, but they brought this on themselves by their ruthless treatment of others.

He attributed the rapid increase of the Jewish population in Alsace in part to their fecund birth rate and their practice of early marriage, and in part to the willingness of certain lords to permit them to enter Alsace from without. He protested the right of these lords to admit them without limit, alleging that it conflicted with "the welfare of the people." Indeed he castigated those nobles for indifference to the welfare of their serfs in permitting "a pernicious race" to prey on them.[19]

He did not ask for expulsion of the Jews or for their mistreatment, but only that they be prohibited to continue their present nefarious practices. He called upon the provincial estates to see to it that every single financial transaction between a Christian and a Jew be made in the presence of a notary, who had personal acquaintance with the peasant before him or else who recorded a description of him, so that no trickery could later be employed by the Jew, and that usury be ended as nearly as possible. He would have laws of greater severity passed to deal with the usurer.[20] He would also call for stricter enforcement of the marriage laws. The populace of Alsace, he stated, was indignant against the Jews.

Like Voltaire and Malouet, Hell called the Jews a nation within a nation. He asserted that they occupied a privileged position in Alsace, with the right to hold assemblies, have their own judges, and largely to run their own civil affairs. They acted moreover as a bloc. If a Christian insulted a Jew, Hell said, the whole Jewish nation arose crying for vengeance, and usually got it—the Christian being deserted by his fellows. On the other hand, the Jews went about on Sundays and other Christian holidays engaging in commerce and delighted at insulting Christianity. He predicted a revolution in France as inevitable, and indeed wished for one.

Hell lived to see his wish fulfilled, and in fact had an active

[19] *Ibid.*, 74-75, 84-88.   [20] *Ibid.*, 132-36.

part in it as a deputy from the Alsatian town of Hagenau to the National Assembly of 1789-1791. There he had a part in discussing the Jewish Question which came up for political action and in seeing that curbs were put on the usurious methods of the Alsatian Jews. In this pamphlet he called himself a patriot, and he thought of himself as a humanitarian espousing the cause of the peasant.

Other pre-Revolutionary writers favored the Jews. Among them, Pierre-Louis Lacretelle, a young lawyer born at Metz, espoused their cause in 1775 in a brochure entitled *Plaidoyers*. He described the Jews as established in all the French provinces, engaged in useful work, law-abiding, loyal to the king, and settling difficulties in the courts.[21]

The gallicized German Baron Jean du Val-de-Grace Cloots, who during the Revolution sat in the National Convention and took the name "Anacharsis Cloots, Orator of the Human Race," published at Berlin in 1782 a ninety-page pamphlet entitled *Lettre sur les Juifs, à un ecclésiastique de mes amis*, in which he claimed that the Jews had always carried prosperity to countries. They had been a commercial and financial people. Had they been agriculturists, they would have been stamped out or coerced into amalgamation with other people, but by being merchants they had been able to maintain their independence.[22] During the Middle Ages they furnished some physicians to Europe. He entered into controversy with Court de Gebelin, a Protestant writer, for saying that the Jews were more stockjobbers than merchants, and more usurers than stockjobbers. Cloots was a friend of the Jews, even as he was an admirer of the Mohammedans. He was silent, however, on the matter of giving them civil rights. Though published in Prussia, the book was evidently designed in part for the French public.

The year 1782 saw another German pamphlet on the Jews designed for French readers, *De la réforme politique des Juifs*, published at Dessau. Its author, Christian Wilhelm von Dohm, was a man of some importance in the Prussian government, holding the positions of councilor of war and archivist and secretary

---

[21] Liber, "Les Juifs et la convocation des Etats Généraux," LXIII, 197 n3; LXIV, 247-48.
[22] *Lettre sur les Juifs*, 67.

of the department of foreign affairs. He was influential with Frederick the Great and dedicated the little book, which he had long been planning, to the sovereigns of Europe, whom he hoped to influence by it. Written in German, it was translated into French by the distinguished Swiss mathematician at the Prussian court, Jean Bernoulli, who listed his membership in the Académie Royale des Sciences and said that his translation of the work was undertaken out of desire to help the Jews, a people in whom he had long been interested. Bernoulli thought the little book an excellent one.

Dohm was interested in seeing the Jews obtain full civil liberties. He wished to see them better housed and permitted to live in cities where they chose, not in *juiveries* or ghettoes. He wanted to see them permitted to own land and cultivate farms, not large farms but small ones, and he considered the money spent by some states on colonists would be better employed if it were used for building homes and buying small farms for Jews and aiding them with loans.[23]

Dohm sharply criticized the crowded, insanitary conditions of the Jews in French and other cities. In these *juiveries* the Jews were heaped in masses, with the result that they lived in filth, stench, sickness, disorder, and constant risk of fire. At Frankfort-à-Main, he said, they lived on a single street which was closed each evening.[24]

He commented that every state in Europe, though desirous to increase its population, ironically sought to restrain increase of the Jews, whom he designated "unfortunate fugitives from Asia." He discussed the well-known disabilities under which the Jews lived and the refusal of some states to receive them at all.[25]

Dohm thought that it would require more than one generation for the Jews to acquire the moral and civic qualities needed in the modern state, but he wished to see them given citizenship and believed that they would prove themselves worthy of it.[26]

When the Revolution came and the Jewish Question was thrust into prominence, a second French edition of Dohm's book was published, and it was reviewed at some length in the *Mercure de France*.[27]

[23] *De la réforme politique des Juifs*, 152-54.   [24] *Ibid.*, 154-55.
[25] *Ibid.*, 7-14.   [26] *Ibid.*, 193-97.   [27] Issue of March 6, 1790, pp. 11-15.

Prior to Dohm, the great German playwright Lessing had written two plays, *The Jews* (1749) and *Nathan the Wise* (1779), pleading for racial and religious toleration. In each a Jew was the hero—magnanimous, courageous, and modest. Christian antipathy for the Jews was exposed as based on hearsay and prejudice. Lessing revealed that nobility of character might be found among the Jews, even as among the Christians. The earlier of these plays, published in German in 1754, was republished at Paris in a French translation in 1781, and may have had some influence in France.

While in Berlin in 1786, Mirabeau wrote a book pleading for Jewish reform. It was published the next year at London under the title *Sur Moses Mendelssohn, sur la réforme politique des Juifs, et, en particular, sur la révolution tentée en leur faveur, en 1755, dans la Grande-Bretagne.* In this treatise, republished in 1788, Mirabeau began with a eulogistic account of Moses Mendelssohn, who had died in January, 1786, at the age of fifty-seven after a remarkable career. Born of a despised race, deformed, sickly, and of a poor family, Mendelssohn nevertheless rose to become a philosopher and scientist of significance and a man of lovable personality. Mirabeau described Mendelssohn's various writings, particularly his *Jerusalem,* a work translated into many European languages, in which he pleaded for religious toleration. After the laudatory account of Mendelssohn, Mirabeau proceeded to make a plea for more humane treatment of the Jews, a people he described as loaded down almost everywhere with prohibitions and persecutions. Only in Britain and Holland had they been given much opportunity to contribute to society; there, he said, "they are laborious, wise, regular, loyal, because they are left tranquil and free, because they are permitted to be happy." He wished to see the Jews unfettered and permitted to live under the same conditions as other men. The idea of writing the book was suggested to him by Dohm.[28]

The book may have induced the Academy of Metz to take it as the subject for an essay prize in 1788: "What Are the Means for Rendering the Jews in France Happier and More Useful?"

[28] *Mémoires biographiques, littéraires et politiques de Mirabeau,* IV, 294, 297, 312-18. Mirabeau also published a *Lettre à Frédéric Guillaume II, roi régnant de Prusse le jour même de son avènement au trône* (Berlin, 1787), in which he requested the Prussian king to give the Jews of Prussia full civil rights.

Prize contests on literary, scientific, and judicial questions were then the vogue with the numerous academies in France, and they did much in provoking thought. The competition in this instance was strong, and three papers were designated as deserving of distinction: those by Zalkind-Hourwitz, a Polish Jew who had come to France, by Henri Grégoire, curé of Embermenil, and by a lawyer of Nancy named Thiery. The three essays were published as pamphlets in 1788-1789, and exerted much influence both in bringing the Jewish Question to the fore in 1789-1791 and in determining the settlement of the matter. By this time, however, the issue had come to be a burning one; thinking persons throughout France and Europe were discussing it with vigor.

The removal of restrictions on the Jews would clear up all the difficulties, according to Zalkind-Hourwitz. The anti-Jewish criticisms, as he saw them, narrowed down to two—usury and swindling. He was unwilling to admit that only Jews might be charged with these faults, but said that if they were more guilty than others, it was because all professions other than that of merchant were closed to them and because they were heaped together on a single street where rents were high and conditions insanitary. Correct this state of things, he proposed, and the Jews would be different persons.[29]

As for the charge that the Jews ruined the trade of a country, he replied, "What impudence! Has experience effectively proven that the commerce of Amsterdam, London, and Bordeaux was ruined since the establishment of Jews in these cities?"[30]

Certain Jewish critics had asserted that the Talmud bade them employ nefarious practices against other peoples. "See the Talmud," they had written. Zalkind-Hourwitz criticized them for giving no particular citation in the Talmud. The Talmud, he said, "is a work of twenty-four large volumes, written without vowels in a language of which these writers and the most of their readers understand not a word."[31]

He admitted the charge that the Talmud virtually rendered it impossible for the Jews to enter military service because of its prohibition for them to walk more than two thousand steps on their Sabbath; but in their defense he asked if the Quakers who also were pacifists were not good citizens.

[29] Zalkind-Hourwitz, *Apologie des Juifs* (Paris, 1789), 15-20, 35-41.
[30] *Ibid.*, 7. [31] *Ibid.*

He gave a different picture of the sources of income of the Alsatian Jews from that presented by Hell and others. Instead of ascribing it to usury, he attributed it chiefly to colportage, animal trading, and goldsmithing. He also told of the competition and vicissitudes of these trades, and painted a picture of small returns (rather than great ones) for most Jews.

The criticisms of the Jews, he said, had arisen out of fanaticism, not out of patriotism or out of humanitarianism. Twice he referred to Voltaire, whom he regarded as the most vicious of those who had attacked the Jews. Nevertheless he recognized a debt of gratitude that his race owed Voltaire, because his many books against fanaticism had promoted a spirit of toleration which indirectly had helped the Jewish people. He expressed his delight in being among the winners of the prize, saying in part, "it is unfortunately very rare that one renders justice to a man of my nation."[32]

The pamphlet by Thiery is not to be found in the Bibliothèque Nationale, but it was reviewed in the *Mercure de France* of April 3, 1790. Thiery indicated that the Jews everywhere else were happier than in France. To render them happy, he recommended the removal "of all the humiliating signs" imposed upon their dress. He would permit their children to attend the public schools and would open to them the same economic opportunities that other subjects enjoyed.

Grégoire devoted his pamphlet to a consideration of the many charges against the Jews, showing that some were baseless, and that though others were true, they should not be allowed to stand in the way of cordial interracial relations. He stated facts and was not unduly sentimental. He had read numerous treatises on the Jews. His general attitude was that of the enlightenment— that of the humanitarian. In his concluding chapter he mentioned that much already had been done for the Jew during the century by Louis XIV, Gustavus III, and Joseph II. He pleaded with opponents of the Jews not to insist on their transformation before innovation was attempted, but to consider the Jews as also of the human race and children of the Heavenly Father.[33]

He did not attempt to defend the Jews of Alsace against the accusation of usury; rather he admitted, for argument's sake, that

[32] *Ibid.*, 3-6, 13.
[33] *Essai sur la régéneration . . . des Juifs,* 193-94 *et passim.*

some were guilty. These, and not the whole nation, should be punished.

Grégoire advocated permitting Jews to enter the scientific and literary academies, the colleges and universities, to own property, to lease and sublet farms, to intermarry with the French at will. He would open to them the hospitals, the charity schools, and other vehicles of philanthropy.[34] In short, he would remove all fetters against them, religious, economic, social, cultural, and then expect them to do their part. It was but the beginning of Grégoire's enormous activity in behalf of the Jews—activity destined to be crowned shortly with complete success.

While the contest was under way at Metz and the papers were being printed, much was happening elsewhere in France. Louis XVI had become interested in the matter from reading Mirabeau's treatise of 1787, and in 1788 he appointed a commission headed by Malesherbes to study the Jewish Question and report to him. Seated on the commission with Malesherbes were several retired intendants from provinces where the Jews were numerous. This body called before it for interviews a number of Jewish leaders from Bordeaux, Bayonne, Paris, Alsace, and Lorraine. Roederer, a prominent lawyer of Metz interested in the issue, also was called in. But before the commission made its report, the Revolution had broken out and the National Assembly had taken the Jewish Question into its own hands. Thus the commission never drew up a report.[35] It is interesting, however, to know that the king of France was concerned to do something for the Jews, and anyone acquainted with the humanitarian attitude of Malesherbes and his attentiveness to a task will be inclined to believe that he would have submitted a report offering some betterment of conditions for them, although it would not have gone as far as the National Assembly of 1789-1791 did in fact go. Allison, his biographer, has reported that Malesherbes made a careful study of the Jewish Question, collected "several dossiers of notes," and passed on "some of his information" to Mirabeau for use in his espousal of the cause.[36]

In summary, it can be said that the cause of Jewish civil rights,

[34] *Ibid.*, 164-70, 185.

[35] Gabriel Hemerdinger, "Le dénombrement des Israélites d'Alsace (1789)," *REJ*, XLII (1901), 258-59; Ferdinand-Dreyfus, *Misères sociales*, 225, 227.

[36] John M. S. Allison, *Malesherbes, Defender and Reformer of the French Monarchy, 1721-1794* (New Haven, 1938), 117.

like that to better conditions for the Protestants, was championed
in the first instance by thinkers outside their own group, and indeed that members of their own had but a negligible part in the
agitation throughout. The need for reform was sponsored first
by the *philosophes*, and the subsequent promoters were in large
part writers directly or indirectly influenced by them. Protagonists of the movement naturally aroused the conservatives to
reply, as happened in other causes of reform. This clash of
opinion not only has provided the student of today with details
of the situation, it aided in clarifying minds of that day on both
the issues and the needed solution to the problem. That the matter was settled in a commendable manner within the short space
of two years after the Revolution began was probably in no small
degree due to the pre-Revolutionary discussion. It is further of
interest that in this movement for bettering Jewish conditions
the king manifested sincere interest, and that the nobility were
more willing to support it than were the bourgeoisie.

It was after the Revolution began that the Jewish Question
became one of vital significance in France. In January, 1789, the
king summoned the Estates General to meet at Versailles in May
and requested cahiers of grievances from the electorate throughout France. In all places where the Jews were established, the
Jewish Question received mention in the cahiers; other regions
in general were silent. Throughout Alsace and Lorraine the larger
number of cahiers were hostile to the Jews and asked for more
effective curbs on them, especially on their economic and marital
activities. There were too many Jews in the first place, and they
bled the country through their usury. The cahiers of Lorraine
expressed a wish that every loan made by a Jew should be registered by a notary, and similarly that every payment of interest
to a Jew should be registered. This had been specified in the
regulation of 1784 in Alsace, but it had never worked well, being
shunned from the first. The clergy, no less than the other two
estates, complained of the Jewish usurers. Some of the cahiers
were bitter, others moderate, but a few asked that they might
participate freely in the professions, the arts and trades, and in
agriculture.[37] The nobles of Nomény stated bluntly that the Jews

[37] Seligman, *La justice en France pendant la Révolution*, 160-64; Liber, "Les
Juifs et la convocation des Etats Généraux," LXIII, 194, 201-207; LXV, 104.
Liber has made a minute study of the cahiers on the Jews.

either should be chased from the kingdom or be given full civic rights.

The nobility of Paris *intra muros* requested that the Estates General act to better "the lot of the Jews." This action might have been suggested by Zalkind-Hourwitz, who sent them a copy of his essay that had been honored by the Academy of Metz.[38]

The cahiers of Bordeaux appear not to have included mention of the Jews, but the people there were very favorable to the Jews and came within a few votes of electing a Jew, David Gradis, as a deputy to the Estates General. De Sèze, who was elected, was friendly toward them and before the National Assembly spoke in their favor. At Bayonne two Jews sat with ten Christian delegates in drawing up the cahier from that city. Elsewhere, however, they were denied this privilege by the Garde des Sceaux.[39]

The Abbé Grégoire in February, 1789, wrote to his friend Isaie Bing, a Jew of Metz, suggesting that the time was opportune for the Jews of France to obtain civil rights, and that they concert themselves to press for this action. It is doubtful that a people who in 1717 had engaged an agent to represent them and for a decade or two prior to 1789 had employed Pereire to represent them as agent in Paris were in need of a suggestion of this sort. The Jews did act quickly, engaging a bright young Parisian lawyer, Jacques Godard, to act as their propagandist and lobbyist. Also they requested permission to send a cahier to the Estates General, which was granted. The Jews of Bayonne and Bordeaux, however, had no part in it, for the reason that they had participated in drawing up of the general cahiers from those places.[40] In their cahier the Jews demanded the rights of full citizenship: the right to enter any profession or trade, to own land, to engage in agriculture; the right to dwell anywhere in France; exemption from special taxes; the right to maintain their cult, cemeteries, marriage customs, and syndics; the right of marriage for all (and not for the eldest son alone); and the right to send their sons to colleges and universities. In 1789 Grégoire published another brochure entitled *Motion en faveur des Juifs,* in which he called anew upon the French to grant full liberties to the Jews. He proposed a law which would exempt all Jews born in France from

---

[38] Liber, "Les Juifs et la convocation des Etats Généraux," LXIII, 203, 209.
[39] *Ibid.,* LXIV, 251-52, 254-57, 262-65, 277.   [40] *Ibid.,* LXIV, 265.

special taxes, and would permit them to go and settle wherever they wished in France; to enter the arts and trades; to own and cultivate land; to practice their religion and its cult; to be free from insult. He implied that he would even permit Jews to hold public office, citing instances of Jews in various countries who had served well in public roles. He would admit them to colleges, universities, and learned societies, and mentioned the case of a Negro who had been made a corresponding member of the Académie Royale des Sciences. Had not the academy honored itself by its action? By permitting the youth of the two races (Jews and French) to grow up together in association, he thought that better race relations would result.[41]

If the French granted citizenship to the Jews, would it not lead to a great Jewish influx into France? He replied negatively. The French would not permit this influx to take place.

He took issue with those who asserted that the Jews were never patriots and that they were beset with vices. If hitherto they had been inactive as citizens, he said, it was because the monarchies in which they dwelt had not permitted them to be active citizens. And as for their vices, he declared that in Holland not a Jew had been executed for two centuries. The Jews of Bordeaux and of Alsace, on their part, had contributed definitely to France in wars of the last two centuries as provisioners of animals and supplies.[42] He recognized that most of the cahiers to the National Assembly from the Three Bishoprics and Alsace and Lorraine were opposed to the Jews, but made light of them.

Not only as a pamphleteer did Grégoire enlist in the cause of the Jews, he spoke before various audiences, often hostile, and led their fight on the floor of the National Assembly. On August 3 he addressed that body in behalf of relieving the Jews of Alsace from persecution. The clergy of his bailliage, he said, had expressed a wish that something be done for them.[43] No immediate action resulted, but on August 27 the Declaration of the Rights of Man and the Citizen was adopted by the assembly, paving the way for granting of civil rights to depressed groups of France. The Jews of Bordeaux recognized the implications of this declaration and on August 14, 1789, while it was still being drafted, they

---

[41] *Motion en faveur des Juifs*, 36-37 *et passim*.   [42] *Ibid.*, 22-24.
[43] *Réimpression de l'ancien Moniteur*, I, 270.

wrote a letter of appreciation to Grégoire, acknowledging his services for them. They commented that at Bordeaux they fraternized with the Christians, assembled with them in churches for the formation of National Guard units, and that one or more of their number had been elected captain in the Guard.

On September 2 Grégoire made an impassioned speech before the assembly on behalf of the Jews. On October 14 a Jewish deputation from Alsace and Lorraine appeared before the assembly, and their leader, Bern-Isaac-Berr, made a plea for relief from persecution and ill treatment. Grégoire followed him with a motion that the matter be considered during the current term of the assembly. It was voted down, but Grégoire was not dejected; his aim was to advertise the matter through repeated discussion.[44]

Subsequent deputations of Jews came before the National Assembly with the design of influencing legislation in their behalf. The same policy was followed in respect to the cause of the Negroes; perhaps the reason for the parallel lines of strategy lay in the fact that, as Grégoire stated, the partisans of one were very largely partisans of the other. Most of the leaders of both movements were members of the Amis des Noirs. It may be observed also that most of those supporting the Protestant cause also supported these other two causes.

Not all, however, had been smooth sailing for the Jews in France in 1789. Following the sacking of the Hôtel de Ville of Strasbourg on July 21, instigated by the capture of the Bastille, there was a wave of rioting and vandalism in Alsace, in which Jewish homes were burned and some chateaux and abbeys sacked. Rochambeau was the new military commander of the province, but his troops were unamenable to discipline and some took part in the rioting.[45] Among the Jewish establishments attacked was a textile factory near Nancy bought by Cerf Berr in 1786 and employing Jewish workmen. Here oddly enough was a Jewish estate existing in pre-Revolutionary France, a complete anomaly save for the fact that the royal court had recognized Cerf Berr as a citizen and a *seigneur,* and he was qualified to own it. Rumor

[44] Liber, "Les Juifs et la convocation des Etats Généraux," LXVI, 202; Grégoire, *Motion en faveur des Juifs,* xiii-vi.

[45] Jean Edmond Wheelen, *Rochambeau, Father and Son: A Life of the Maréchal de Rochambeau,* tr. by Lawrence Lee (New York, 1936), 129-30; Gaston Zeller, *L'Alsace française de Louis XIV à nos jours* (Paris, 1945), 52.

spread that he had participated in grain speculation, and in February, 1788, his barns had been pillaged and windows in his home and in other Jewish homes had been broken by a mob, quelled at length only by the calling out of troops. Bitter charges against his exploitation of the public lingered in the summer of 1789. The riots, in fact, did not end in 1789 but continued into 1790. Many Jews in fear fled to Switzerland, and in April, 1790, some of those remaining in Alsace wrote asking special protection of the National Assembly. On April 16 action to this effect was taken, by a vote almost unanimous. All persons were prohibited to molest them, and all cities and national guard units were ordered to render them protection.[46] With this the disturbances ceased.

Several pamphlets against the Jews appeared within this period, designed to influence the National Assembly to tighten restrictions on them. Among them was a twelve-page brochure by Hell, deputy from Hagenau and bearer of a cahier calling for more restrictions. Depicting the Jews of Alsace as usurers, he proposed a law to meet the situation. It would grant the Jews born and domiciled in France full citizenship, with the right to own property, even agricultural property provided that they themselves would till it, and with the right to enter any trade. They, in turn, would give up their special status as an organized body within the state—their syndics, judges, notaries, and police. All their contracts in the future must be in French or German, and witnessed by legal officials. They would pay the same taxes as other citizens, and in addition the tax or taxes for protection as Jews. They might marry and settle in a place only on the permission of the provincial estates. Moreover, marriage would be permitted only to those who followed a trade, farmed, sewed, knitted, or spun. And then by way of a double safeguard, no French citizen might be held accountable for a loan for more than twice the sum he paid in taxes, nor might he buy or sell landed property except before an officer of the municipality where he lived and with the consent and in the presence of five relatives or friends.[47]

<hr/>

[46] Liber, "Les Juifs et la convocation des Etats Généraux," LXIII, 202-203; *Réimpression de l'ancien Moniteur*, IV, 132-33; *AP*, XIII, 76-77.

[47] François Joseph Antoine de Hell, *Mon opinion sur les Juifs, extrait des cahiers dont je suis le porteur* (Paris, 1789), 1-12.

Another anti-Jewish pamphlet of 1789 was by Captain, later General, Philippe François de Latour Foissac, an Alsatian stationed at this time with the National Guards at Phalsbourg. Taking the same slant as Hell and Malouet, he criticized the Jews above all for their usury and swindling, citing instances that he had known. Like Hell, he posed as a humanitarian, a champion of the oppressed peasantry. He made the Jew a villain, totally unscrupulous. After presenting a damning case against the Jew, Latour-Foissac set forth his proposals which would permit the Jews to remain in France but only after their fangs had been pulled. This he would accomplish by abolishing the practice of usury. "These vampires" he would force to work. The existing loan contracts in their favor should all be repudiated, as having been made in bad faith.[48]

Other brochures against the Jews of this period included the anonymous *Révolte des Juifs d'Avignon,* denounced by Grégoire as scurrilous, since it charged the Jews of Avignon with plotting the assassination of various persons, and also a second edition of *Le cri des citoyens contre les Juifs,* by J. B. H. Aubert du Bayet, a cavalry captain at Metz. The latter pamphlet, first published in 1788 at Paris, was marked by Voltairean banter and attitude and made some impression. Several replies reportedly were made to it.[49]

Meanwhile the Jews and their protagonists had not been idle. In August they published at Paris a nine-page *Adresse presentée à l'Assemblée Nationale, le 26 août, par les Juifs residans à Paris,* deploring their conditions and asking for religious toleration and full rights.[50] The Jews of Alsace about the same time submitted to the assembly a petition requesting the same objectives which was considered in the meeting of September 3. The matter was sent to committee.[51] Then on October 14 several Jewish representatives from Alsace, Lorraine, and the Three Bishoprics appeared before the assembly to deplore the tribulations under

[48] *Plaidoyer contre l'usure des Juifs des Evêchés, de l'Alsace et le Lorraine,* 1-17, 30-31, 38, 46-47, 49-50.
[49] See article on Aubert du Bayet in *Nouvelle biographie générale,* ed. by J. C. F. Hoefer (Paris, 1853-1866) (hereafter *NBG*), III, 566-67; Grégoire, *Motion en faveur des Juifs,* xiii.
[50] To it the Curé Thiebaut, deputy for the clergy of Metz, published a reply.
[51] *Réimpression de l'ancien Moniteur,* I, 420; Farges, "La question juive," XI, 145.

which they lived, the most recent of which were the riots of 1789.[52]

The subject was now one of general interest and discussion. Camille Desmoulins in the December 28 issue of *Révolutions de France et de Brabant* had an article favoring the Jewish cause, to which Rewbell, a deputy from Alsace, wrote a reply not published.[53] In early January, 1790, one of the Jewish leaders informed the Abbé Maury, a deputy, that he was sending him two pamphlets on the Jewish Question which he hoped would lead him to favor the Jewish side henceforth in the assembly. The Abbé replied that he would not change his position but that he would always advocate humanitarian treatment of the Jews.[54]

On January 28, 1790, a deputation of fifty Parisian Jews presented themselves before the commune of Paris and asked for active citizenship. A speech in their behalf was made by their lobbyist Jacques Godard, prominent lawyer and member of the commune. He stated that during the Revolution the Jews had shown themselves patriotic and loyal. Among the delegation was Zalkind-Hourwitz, the Polish Jew who now was interpreter in Oriental languages at the Royal Library, and who agreed to give thenceforth one-fourth of his salary of nine hundred livres to the state as a patriotic gift.[55]

This same day was marked by a stormy debate on the Jewish Question in the National Assembly and the extension of civil rights to the Portuguese, Spanish, and Avignonese Jews of southern France. It was precipitated when Talleyrand read a report for the Committee on the Constitution on the situation of the Jews of Bordeaux. Friends of the Jews were clearly in control of the committee and had waited in presenting their report until the Protestant Question had been settled on December 24. They further revealed deft handling of the problem by splitting the Jewish Question into fragments and considering first the case of the Bordeaux Jews who were popular and already enjoyed greater privileges than their fellows in other parts of France. Rewbell

[52] *Réimpression de l'ancien Moniteur*, II, 62; *Mercure de France*, Oct. 24, 1789, p. 279.

[53] Raymond Guyot, *Documents biographiques sur J. F. Rewbell (1747-1801)* (Tours, 1911), 70.

[54] Weisly, *Instruction salutaire*, 3-10.

[55] *Réimpression de l'ancien Moniteur*, III, 263; Ferdinand-Dreyfus, *Misères sociales*, 246-47.

and Maury led the opposition, supported by Noailles, De Sèze, Chapelier, and others. Talleyrand and Grégoire championed the Jewish side. At length the decree proposed by Talleyrand and reworded by Grégoire was passed by a vote of 374 to 224, and it was stipulated that this action was not to prejudice the case of the Jews elsewhere in France, which would be considered later.[56]

When the edict was announced to a crowd of more than eight hundred persons in Bordeaux, they cheered loudly. With the inhabitants there the decision was popular.[57]

In no wise was there a lessening of activity following this edict, either by the Jewish party or their opponents. Their opponents in the assembly tried repeatedly to have a vote on the question of civil rights for the remainder of the Jews in France, but in vain, as the proponents played for time and succeeded always in postponing the question.[58] The city of Strasbourg in April submitted an appeal to the National Assembly asking that Jews not be admitted to citizenship, and that the few Jewish families already established in the city by royal influence be expelled.[59] This request made a great impression throughout France. A wave of anti-Semitism spread to other countries. In France nasty rumors were spread, and libels and defamatory songs written. Cerf Berr was charged with spending great sums in Paris to influence public opinion. Grégoire was designated "The Rabbi" and compared to Judas Iscariot. Even the king in 1791 was criticized in a pamphlet in whose title he was referred to as "king of the Jews and the French."[60]

A sharp, twenty-page pamphlet, succinctly stating the matter from the angle of the opponents of the Jews, was published by Jean-Adam Pflieger, an Alsatian deputy to the National Assembly.[61] He stated that if the Alsatians and their laws were so severe, the Jews would emigrate. Not the Jews, but the Alsatians, had been migrating. They had done so in large numbers for thirty years, and Pflieger attributed their action to the Jews. No longer would anyone but a Jew enter livestock trading. The Jews

---

[56] *Journal de Paris*, Jan. 29, 1790, pp. 114-15; Farges, "La question juive," XI, 148-50; *Réimpression de l'ancien Moniteur*, III, 251-52, 255-56.

[57] *Ibid.*, III, 334.   [58] *Mercure de France*, March 22, April 3, 1790.

[59] *L'adresse de la commune de Strasbourg à l'Assemblée Nationale contre les Juifs (avril 1790)* (Paris, n.d.), 19.

[60] Ferdinand-Dreyfus, *Misères sociales*, 243-44.

[61] *Réflexions sur les Juifs d'Alsace* (Paris, 1790).

had hurt agriculture and commerce. They were detested through-out the province, and he declared that the present moment was inauspicious for conferring on them citizenship. He described them as a very unsocial people, and predicted that they would never mix with the French. That, however, was what he would have them to do. He would take away their syndics and other elements of special status; he would have them treated like the other inhabitants; and finally he would have them intermarry with the French, rather than among themselves. He would ex-terminate them by absorption.

The Jews on their part were active. They saw to it that their young men enlisted in the National Guard; they contributed lib-erally to the *don patriotique;* and they failed not to let these pa-triotic actions be known. They attended the political meetings, and in Paris and Strasbourg they gained the favor of the Com-mune.[62] They continued to send petitions to the National Assem-bly, usually in the form of brochures. One such, drawn up by Godard, their lobbyist, and signed by seven Jewish leaders, in-cluding Cerf Berr, appealed to the "Illustrious Representatives of the Nation" for full citizenship at once.[63] The pamphlet pre-sented an elaborate summary of the Jewish position, their afflic-tions, and their hopes. Godard was an able writer and did a good job for the Jews.

Another pamphleteer enlisting in the cause was a member of the commune of Paris, J. C. A. de Bourge, who fired, as it were, two volleys for it. The first was a fifteen-page *Discours,* or speech, given before the commune on January 30, in which he appealed for the commune's support before the National Assembly, and mentioned among other grounds for this support that one hun-dred of the five hundred Jews living in Paris were enrolled in the National Guards.[64] His second pamphlet, published under date of May 19, 1790, was addressed to the Committee of the Constitution of the National Assembly, in an attempt to influence

[62] Ferdinand-Dreyfus, *Misères sociales,* 244; Grégoire, *Motion en faveur des Juifs,* 34; Paul A. Hildenfinger, "L'adresse de la commune de Strasbourg à l'As-semblée Nationale contre les Juifs (avril 1790)," *REJ,* LVIII (1909), 113-15.

[63] *Pétition des Juifs établis en France, adressée à l'Assemblée Nationale, le 28 janvier 1790, sur l'adjournement du 24 décembre 1789* (Paris, 1790), 104-107.

[64] *Discours prononcé, le 30 janvier, dans l'Assemblée générale des représentans de la Commune, par M. Debourge, l'un des représentans de la Commune, à l'oc-casion de la demande faire, le 27, par les Juifs de Paris* (Paris, 1790?).

it on behalf of the Jews. He charged the opponents of Jewish civil rights with religious intolerance, denied the repeated complaint that the Jews were unsociable, and charged that "interested parties" had incited the recent riots in which Jewish homes and property had suffered. He admitted Jewish usury, saying that they were forced into commerce, in which it was impossible to have a clean role. The commune had requested freedom for the Jews, and he hoped that the National Assembly would be quick to give it, lest they be anticipated by the British.[65]

The same fear of British anticipation was voiced by another pamphleteer, a woman of Belgian birth, the Baroness de Vasse. "There is not an instant to lose," she wrote. If France should hesitate, some other nation would act first. The British were considering such a step. If France were anticipated, the Jews would leave with their money and France would have lost her golden opportunity. She pointed to the loss that France had suffered through emigration of the Huguenots. It is puzzling that a Belgian woman should have been so solicitous about the welfare of France. She must have been a French citizen.[66]

On at least two occasions demand was made on the floor of the National Assembly that civil rights be extended to the remainder of the Jews in France. On February 25, 1790, a deputation from the commune of Paris made a visit for this purpose, and the Abbé Mulot spoke in favor of it. No vote was taken.[67] Again at a night meeting January 18, 1791, active citizenship was proposed by Martineau, a deputy from Paris who earlier had been active in getting toleration for the Protestants. Several speakers participated in a warm debate, the Prince de Broglie making more extended remarks than any other. He charged that the whole matter, as far as the Alsatian Jews were concerned, was being promoted by four or five rich Jews of the department of Bas-Rhin. One of them had acquired great wealth at the expense of the state, and he, along with others, had "spent considerable sums in this capital to get protectors and supporters." Strasbourg

[65] *Lettre au Comité de Constitution sur l'affaire des Juifs* (Paris, 1790), 45.
[66] *Mémoire à l'Assemblée Nationale, pour démontrer aux François les raisons qui doivent les determiner à admettre les Juifs indistinctement aux droits de citoyens* (Paris, 1790), 9. It was published by the National Assembly, as were wellnigh all such manuscripts sent it.
[67] *Journal de Paris*, Feb. 27, 1790, pp. 230-31.

had long been in ferment on this Jewish Question. To vote civil rights for Jews would produce a storm in Alsace and Lorraine. He succeeded in shelving the matter by having it sent to the Committee on the Constitution.[68]

Throughout 1791 the matter appeared to die down, so far as pamphlets were concerned. But it was merely transferred to the political arena, and it was far from dead. Within Jacobin circles and on the floor of the assembly it continued to come up. On July 20, 1790, the assembly had abolished the tribute money that had been paid by the Jews of Alsace to the House of Brancas.[69] This encouraged the Jewish partisans to hope for more.

They chose their moment well. It came at the night meeting of September 27, 1791, in the last days of the assembly. Seeing that their proponents constituted a majority present that night, Adrien Duport, deputy for the nobility of Paris and one of the leaders of the reform movement in the assembly, brought the matter up for consideration. Saying that "Turks, Moslems, [and] men of all sects are admitted to enjoy in France political rights," he proposed the adoption of a decree "that the Jews in France will enjoy the rights of active citizens." There was applause. Rewbell arose to speak against the motion, but its supporters succeeded in suppressing debate and in calling for the question. The vote was taken and the motion passed.[70]

This mode of procedure of course was most unusual. It was tricky and undemocratic, but it was the only way that its followers thought that they could succeed with it, and time was fast running out. Incidentally the same body of men (in general, the Amis des Noirs) used very much the same trick two and a half years later, in February, 1794, to abolish slavery in the French colonies.

But why, one may ask, did not the opponents of the measure bring it up in a subsequent meeting and reverse the decision? They did bring it up the next day. But it is more difficult to have a parliamentary body reverse a decision than adopt it in the first place. The burden was now with the opponents of Jewish civil rights. Fearing that they could not obtain a reversal of

[68] *Réimpression de l'ancien Moniteur*, VIII, 167.
[69] Farges, "La question juive," XI, 150, 209.
[70] *Réimpression de l'ancien Moniteur*, IX, 791.

the decision of the previous night, Broglie and Rewbell satisfied themselves with some amendments, which were adopted. Broglie proposed that the Jews must take the civil oath before obtaining citizenship. This met no opposition. Rewbell then castigated the assembly for its procedure of the previous night, and amid complaint from its opponents proposed that Jewish creditors in Alsace be required to submit to district officials within a month lists of their debtors and details of the debts, and that the district and departmental officials take steps for the liquidation of these debts. After accepting this amendment also, the assembly then adopted a motion by Duport which had the effect of embodying these amendments with the decree of the previous evening. Following this action, the assembly adopted a motion by Emmery, providing "that every man, of whatever color, whatever origin, of whatever country he be, will be free and will enjoy the rights of an active citizen in France, if he meets in other respects the conditions required by the Constitution." Thus on September 28, 1791, the National Assembly granted not only Jews but also Negro slaves and other unfranchised persons residing in France the rights of active citizenship, provided that they took the civic oath and met other technicalities that the laws specified.

A detailed study, as this, of the movement to obtain civil rights for the Jews must necessarily uncover a great deal of the "jockeying" by propagandists and politicians to win persons of influence or to obtain a favorable setting for a vote. Such scenes often seem to go strangely with the movement we call humanitarian. They may not have been idealistic, but the idealistic is dependent upon the practical for attainment; and politics are as essential in this world as philosophy. The story here recorded is therefore a story of men of various types and methods who consciously or unconsciously concerted themselves for bettering the conditions of life in France for many thousand Jewish people. The victory was a great one, and today one can see the wisdom of the choice made by the National Assembly. It had been amply justified by the subsequent history of France. One must not, however, adopt the attitude that its proponents alone were humanitarians, and that its opponents were not. As oddly as it may seem, these latter declared repeatedly that they, too, were motivated by humanitarianism. The one group was motivated to help the Jew; the other, the peasant. Idealism was the common atmosphere of both.

One must not think moreover that the decree of September 28, 1791, brought a new heaven and a new earth for the Jews in France. Such did not happen. Throughout the 1790's they continued to have tribulations. Amid the vicissitudes of the Revolution—the Terror and the war—they found that life continued to hold out perils for them. While they claimed to be ardent revolutionists, and in general they were, their loyalty was often challenged. Some were thrust into prison, charged with treason or crime. Their sons were forced or drafted into the Revolutionary armies, and they did not revolt. Their public worship was interfered with during the Terror, as was that of the Catholics and the Protestants. Their synagogues were closed, their candlesticks were taken, and attempt was made to force their rabbis to renounce their calling. The severe famine of 1794-1795 brought a renewal of charges that they were exploiting it to their own economic advantage. During epizootics of 1796 and 1798-1799 they were accused of selling to the French armies the meat of diseased cattle.[71] A citizen of Metz in 1796 complained that though the Jews of that city had been given citizenship, they had done very little to carry out the basal conditions, and that they continued to live as a Jewish community, putting racialism above citizenship. The Jews of Metz on their part complained that during the Terror their synagogue, like churches, was used to stable animals being sent to the armies.[72] By the mid-1790's five thousand Jews reportedly had moved into Strasbourg and were doing a profitable business supplying the armies.[73] That Jews still were not popular in Strasbourg is seen by an eighteenth-century Dreyfus case. Simon Dreyfus, a Jew, was arbitrarily condemned by Strasbourg revolutionists to six years' imprisonment in irons on November 16, 1793, and was kept thus until the National Convention on January 18, 1795, ordered his release.[74] In a multitude of ways the Jews continued to find life in France

[71] Reuss, "Quelques documents nouveaux," LIX, 266-67.

[72] Puyproux, l'ainé, Encore un mot pour les créanciers des Juifs de Metz (n.p., 1796), 4. Puyproux was the author of three pamphlets on Jewish finances in the late 1790's.

[73] Wolfson, "Le Bureau de Commerce," LXI, 266.

[74] [Perroud] "Une affair Dreyfus en l'an III," RF, XLVI (1904), 544.

exasperating, and the French to find the Jews equally exasperating.[75] Considering the violence of the times, it doubtless was
remarkable that the two races got along without more trouble
than did occur.

Much has been written of this subject, all of it by Jews, who
with few exceptions have had a martyr complex. The late Professor Aulard, in his review of Robert Anchel's doctoral treatise
Napoleon et les Juifs, charged that Anchel accentuates the idea
of persecution. He denied that anti-Semitism existed during the
Terror.[76] To deny or approve this position might involve one in
semantics on anti-Semitism. Aulard insisted that the French in
general were friendly to the Jews during the 1790's. The Jews
prior to the Revolution were subject to harsh laws in France—
laws that no reasonable person today would condone—but they
partly brought them upon their own head. There were distinctly
two sides to the situation. The Jews perhaps treated their victims as badly as they themselves were treated. A change in the
situation from both angles was very desirable, and to the credit
of the French they took the initiative, in 1790-1791, in extending
the hand of friendship.

[75] Robert Anchel, *Napoleon et les Juifs* (Paris, 1928), 14-25; Moïse and Ernest
Ginsberger, "Contributions à l'histoire des Juifs d'Alsace pendant la Terreur," *REJ,*
XLVII (1903), 283-99; Jacques Godechot, "Le comité de surveillance révolu-
tionnaire de Nancy (2 avril 1793—1er germinal an III)," *RF,* LXXX (1927), 254;
Alexandre Tuetey, *Répertoire général des sources manuscrites de l'histoire de Paris
pendant la Révolution française* (Paris, 1890-1914), IX, 235-36, 422; X, 551; XI,
158-59; Reuss, "Quelques documents nouveaux," LIX, 235-37, 251, 260, 265-66.
[76] *RF,* LXXXI (1928), 271-72.

CHAPTER FOUR

Antislavery Sentiment
Prior to 1789

IT IS SURPRISING that the movement in France against
slavery and the slave trade was so large when the colonies
affected were so few and small. The fortunes of war in the
eighteenth century, however, led France to encourage slavery.
In the wars of the Spanish Succession (1702-1713), the Austrian
Succession (1740-1748), and the Seven Years (1756-1763), she
lost to Britain nearly all of her previous vast empire, retaining
only the islands of Saint-Pierre and Miquelon off the Saint Lawrence; the West Indian islands of Santo Domingo (then called
Saint-Domingue), Martinique, Guadeloupe, and certain smaller
ones in the Antilles, a part of Guiana; the islands of Réunion and
Isle de France, to the east of Madagascar; and five trading sta-
tions in India. Most of these possessions were in the West Indies
and in the Indian Ocean, and the crops were chiefly sugar, tobacco, indigo, and manioc, for which slave labor was a great
asset in cultivation, harvesting, and processing. The leading
sugar island, Santo Domingo, now Haiti, came to dominate
French attention in regard to emancipation as the century pro-
gressed. Had Britain at the end of her victorious wars with
France during the century insisted on obtaining possession of
the French sugar islands, and left to her enemy some of the
"acres of snow" in Canada, the French would have had no great
problem with slavery.

In the seventeenth century French colonization became definitely established and the French adopted slavery. It grew slowly
but steadily and with such severities that Louis XIV, in 1685,

considered it advisable to enact legislation setting forth certain rights to which slaves were entitled and the limits beyond which slaveowners must not go. This legislation, possibly suggested by Madame de Maintenon, who had lived several years in Martinique and seen the cruelties attending slavery,[1] was known as the Code Noir, which with a few modifications and additions, made in 1724 and 1784, continued in effect to the Revolution.[2] As these successive measures went into effect, it became customary to refer to them all by the term Code Noir. Other enactments affected the slave trade, commonly in the form of treaties between the French government and the exploiting company or companies that were to obtain and transport the slaves. It is deserving of attention at the outset that so essential did the government consider the need of slave labor to cultivate the plantations and manufacture their products in the colonies that it undertook to subsidize heavily the slaving companies, at a certain sum per slave and at so much per tonnage of the vessels engaged. Thus, in 1713, for every Negro imported into the West Indies, the Compagnie de Guinée was to receive thirteen livres, but by an order of council of 1784 it was ten livres.[3] These subsidies for 1789 amounted to 865,000 livres.[4] Nevertheless, Lamoignon, keeper of the seals, in a speech before the Estates General in May, 1789, indicated that governmental expenditure for the introduction of slaves amounted to 2,400,000 livres annually.[5]

The number of African slaves brought to the western world until the termination of slavery in the mid-nineteenth century has been estimated by Père Dieudonné Rinchon at 13,250,000. Yet at the end of the eighteenth century there were living only about 2,627,833. Such was the severity of life for the slave. Of

[1] Carl Ludwig Lokke, France and the Colonial Question: A Study of Contemporary French Opinion, 1763-1801 (New York, 1932), 32.

[2] Promulgated in March, 1685, and entitled "Code Noir, touchant la police des îles de l'Amérique," it is reproduced by Isambert, Recueil général des anciennes lois françaises, XIX, 494-504. Isambert did not consider the terms of the 1724 edict important enough to reproduce them (ibid., XXI, 261), but he did reproduce those of 1784 (ibid., XXVII, 533-41).

[3] A. de Boislisle, Correspondance des controleurs généraux des finances avec les intendants des provinces (Paris, 1874-1897), III, 507; Gaston Martin, Nantes au XVIIIe siècle (Toulouse, 1928-1931), II, 326; André Ducasse, Les négriers ou le traffic des esclaves (Paris, 1948), 63.

[4] Etienne Pollio, "Le commerce maritime pendant la Révolution," RF, LXXXVI (1933), 269-70.

[5] Mercure de France, May 23, 1789, p. 190.

these two and a half million, slightly more than a third were in the French West Indian islands. The others were in Brazil and the United States, 600,000 in the former and 697,397 in the latter. Rinchon reckoned at 2,200,000 the number of Negroes imported to Santo Domingo during the latter half of the eighteenth century. The estimated mortality there was around 30,000 a year, which, if accurate, would accrue to 1,500,000 in fifty years. Births and importations, however, amounted yearly to about 44,000, and so the population slowly increased.[6]

The slave trade brought great wealth to the cities of Nantes, La Rochelle, Bordeaux, Rouen, Saint-Malo, and Le Havre. The families engaged in it were enriched and ennobled.[7] It is said that on the French slave ships the Negroes were turned free to move about the vessel at will after they had been out at sea three or four days. This contrasted sharply with the British, Dutch, and Danish practice of keeping the men in irons and the women handcuffed. The French action was daring in view of the fact that there were instances in the eighteenth century in which the slaves massacred the crew and seized the ship.[8]

In the colonies the slaves were consigned to miserable huts, but they were probably as well off in this respect as they had been in Africa. They might not leave the plantation, either by day or night, without written permission from their master. Gatherings of slaves at night were distinctly forbidden, lest they lead to uprisings or trouble. For that matter, neither were meetings of citizens in France permitted without authorization. Slaves could hold no public office or employment, nor might they own property. Masters might, however, if they chose, permit them to earn small amounts of money and keep it. This the government encouraged. Slaves might not qualify as witnesses in any court, whether in a matter civil or criminal, but their testimony might have auxiliary value in clearing up confused points for the judge.[9]

[6] He gives estimated figures for the period around 1780: Santo Domingo, 452,-000; Martinique, 76,000; Guadeloupe, 90,000; Saint Lucie, 20,000; Marie Galante, 10,000; Tabago, 15,000; Cayenne, 10,000; Saintes, Sainte Marie, and La Désirade, 500. This he totals at 673,500 slaves. P. Dieudonné Rinchon, *Le traite et l'esclavage des Congolais par les Européens: histoire de la déportation des 13 millions 250,000 noirs en Amérique* (n.p., 1929), 96-98.

[7] Martin, *Nantes au XVIIIe siècle*, II, 179, 427-28.

[8] Rinchon, *Le traite et l'esclavage des Congolais*, 201.

[9] Isambert, *Recueil général des anciennes lois françaises*, XIX, 496-99 (Code Noir of 1685, arts. 16, 17, 28-30).

A slave might not sell sugar cane for his master without his permission, on penalty of scourging. Theft was to be punished according to the nature of the goods taken, from scourging and branding with the fleur-de-lis to the death penalty. Masters were held responsible for making good the losses to other citizens from thefts committed by their slaves, although they might renounce a slave and turn him over as indemnity to the damaged party. A runaway slave who had been gone a month would be branded with the fleur-de-lis and his ears clipped; and if the offense were repeated, he would be hamstrung and a fleur-de-lis branded on each shoulder. Under the Old Regime there were many runaway slaves, called *marrons* (after the Spanish word *cimarron*, runaway). Perhaps the worst offense of which a slave could be guilty was that of striking his master or mistress or a member of their family. For this, if blood had been shed or even a bruise made, he was to be condemned to death.[10]

These penalties were to be inflicted by the court, not by the masters, and it should be borne in mind that penalties in France at that time were similarly severe. The common beggar, for instance, might be branded for a first offense and sent to the galleys for a second. Robbery was punished by branding and a sentence to the galleys, or by death if made in a home. The slaveowner was permitted only to chain or scourge his slave; he could not torture, mutilate, or execute him. This prohibition of torture by the master was repeated in a royal ordinance of December 30, 1712, after reports that torture had been used and that some colonists had not fed their slaves well.[11]

The Code Noir also carried clauses on the food and clothing the master must provide each slave, and on the religious care he must give to the slave. The slave must be baptized and instructed in the Catholic faith within a week after his purchase, on penalty of a fine. Catholic rites were to be followed in all marriages between slaves or between slaves and free Negroes. Sundays and feast days were to be scrupulously observed, and no work permitted. While no slave might be married without his master's consent, no master on the other hand might force a slave to marry against his will. Several articles at the outset of the

---

[10] *Ibid.*, 497, 499-500 (arts. 18, 33, 35-38).
[11] *Ibid.*, 500-501 (art. 42); XX, 582-83; XXI, 260-61.

code illustrate the Grand Monarch's fear lest Protestantism spread to the colonies.[12]

All in all the Code Noir was designed to protect the slave by designating his rights and obligations. The peaceful slave ought to experience no difficulties, unless his master was unjust. That masters and officials were scrupulous, however, to follow the wording and spirit of the code there can exist only the gravest doubt. Evidently some did; others did not. The penalties of course strike us as brutal. Flogging, branding, and death by breaking on the wheel were common penalties in eighteenth-century France and throughout Europe in that day, but they were heartless inflictions. Their imposition on the slave was all the more cruel because he was deprived of his liberty and forced to labor for the welfare of a master.[13]

While an occasional thinker before and during the early eighteenth century had expressed criticism of slavery, they had made little impression on the public, and it may be said that the development of the movement that was to influence public opinion was due, in origin, to the French *philosophes,* of whom Montesquieu was the first to speak out, in his *Lettres persanes* (1721) and *Esprit des lois* (1748). In the former were a few passing criticisms of the transportation of Africans from their own climate to one less healthy, of their being compelled to labor, on land or in mines, for the riches of other men, and of the terrible mortality to which they were subjected.[14] He contrasted ancient and modern slavery, to the advantage of the former, and censured Christians for using it. Actually he was more critical of slavery in his earlier work than in his *Esprit des lois,* where he gave it more extended treatment. So mild there were his criticisms that some later and more ardent abolitionists considered him flippant. He treated the subject objectively, with no expressed sympathy or antipathy. He attributed Negro slavery to an economic motive. He argued that there was no work in any climate that free men could not perform. He admitted that slavery had advantages

[12] *Ibid.,* XIX, 494-95 (arts. 2-6, 8, 10-11). Article 1 moreover specified that all Jews were to be chased from the colonies "as declared enemies of the Christian name."

[13] While Louis XIV permitted clipping of the ears, this penalty appears to have disappeared from practice in Europe in the eighteenth century. It was not listed in the revision of the penal clauses of the Code Noir in 1784.

[14] Letters, 75, 115, 118, 121, 122.

for a small, luxurious group, but denied that it was beneficial to a nation as a whole. Actually, he said, it was "useful neither to the master nor to the slave," for while the master might benefit economically, he would be harmed morally. Interestingly enough, it was in this section on slavery that Montesquieu made his famous assertion that "all men are born equal." He declared that under a despotism slavery might be an institution of protection, but that under a monarchy, and even more so under a democracy, it had no place.[15] In appraising Montesquieu's significance, it should be mentioned that his two books were among the most popular of the eighteenth century, each undergoing many editions and being translated into the other important languages of the day. In a very real sense, therefore, he set Europeans thinking.

Voltaire, like Montesquieu, was so mild an opponent of slavery as to be criticised by subsequent abolitionists. He did not crusade against it, as he did against certain other social injustices; nevertheless in several of his writings, such as *Alzire*, *Candide*, the *Essai sur les moeurs*, and his *Dictionnaire philosophique*, he made biting criticism of slavery, more particularly as the Spanish had used it in the New World.[16] Like Montesquieu, he considered the Negro handicapped by color, appearance, and intelligence, inferior to the white man.[17]

Rousseau, fervent lover of liberty, made only a few passing remarks on slavery, all condemning it, in his *Discours sur l'orgine et les fondements de l'inégalité parmi des hommes* (1755), *La Nouvelle Héloïse* (1762), and the *Contrat social* (1762). In the first and third of these writings he questioned the right of one man to sell another. In the *Contrat social*, he opened with the fulminating statement that man though born free is everywhere in chains. He included in the book a short chapter condemning slavery, saying that no man has the right to own or to force another to do his will.[18]

[15] *De l'esprit des lois par Montesquieu, avec des notes de Voltaire, de Crévier, de Mably, de La Harpe, etc.* (new ed., Paris, 1922), I, 236-63. All of Book XV, consisting of nineteen short chapters, in the *Esprit des lois* deals with slavery.

[16] Edward Darbyshire Seeber, *Anti-Slavery Opinion in France During the Second Half of the Eighteenth Century* (Baltimore, 1937), 38-40.

[17] Lokke, *France and the Colonial Question*, 43-44; Montesquieu, *Esprit des lois*, I, 239-40. The Abbé Royou was challenged in the *Mercure de France*, Sept. 10, 1791, p. 80, for calling Voltaire a supporter of slavery.

[18] Seeber, *Anti-Slavery Opinion*, 63-64; Lokke, *France and the Colonial Question*, 36-37; Rousseau, *Contrat social*, ch. IV.

Diderot, though no crusader for the cause, was hostile to slavery and the slave trade, as seen by the inclusion of several articles in the *Encyclopédie*. The articles "Esclavage" and "Traite des nègres" by his assistant Jaucourt and "Nègres" by Formey may be cited. That of "Esclavage," lengthy and historical in scope, portrayed slavery as a relic of man's greed, ambition, desire of conquest, love of ease, and cruelty. It was utterly inconsistent with the sentiments of humanity. Though slavery in the French colonies was not denounced, its disapproval was tacit. The article "Nègres" set forth an elaborate summary of the Code Noir and its revolting terms. The *Encyclopédie*, however, though critical of slavery, was not bitter on the subject; its articles were primarily informative.[19]

More pronounced was the condemnation of slavery by the Abbé Raynal in the *Histoire philosophique des deux Indes*, a voluminous work published in 1770 that went through a score of printings before the end of the century and was translated widely. The Europeans of the eighteenth century were exceedingly curious to learn about distant peoples and countries, and the *Histoire philosophique* appealed greatly to this taste for exoticism. The book contained the idea that civilization carried a blight with it, and that the Spanish and other European peoples had transported to the New World despotism, injustice, and greed. It was much more critical of the Spanish and other slave traders than of the French. The over-all picture in the book was a sharp condemnation of slavery. Turgot and Dupont de Nemours, other antislavers, however, considered that the author straddled the fence,[20] while Brissot, at a later date, because of Raynal's dislike of the Revolution, considered him a downright turncoat.[21] The charge that Diderot, Condorcet, the Abbé Martin, Péchmaja, and perhaps others of his friends aided drastically in the preparation and revision of his manuscript has not added to the Abbé's reputation. Many errors, too, had their entrance, and critical readers have not regarded the work as accurate.[22] Some of the sharper criti-

---

[19] *Encyclopédie*, V, 873-82; IX, 69-76; Seeber, *Anti-Slavery Opinion*, 46, 49, 50, 56, 61-63, 82.

[20] Seeber, *Anti-Slavery Opinion*, 94.

[21] Brissot, *Mémoires (1754-1793)*, II, 84-86.

[22] Lokke, *France and the Colonial Question*, 112, 152; Seeber, *Anti-Slavery Opinion*, 42.

cisms of slavery were made in revised editions of the book and were regarded as the work of others than Raynal. Quérard, who discusses the charges of collaboration in the book's authorship, states that Péchmaja claimed to have written the part on the slave trade and slavery.[23]

Raynal admitted that masters might often be kind to their slaves. He gave the French credit for treating their slaves better than did the British. The Dutch and Danes, like the English, chained their slaves in transit, because of the small number of their crews. The churches he criticized, saying that the Protestants left the slaves in Mohammedanism or whatever religion they brought from Africa. The Catholics, though careful to baptize them and give them some religious instruction, did no more for them.[24] Surprisingly little criticism of the church was made by the opponents of slavery, although they considered it as inconsistent with Christianity. This escape from criticism was perhaps due to the church's acting as a moderating force, insisting on kindly treatment of the slave. It appears often to have taken the side of the slaves rather than that of the owners, although reportedly some of the Catholic orders themselves had slaves.[25]

The mortality of the slaves Raynal described as frightful. Aside from the large number that died in transit, about one-seventh of them died each year in the New World. One million four hundred thousand slaves in the colonies were all that remained, he declared, of nine million who had been transported there.[26]

Raynal condemned not only the slave trade but also slavery. The existence of slavery, he asserted, led to "all sorts of crimes." No reason for its existence could be set forth to justify it; but until some great revolution should come, he could see no way to terminate it. He called upon the sovereigns of the world to bring this revolution about. By uniting in a decision to refuse the continuance of this trade, it would cease. He hoped that some Negro leader would arise and lead the Negroes "to vengeance and

[23] Quérard, *La France littéraire*, VII, 473-75; Brissot, *Mémoires*, II, 84; Seeber, *Anti-Slavery Opinion*, 152-53.

[24] G. T. F. Raynal, *A Philosophical and Political History of the Settlements and Trade of the Europeans in the East and West Indies* (Edinburgh, 1782), IV, 41, 45-46.

[25] V. P. Malouet, *Collection de mémoires sur les colonies, et notamment sur le régime colonial* (Paris, 1801/1802), IV, 94-95.

[26] Raynal, *A Philosophical and Political History*, IV, 48.

slaughter." "Till this revolution takes place, the Negroes will groan under the yoke of oppression."[27]

The latest and most forceful opponent of slavery among the *philosophes* was the Marquis de Condorcet, who in 1781, under the pseudonym of Pastor Joachim Schwartz, published at Neuchâtel a scorching brochure entitled *Réflexions sur l'esclavage*. Why the staid mathematician and academician chose a pseudonym and a foreign city for publication is not clear, for opposition to slavery and the slave trade had become so widespread among thinkers of the era as to be almost universal; it was a tenet of enlightened despotism; and the French government so far as I know condemned no book or punished no author for attacking slavery. Since, however, he was member of two royal academies, Condorcet might have thought that he should not openly attack an institution that was supported by the government. Whatever the explanation, the little book made a vigorous impression, provoked a careful reply from Malouet, one of the ablest defenders of slavery, and went into a second and revised edition, at Paris, in 1788.

The year 1780 has been designated by C. L. Lokke as the dividing date in the century between the passing critical reflections and the concerted treatises attacking slavery and the slave trade.[28] The observation, although it may not hold in all cases, is a judicious one, and Condorcet's treatise may be considered among the earliest French antislavery pamphlets. It was dedicated, appropriately, to the Negro slaves, whom he addressed as "My friends" and called the victims of injustice—exploited, insulted, calumniated.

Condorcet chose no soft words. The transportation and ownership of slaves he called crime. He considered it worse than robbery. The masters as well as the slave traders were guilty of the most horrible cruelties. They were bestial in appetites. He even questioned whether persons upholding the cause of slavery deserved the designation of "men." He admitted that he had never visited the colonies, but this did not deter him from describing conditions that he believed to exist in them. He denied the common assertion of the defenders of slavery that labor in the colonies was too severe for the whites. He denied the claim that the slaves

[27] *Ibid.*, 54-61.   [28] *France and the Colonial Question*, 90.

were better treated in the colonies than they had been in Africa. He expressed wonder that the clergy did not deny the colonists the eucharist and absolution because of their barbarity, and he praised the courage of one unnamed French monk who had denounced the evil.[29]

To remedy the situation, he would end the slave trade at once and proceed toward gradual emancipation of the slaves according to a scheme that he set forth. To free all the slaves at once would be calamitous; the action should be gradual. Older Negroes, the crippled and incapacitated should be freed first; all slaves over fifteen years of age at the time of emancipation should be liberated at the age of fifty, unless they chose to continue working for their masters, and even then they should be paid for their labors; children of slaves under fifteen should continue in slavery until they reached the age of forty, when they should go free. Infants born to slaves after the emancipation date would be freed at thirty-five, and given six months' maintenance and food for life if crippled. Mulattoes were to be emancipated at birth, on the assumption that they were the children of the owner, and any slave woman who became pregnant by her master and any slave mistreated by his master was to receive immediate freedom and expense money. In addition to this, Condorcet would make it possible for a slave to buy his freedom prior to the normal time for emancipation under his scheme.[30]

The masters would receive no reimbursement whatever, since they had no right to exercise dominion over others. He did propose that the state float bonds and acquire funds for the needs of freed slaves in distress. In this category he would place Negro orphans, aged and disabled Negroes, and the victims of unemployment. To repay these bonds, the former masters would be subjected to a tax.[31]

Of course this scheme would have had no appeal to the slave traders and slaveowners. Condorcet was unwilling to recognize that they had heavy economic investments at stake. It is surprising to find the academician and *philosophe* so unwilling to see more than one side of the question. Herein he differed from

[29] *Oeuvres de Condorcet*, VII, 69-70, 82, 90, 96-97, 100, 102, 109, 111 and n., 120-25.
[30] *Ibid.*, 95-101, 104-105.   [31] *Ibid.*, 91-92.

the earlier *philosophes,* and one can detect a transition from the Age of Reason to the Age of Revolution. For Condorcet and other abolitionists of the 1780's began to insist on force as a means to action. It should be observed, however, that Condorcet was the first abolitionist of the period who had a clear-cut plan for emancipation. The others dealt in generalities. They advocated emancipation but wished it to be gradual. They had no set plan. Save for one other, none of the abolitionists had a scheme of monetary reimbursement for the owner such as the British later adopted in 1833; but then the British had the French Revolution to look back upon as a warning.

As editor of one or more journals early in the Revolution, and as a deputy to the National Convention, Condorcet had a chance to play a continued role in the movement. Unfortunately his active membership in the Girondin party led to his forced exile and suicide in the Reign of Terror, and he was unable to participate in the emancipation of the slaves in February, 1794. Before his death he wrote a book, posthumously published, entitled *Tableau historique des progrès de l'esprit humain,* a philosophical sketch of the history of civilization wherein he criticized modern slavery as worse than that of the ancients, and he praised the English and French philosophers of his age for espousing the cause of the Negro slave and demanding for him the consideration of a human being.[32] Condorcet must be rated as one of the most forceful opponents of slavery. He was confident that within a few generations the Negroes would enjoy the same privileges as the whites, and that only the matter of color would separate them.[33]

Closely associated with the *philosophes,* Turgot, intendant of Limoges, wrote a treatise in 1766, published three years later,[34] in which he sharply criticized slavery as inhumanitarian, unjust, and unprofitable. It was founded wholly on violence. The chief purpose of wars in ancient times, he wrote, "was to raise slaves that the conquerors forced to work for their own account or that

[32] Edition of 1900, pp. 100, 131.

[33] *Oeuvres de Condorcet,* VII, 113.

[34] *Les réflexions sur la formation et la distribution des richesses.* Seeber (*Anti-Slavery Opinion,* 101-102) says that it was first published in 1769 in *Ephémérides du citoyen,* and that Dupont in editing it took liberties of which Turgot disapproved.

they sold to others." He denounced modern slavery. In a letter to his friend Dupont de Nemours in 1770 he called it "an abominable and barbarous practice." He recognized that it might be beneficial to the slaveowner, though he considered it detrimental to society. He wished to see the slaves emancipated by a gradual process, through growth of enlightened public opinion rather than by government decree. He rejected the request of a wholesale merchant to permit the naming of a slave ship after him.[35] In his letter to Dupont he expressed his intention to write a longer treatise against slavery at some future date, but the demands on his time and his early death in 1780 did not permit the realization of his plan.

Other followers of the *philosophes* that attacked slavery were Mercier and Brissot. Mercier opened his attack in a book about the future, entitled *L'an deux mille quatre cent quarante* (1771), in which he pictured a magnificent statue erected to the memory of a great Negro hero who had arisen and removed the shackles from his compatriots in the New World "oppressed under the most odious slavery." These had rallied around him and had smitten their oppressors—French, English, Dutch, Spanish, and others. Mercier rejoiced.[36] He pictured the Negro as hating the white man, and the Negro woman as destroying her offspring rather than rear them to slavery. He described the master, on his part, as carrying fear in his heart and as enjoying no real happiness. He blamed "the virtuous Las Casas" for having introduced Negro slavery in the New World, but said that he did so in an attempt to aid the Indian, not realizing that it would be used against the African to such an extent. He praised the Quakers for having freed their slaves, and Philadelphia for being without slavery. He suggested further emancipation, by the owners themselves.

He feared, however, that emancipation could come only through violence. He reported that many runaway slaves had gone into the northern parts of North America, there formed communities, and would sooner or later seek revenge. As for the slave trade, which every year sent about one hundred thousand

[35] *Oeuvres de Turgot et documents le concernant*, II, 533-34, 545-48; III, 378; IV, 90.
[36] London edition of 1771, pp. 147-48.

unfortunate beings across the sea, he hoped that some Negro leader would arise in Gambia or Senegal to end it.[37]

He was one of several who denounced the use of slavery for the production of Europe's sugar supply. Both Negroes and sugar cane, he said, came from Africa, and neither did so well in the New World as in Africa. He pictured the world's sugar supply in the year 2440 as coming from Africa, where cane grew luxuriantly without cultivation.[38]

A fecund writer, Mercier produced many plays, but his reputation was made by *The Year 2440* and the *Tableau de Paris,* both of which went into repeated editions. He also was a journalist in the Revolutionary period and a member of the National Convention. His role as an advocate of emancipation was displayed in several of his writings and also in his political career.[39]

Brissot was an admirer of Rousseau, and like him the victim of a persecution complex. He wanted to rectify the evils of the world and to make a name for himself. Though an admitted follower of the *philosophes,* he criticized them in his *Mémoires* as hypocrites in their claims to humanitarianism, saying that in the showdown they stood by their self-interest. His first attack on the slave trade was in his prize essay of 1781, the *Théorie des lois criminelles,* in which he gave a passing slap at "the infamous traffic in slaves."[40] In 1788 he took the leading part in forming in Paris, on the model of a body he had seen in London, the *Amis des Noirs,* the abolitionist society that was to play so vital a role in the Revolution. In 1788, in order to assure himself that his opposition to slavery had some foundation, he made a visit to Philadelphia, and came back more resolute than ever to attack the evil. Thenceforth he played the part of Saint George against the dragon, but this story must be related with events of the Revolution. He did issue, prior to the Revolution, a caustic reply to the Marquis de Chastellux, who proposed to solve the problem by exporting most male Negroes and encouraging marriages be-

[37] Paris edition of 1799/1800, III, 77-81.

[38] *Ibid.,* 7-8.

[39] In 1791 he was coeditor with Carra of the *Annales patriotiques et littéraires de la France, et affaires politiques de l'Europe.* This journal in its issue of Feb. 8, 1791, carried a long article on the "Colonie de Cayenne," in which the blame for all the colonial disorders was placed on the governors.

[40] *Mémoires,* I, iii, 38, 122-23, 147-48, 220.

tween white males and the Negro women, setting free every slave woman who so married.[41]

The *philosophes* and their imitators were far from being the only ones to espouse the cause of the slave, but they deserve prior attention in this chapter because unquestionably they were the leaders in the French antislavery movement of the eighteenth century. The score or two of other writers who participated are given some description in the able doctoral dissertation by Professor Seeber, already cited, which though inclining toward brevity treats the subject rather completely save for the mass of allusions in periodical literature of the period. That is barely touched and would perhaps be significant enough for a doctoral dissertation in itself. In the brief limits of this chapter only the more important figures and phases can be considered.

In the interest of setting forth the role of the *philosophes* I have done some violence to chronological considerations. Among those that took an active role prior to certain of the *philosophes* was Bernardin de Saint-Pierre (1737-1814), the pre-Romanticist author of certain very popular novels, *Paul et Virginie* and *La chaumière indienne*. Bernardin was a wide traveler. Always shy and inclined to disagree with others, he was trained as a youth by tutors. Afterward he received one year's training in the military engineering college at Mezières. Thenceforth he held a series of posts as a government engineer in various parts of the world. Some writing that he did about 1768 attracted the attention of the king, and he was offered a post on the Isle de France, off Madagascar, which he accepted and filled for several years. Because of his attitude on slavery, he was not popular with the other French on the island. Already interested in the slave question, he welcomed the chance to view the slave trade and slavery at first hand. He was confident before setting out that the condition of the slaves was terrible, for in a letter written from Lorient, Brittany, January 4, 1768, prior to his embarkation he told a friend: "I have seen the peasant in Holland rich, at his ease in Prussia, in a supportable condition in Russia, and in extreme poverty in Poland. I shall now see the Negro, who is the peasant of our colonies, in a deplorable situation." This letter,

[41] Seeber, *Anti-Slavery Opinion*, 158-59.

with others written during the next year from the South Seas, was later published in 1773 in a travel account, entitled *Voyage à l'Isle de France*.[42] The book was published anonymously in Switzerland, like Condorcet's some years later.

In a letter of April 25, 1769, from Isle de France, Bernardin depicted the slave trade as he had seen it on Madagascar, and slavery as he had found it on the Isle de France. The slaves he portrayed as simple, happy, hospitable people, not without certain skills, suffering under the most cruel oppression. Flogged unmercifully, both male and female, sometimes even to two hundred lashes on their naked backs, they prayed for their masters and their masters' families, they drank their own blood for wine, they induced miscarriage so as not to bring children into a cruel world, they danced at night in secret assemblies, and dispersed on the approach of any whites. The Code Noir existed as a law to protect them but its terms, he stated, were not enforced. Sometimes when they were old their heartless masters sent them to take their own lives. He told of seeing one cutting meat for food from a dead horse.[43] His language was written to convey deep emotion.

So cruel was the treatment of the slaves, he related, that some took their lives by poisoning, others set out in pirogues without food in an endeavor to return to Madagascar, and still others fled into the forests, chased by posses with bloodhounds. If caught, they were brought back "like savage beasts," scourged, and an ear cut off. After a second offense, they were again scourged, hamstrung, and chained. For a third offense, the penalty was hanging, but he said that their masters forewent this, since they had much money invested in them. He reported having witnessed several executions by hanging and breaking on the wheel. The slaves welcomed even these means of release from life. When runaways could not be captured, they were fired upon, and their heads were cut off and borne back in triumph on a stick. Such scenes he claimed to have witnessed weekly.[44]

He scoffed at the idea that such punishments were necessary. He criticized the clergy for acquiescing in such conditions, and

[42] *Voyage à l'Isle de France, à l'Isle de Bourbon, au Cap de Bonne-Espérance, avec des observations nouvelles sur la nature et sur les hommes, par un officier du roi* (Neuchâtel, 1773), pt. I, 9.

[43] *Ibid.*, 134-37.   [44] *Ibid.*, 138-41.

the *philosophes* (Bernardin was an *antiphilosophe*) for not speaking out more sharply. He reminded his European readers that their coffee and sugar were luxuries produced by slave labor. And he asked why white laborers could not perform the same work. European carpenters, masons, roofers, and other artisans worked in the colonial sun; why could not the whites till the plantations also? The landowners feared to use them, he said, lest they should lose their lands to them.[45]

The attack was continued in his *Etudes de la nature* (1784), an elaborate study on natural history, wherein he reminded Europeans once again that the coffee, sugar, and chocolate which they enjoyed were due "to some Indians totally nude, to some poor peasants, [and] to some miserable Negroes."[46]

In his novels *Paul et Virginie* (1788) and *La chaumière indienne* (1791) he again took up the cause. Both were romances, idealizing people of little education and scoffing at racial and class differences. The former was a drippy story recording the love between a boy and a girl of the widest social differences who had been taken to Isle de France, and who persisted in love despite the fact that the girl was sent back to France to receive a "finishing" education. Pictures of slavery appeared incidentally in the book. Paul's and Virginia's mothers were generous toward their slaves, and in consequence were beloved, in contrast to other slaveowners. The book's popularity was enormous, and readers wept as they read. To call it an eighteenth-century *Uncle Tom's Cabin* might be an exaggeration, but it tended in that direction. *La chaumière indienne* gave promise of the same success, for within eight or ten days after its publication a pirated edition appeared in Paris.[47] Summarizing, it may be said that Bernardin de Saint-Pierre must be rated as a major advocate of removing the shackles of slavery and the slave trade.

A different approach to the problem was made by the Marquis de Lafayette, who resorted not to propaganda but to experimentation. In 1785, shortly after the American Revolution, he suggested to Washington that they buy a farm together in the American colonies and experiment at emancipating slaves. If success attended the enterprise, he would carry the plan to the

[45] *Ibid.*, 141-44.   [46] *Etudes de la nature* (new ed., Bar-le-Duc, 1878), 20.
[47] *Mercure de France*, Feb. 19, 1791, p. 111.

French West Indies and work to make it popular there. Washington, however, did not share his interest, and the plan was not tried. Later, in February, 1786, he wrote Washington that he had purchased a plantation and sixty slaves at Cayenne, French Guiana, and would experiment there. His wife, who shared his zeal, assumed direct control of the enterprise, and a Frenchman called Richepry, also an enthusiast, offered his services free to oversee the farm. It was Lafayette's design to free the slaves gradually; he considered that it would be folly to free them at once. He still held his farm and slaves when the Revolution occurred, and he was censured as a hypocrite in May, 1791, by one of the aristocrats in a debate before the National Assembly affecting the race question. Lafayette held his silence, but reply was made for him the next day by Victor Henry, brother of Richepry, in a letter published in the *Moniteur universel*. Henry assured the public of Lafayette's noble intentions, and cited as witness a certain Lescalier of the colonial office who had been directed by De Castries, minister of the marine, to protect the experiment. The enterprise indeed had no influence: the Revolution came too swiftly. Lafayette, however, did exert some influence indirectly as an active member of the Amis des Noirs.[48]

The French Protestants are reported to have taken divergent stands on the slave question.[49] Those who resorted to writing appear to have opposed slavery and the slave trade. Necker in his *Administration des finances* denounced the two institutions as inhumanitarian, but declined to advocate their abolition lest the British might benefit at France's expense in international trade. He suggested that the slave trade should be abolished by concert of all the nations.[50] Jaucourt, Diderot's Protestant assistant, contributed certain articles to the *Encyclopédie* that were critical of the twin institutions. André Daniel Laffon de Ladebat, son of a Bordeaux shipowner and a graduate of the Dutch Uni-

[48] Henry Dwight Sedgwick, *Lafayette* (Indianapolis, 1928), 128-45; *Mémoires, correspondance et manuscrits du Général Lafayette*, II, 139-40, 152; III, 72; *Correspondance inédite de La Fayette, 1793-1801: lettres de prison—lettres d'exil; precédée d'une étude psychologique, par Jules Thomas* (Paris, 1903), 195; *Réimpression de l'ancien Moniteur*, VIII, 374, 433-34. Later he served as vice-president of the American society for colonizing Liberia with mulattoes.

[49] Henri Lohr, *Les Protestants d'autrefois: sur mer et outre mer* (Paris, 1907), 57-58.

[50] *Administration des finances* (n.p., 1785), I, 332-34; Lokke, *France and the Colonial Question*, 77.

versity of Franeker, published an abolitionist pamphlet in 1788;[51] and the famous American Quaker, Anthony Benezet, born in Picardy, was the author of several antislavery pamphlets, some of which were translated into French for influence in France. The most notable of the Protestant writings on the matter, however, was a two-volume treatise by Benjamin Sigismond Frossard published at Lyons in 1789, entitled *La cause des esclaves nègres et des habitans de la Guinée.*

Of Swiss birth like Necker and Clavière (also opponents of slavery) Frossard had been educated at the University of Geneva and had come to Lyons as pastor of a Huguenot church. There in 1782 Brissot had visited him, as the latter recorded in his *Mémoires,* and attended a Protestant service at which Frossard presided. When the central schools were set up in the 1790's he became a teacher in that at Clermont-Ferrand, and in 1809 he became dean of the faculty of theology at Montauban. Already in 1789 he was a recipient of many high honors, among them a doctorate in laws from Oxford University.

His treatise well exhibited his abilities. It was not only the longest but in several respects the ablest of the French antislavery writings of the period. It was as much the work of a scholar as of a propagandist. Remarkably well organized and written, the piece began with a historical account of slavery before discussing the various economic, political, and moral aspects. He sought always to be fair, and alone among those who would see slavery destroyed he would reimburse the slaveowners.[52]

He did not think that the time had yet come for emancipation. The slaves were too uncivilized. They needed both educational and religious instruction first. They must be taught the duties of citizenship. The civilization of which they stood in need did not have to be great, but enough that they might become satisfactorily integrated into society. The whites, too, must learn to regard the Negroes as their equals. They should receive instruction on this point.[53]

---

[51] Alfred Leroux, "Histoire externe de la communauté des religionnaires de Bordeaux de 1750 à 1789," *BSHPF*, LXVIII (1919), 40-41. Laffon's brochure was entitled *Discours sur la nécessité et les moyens de détruire l'esclavage dans les colonies.* Laffon was a writer on economic matters and a member of three academies.

[52] *La cause des esclaves nègres*, II, 257-60.   [53] *Ibid.*, 251-54.

In regard to emancipation, he suggested that slaves born in the colonies be freed first, since they would be more content to remain. He thought that a scheme of gradual emancipation by which slaves might be enabled to purchase their own freedom within a period of fifteen years might be practical. A law should be made to this effect and the government oversee its workings. He would set up a bank to handle the savings of slaves and to make payments to the masters. He would free all slaves who had borne five children in marriage while in their master's service, since Frossard considered that the master was amply reimbursed in the children. As for the children born in slavery, he would have them serve their master until he was recompensed for their rearing. Similarly he would free all Negresses who had borne three living children, after they had served their master fifteen years or after they had purchased their freedom (at the rate fixed by law). Every mulatto child he would free on birth, and the father if known should be compelled to bear the expense of rearing him.[54] Slave children should be freed with their parents if they had been at no cost to the slaveowner. Thus can be seen Frossard's attempt to be fair. Max Weber might have commented that it was not by accident that these economic considerations should have been made by a Calvinist.

Travelers contributed to the antislavery literature. Père Labat, around 1728, had published a five-volume *Relation de l'Afrique occidental,* in 1730 had edited the *Voyage du chevalier Desmarchais en Guinée, îles voisines et à Caienne,* and in 1735 had translated and published in France Antoine Cavazzi's *Relation historique de l'Ethiopie occidentale.* Although he held no high opinion of the Negro and was a slaveowner himself, each of these works had its criticisms of slavery or the slave trade. Operating also to discourage a dislike for slavery was Pierre Raymond de Brisson's account of his shipwreck off the west coast of Africa and his captivity among the Arabs. Slavery he painted as cruel.[55] More caustic, however, was the two-volume account of wanderings among the Hottentots and other Negroes of South Africa by François Le Vaillant, published in 1790.[56] A great admirer

[54] *Ibid.,* 256-57, 268-77.
[55] *Histoire du naufrage et la captivité de M. de Brisson. . . . Avec la description des déserts d'Afrique, depuis le Sénégal jusqu'à Maroc* (Paris, 1785).
[56] *Voyage de M. Le Vaillant dans l'intérieur de l'Afrique par le Cap de Bonne Espérance, dans les années 1780, 1781, 1782, 1783, 1784, et 1785* (Paris, 1790).

of the Negroes as simple, happy, hospitable people, Le Vaillant hated the whites as their enslavers. To him the slave trade was a revolting commerce. He disliked the civilization of the white man and considered that it corrupted the Negro wherever the two peoples came in contact.[57] The book was given a long and favorable review in the *Mercure de France* by Carra, who pointed out the author's attitude on the slave question.[58] The *Mercure de France,* the leading French literary journal in the 1780's and early 1790's, gave favorable reviews to a number of abolitionist writings, and thus aligned itself on the humanitarian side.

The travel accounts here designated are but a few of the many published during the century. Books of travel were one of the most popular forms of eighteenth-century literature. Europeans greedily read of the strange peoples in far-off parts of the world and of the experiences of travelers among them. Some of this literature discussed Africa and the Americas; some touched on slavery; but it all tended to make the European interested in the Negro and in the slave question.[59]

A singular contribution to the movement was made by a former slave having some education. He was Ottobah Cugoana, from the Guinea Gold Coast, captured by other Negroes, sold on Grenada in the English Antilles, and in time purchased and liberated by Lord Hoth, who carried him to England. There he obtained employment with the painter Cosway, doubtless as a butler, and was prevailed on to write his experiences and impressions of the slave trade. The book was published at London in 1787 under the title of *Thoughts and Sentiments of the Evil and Wicked Traffic of Slavery,* and a French translation appeared the next year in Paris. The language and style were clearly those of an English "ghost writer" and abolitionist. Cugoana's name was signed merely to give the book more weight. The book abounded in Biblical references and in appeal to the religious spirit. Both the slave trade and slavery were bitterly denounced, and the author appealed for their immediate abolition.[60]

---

[57] Paris edition of 1932, abridged, with introduction by Jacques Boulenger, I, 123, 124. In his introduction (p. xviii), Boulenger says that he has expurgated some of Le Vaillant's tirades on the slave trade and some of his eulogies on the savages.

[58] Issue of March 20, 1790, pp. 57-81.

[59] Several dozen are listed by Seeber in *Anti-Slavery Opinion,* 49.

[60] *Thoughts and Sentiments on the Evil and Wicked Traffic of Slavery* (London, 1787), 26, 118-22, 130.

Actually this was but one of a series of British and American antislavery books translated and published in France shortly before and early in the Revolution. The abolitionist writers in these three countries considered themselves comrades in arms in a cause that they regarded as international in scope. It was common for them to correspond with one another. The French abolitionist society in 1790 reported to the National Assembly that it had translated and published in French thirty-four pamphlets on the slave question.[61] Included were Wesley's *Thoughts on Slavery*, Benezet's *Historical Picture of Guinea* and *A Caution to Great Britain and her Colonies*, Clarkson's *Essay on Slavery and the Commerce of the Human Species*, various sermons, letters, parliamentary reports and debates, and other matters. All were designed to appeal to the cultured class in France that molded public opinion, revealing to it how thinkers in England and America were gravely interested in the same problem.

The chief way in which the British influenced the French movement was in the formation of the Société des Amis des Noirs. In 1787 the English had organized in London an abolitionist society, and Brissot, a foreign correspondent in England, was greatly impressed with it and the next year organized the French group after its model. Though a man with small reputation, he was burning with zeal, and he obtained for the Société within a year or two, through his own solicitation and that of his friends, a membership of 141, for the most part drawn from the influential classes. It came to embrace thirty-three members of the higher nobility, eleven of the lower nobility (important judges), twenty-six financiers, some fashionable women, abbés, writers, journalists, and others. Among its members were Lafayette, Mirabeau, Condorcet, Clavière, Pétion, Grégoire, the Duc de la Rochefoucauld, Lavoisier, Volney, Carra, Bergasse, and Sieyès. Not all were charter members. At the first meeting, on February 19, 1788, only twelve were present, but the number rapidly grew. Brissot induced Lafayette to become one of the earliest members, and in April, 1788, Condorcet. Each of these persuaded a number of high-placed friends to join. Condorcet was president for two periods of several months each in the first two years of the club, although he was not its first president. Ber-

[61] Seeber, *Anti-Slavery Opinion*, appendix, 197-99, reproduces the list.

nardin de Saint-Pierre declined to become a member, as also did Brienne, then controller general of finance, and President Jefferson of the United States. The latter two expressed their personal sympathies but stated that their official positions forbade their joining. Mirabeau, Bergasse, Volney, and Raynal did not long remain members. Brissot charged that Mirabeau used the club merely for his own advantage, and likewise criticized others who declined membership or resigned. Mirabeau, however, was unjustly criticized, for Brissot himself recorded that he was most responsible for the success of the club in its publication of books, British and French, on slavery. Mirabeau likewise displayed activity as a journalist and a deputy to the National Assembly on behalf of the cause. The club corresponded with the British society and with societies in the United States and elsewhere. From its inception it played a very active role. Brissot, in his *Mémoires,* ascribed its founding largely to his republican sentiments and his desire to sweep away the monarchy. He attributed the Revolution in considerable part to it.[62] The Amis des Noirs continued their existence until 1799, after having directed the French campaign against slavery and the slave trade throughout that period.[63]

Brissot, Condorcet, and others of the Amis des Noirs considered that they were directing the movement, but this idea has been challenged in our own day by M. Gaston Martin, leading French scholar on the history of the slave trade. He considers that Brissot and their group gullibly swallowed British economic propaganda designed to cripple French colonial trade. Britain had just lost her American colonies, an important setback in her economic rivalry with France, and the government through its Clarksons, Wilberforces, and Granville Sharpes peddled the soft philanthropic propaganda that would help to readjust the situation.[64] He points out that Britain no longer had need of many slaves, as she had only a few islands in the Caribbean where she could use them. It would be better for her in the future to con-

---

[62] Claude Perroud, "La société française des Amis des Noirs," *RF,* LXIX (1916), 145; Léon Cahen, "La Société des Amis des Noirs et Condorcet," *RF,* L (1906), 482-83; Brissot, *Mémoires,* II, 22-23, 54, 56, 71-110.

[63] Perroud, "La société française des Amis des Noirs," LXIX, 147.

[64] Gaston Martin, "La doctrine coloniale de la France en 1789," *Cahiers de la Révolution française,* III (1935), 38-41.

centrate on commerce, not colonial production. And if she could ruin French colonial production, so much the better.

Prior to the French Revolution, it appeared to be generally regarded, both in Britain and in France, that if the slave trade and slavery were abolished it must be done as a joint undertaking of both countries, lest the country retaining them would enjoy an advantage. Necker expressed the view in his *Administration des finances* (1785). Pitt, the British minister, shrewdly enough in 1787 proposed to Montmorin, French minister of foreign affairs, that the two governments unite in halting the slave trade. Montmorin, in a letter of January 5, 1788, declined.[65] Ironically, though the French abolished the slave trade in 1793 and slavery in early 1794, the British waited until 1807 before abolishing even the slave trade. Lafayette wrote from a German prison to Clarkson on January 27, 1798, expressing his bitter disappointment that Pitt, though he commanded a majority in both houses of Parliament, had neglected to pass a bill ending the slave trade. Clearly he questioned Pitt's sincerity.[66]

It is not without interest that in 1775 De Sartine, minister of the marine, had sent Bégouen, one of the leading shipowners of Le Havre and a native of Santo Domingo, on a mission to discuss colonial commerce and the slave trade with representatives of the colonies and the leading French Atlantic seaports. Bégouen in his report in April, 1776, declared that abolition of the slave trade appeared likely, and that it would be unfortunate for France. He and the representatives with whom he talked agreed that France should revert to a monopoly of her colonial trade, suppressing her free ports.[67] This does not indicate that the French government considered the abolition of slavery but that it was alert to the movements of the day.

Naturally the attacks on slavery and the slave trade provoked

[65] Lokke, *France and the Colonial Question*, 69-70.

[66] *Correspondance inédite de La Fayette, 1793-1801*, 329-31; Lokke, *France and the Colonial Question*, 152-60. The latter discusses some writings by Arthur Young and Jeremy Bentham urging the French to discard their colonies. On the economic importance of the slave trade and slavery to Britain and France, see Michael Kraus, *The Atlantic Civilization: Eighteenth-Century Origins* (Ithaca, 1949), 21-22.

[67] Département de la Seine-Inférieure, *Cahiers de doléances du bailliage du Havre (sécondaire de Caudebec) pour les Etats Généraux de 1789* (Epinal, 1929), 85-86.

reply. Until after 1770, however, the abolitionist attacks were
so scattered and so lacking in bitterness as to be more or less
ignored by the slaveowners. An inane reply indeed was made in
1764 by J. Bellon de Saint-Quentin, a brochure of 174 pages, in
which the author upheld the right to own and buy slaves, saying
that French law permitted it, the Bible permitted it, and natural
law permitted it. He declared that slavery brought the Negroes
greater advantages in the New World than they had enjoyed in
the Old, and that it led to the salvation of their souls. He deplored the cry against slavery and the slave trade, saying that
slaves were "necessary for the cultivation of our colonies."[68] Evidently he was read by the antislavers for they made his arguments targets for demolition in their replies.

A much more able treatment of the conservative position was
set forth in 1776-1777 in a two-volume treatise by Hilliard d'Auberteuil, entitled *Considérations sur l'état présent de la colonie
française de Saint-Domingue.* Born at Rennes in 1751 and trained
as a lawyer, Hilliard was sent by the government to Santo Domingo in a judicial post and spent many years on the island. He
thus was better acquainted with the problem than nearly all the
men who wrote on it, and he made his book very informative.
He described conditions on the island as they actually existed,
and answered questions of every sort that a curious reader might
wish discussed. He described all phases of life, economic, agricultural, police, judicial, and military. One chapter even described the fertilizers that were used. He presented both sides
of the slave question, and some readers regarded him as being
in one camp, while others put him in the opposite. Actually he
was a moderate conservative, who wanted slavery retained but
drastic reforms made. He condemned slavery, saying that it rendered a master "proud, hasty, hard, choleric, unjust, cruel, and
made him insensibly to lack all the moral virtues." The slave, on
his part, had no recourse against ill treatment; he was a slave in
fact not only of his master but also of the public. He described
the Negro in Santo Domingo as a person with much native intelligence, goodness, kindness, and industry, who worked hard
for considerate masters, but under cruel masters was sullen and

[68] *Dissertation sur la traite et le commerce des nègres* (n.p., 1764), 2-3, 21-22,
61-62, 119.

inclined either to flee or commit suicide.[69] The women often produced abortions. Hilliard shared the view of the *philosophes* that the natural man was free of evils, and he said that the Negro's vices had come from contact with the white men. He declared that the whites feared their slaves, but without reason inasmuch as the Negroes were fundamentally good.

The Negroes, he reported, went into all types of work, and not agriculture alone. They did well as carpenters, watchmenders, goldsmiths, and other craftsmen. He did not consider them an inferior race.[70]

He discussed the prices of slaves, their frightful mortality (due, as he thought, to the severe climate rather than to their work), their religious superstition, their loyalty to a kind master, and the mixing of the races. He told of the mixed marriages and their unhappy results, saying that about three hundred white men on the island, some of aristocratic birth, had married mulatto wives. Not only were the wives not accepted by the whites socially, but the husbands who married them also lost caste. Down to the sixth generation a child of mixed parentage was not accepted in social intercourse by the whites. Hilliard was in favor of preventing such marriages by law.

His solution to the unhappy situation on the island was for the creation of the mulattoes as a middle class, between the whites and the slaves. He would render freedom to all mulattoes and would force marriages between them and the free Negroes. No slave might thenceforth marry a mulatto, and no mulatto a white. At the same time, he would tighten the regulations concerning emancipation of slaves.[71]

He considered the political and judicial conditions on the island responsible for the existing unrest, but mentioned no names, and he had no difficulty in getting approval of the ministry of the marine for its publication, the ministry considering that he was actuated by high motives of reform. However, the book produced a storm, the ministry felt compelled shortly to withdraw its approval, a colonist named Dubuisson made a labored reply refuting point by point almost every assertion in the book, and some years later Hilliard was killed. One rumor had it that the assassin was hired by Dubuisson to do the job; another, that he

[69] Hilliard d'Auberteuil, *Considérations*, I, 130-46.   [70] *Ibid.*, 141.
[71] *Ibid.*, 54, 67, 73, 79-80, 83, 87-89, 142n; II, 67-69.

was killed or died in prison, having been put there by the colonists. This was in 1785, when men in disagreement were losing calmness of reason. Hilliard wrote certain other books and was a young man of high type. He wanted reform, and it is on men like him that a country must depend for reform. His book, however, did not die, and was very influential. According to a letter by his publisher, pasted in the copy in the Bibliothèque Nationale, Hilliard spent ten years in research for the book, in the colonial archives and on the island.[72]

Another significant defense of the slaves was published late in 1788 by Pierre Victor Malouet, in reply to the second edition of Condorcet's *Réflexions*.[73] Early in life Malouet had spent five years in Santo Domingo on a government job, and there had married the daughter of a planter, becoming a slaveowner himself. Returning to France in 1773, he was later sent on a mission to Guiana, where he became better acquainted with the colonial problem. At the time of writing this brochure he was intendant of Toulon. Here was a man, like Hilliard d'Auberteuil, familiar with colonial conditions. Like Hilliard, too, he saw the problem from two sides, and was destined to be criticized by some in both groups who considered him in the opposite camp.[74]

Santo Domingo at the time of his sojourn (1768-1773) was governed by a brother of the Cardinal de Rohan, a weak administrator. Idleness, lack of discipline, discontent, and injustice prevailed. Malouet in 1775, with backing from De Sartine, tried, without success, to initiate some reforms. The administrators, however, did not want reform, and he merely acquired the reputation of being "an exaggerated *philosophe*, a friend of the blacks." Later in life he looked back ruefully on the failure, believing that his proposed reforms might have operated to save the colony for France.[75]

---

[72] Dubuisson's reply was entitled *Nouvelles considérations sur Saint-Domingue, en réponse à celles du M.H.D.* (Paris, 1780). Dubuisson wondered how anyone could have spent so long a period in the colony and still be so ignorant of actual conditions. A sketch of Hilliard d'Auberteuil may be found in *NBG*, XXIV, 694-95.

[73] *Mémoire sur l'esclavage des nègres, dans lequel on discute les motifs proposés pour leur enfranchissement, ceux qui s'y opposent, et les moyens practicables pour améliorer leur sort* (Neuchâtel, 1788).

[74] *Mémoires*, I, 31-34; Lokke, *France and the Colonial Question*, 83-85.

[75] Malouet, *Collection de mémoires sur les colonies*, IV, 125; *Mémoires*, I, 370-72.

Malouet agreed that slavery was a cruel institution and eventually must go. For the present, however, it was essential. The climate was too hot for the white man to do the work demanded in the colonies. It was even necessary to continue the slave trade. He would emancipate the slaves by degrees. Even in the unhappy condition in which they existed, the slaves were better off in the colonies than the poor whites. To free them as the abolitionists proposed would constitute a colossal problem. How would they be housed and employed as day laborers? He could see no answer. What was needed, he insisted, was betterment of conditions rather than emancipation.[76]

Malouet lived to become a distinguished man. He was, in turn, a deputy to the National Assembly, a refugee, and briefly under the Restoration, minister of the marine. As deputy to the National Assembly he took an active part in the debates of that body concerning colonial matters.

Thus stood the agitation over slavery on the eve of the Revolution. It had developed rapidly since around 1770, with men of all social ranks and types of training taking part. All of the participants considered themselves humanitarians, even those who advocated continuance of slavery and the slave trade. All or virtually all damned the twin institutions as cruel and undesirable; they would have liked to see them eliminated. But they disagreed on when and how it could be done. The proponents of abolition advocated, almost without exception, immediate cessation of the slave trade, without indemnity to the shipowners and others engaged in it. In regard to slavery proper, none advocated instant, wholesale emancipation. It would be impossible, as it would create for the Negro conditions that would be calamitous. The slaves must be freed gradually. But almost without exception the abolitionists had no concrete plans for this emancipation. Condorcet and Frossard were the only ones with sensible plans, and even Condorcet regarded the matter wholly from the side of the slaves. To the slaveowners, who would lose heavily in their invested funds, he would make no reimbursement whatever. They were regarded merely as some holders of stolen property, which the state should retrieve. The spirit of concession was wholly absent. Frossard took a fairer stand. As the Revolution

[76] *Collection de mémoires sur les colonies*, IV, 8, 11-13, 125, 136.

approached, the spirit of bitterness and intolerance became more and more evident. The abolitionists already were considering that the slaveowners were part and parcel of the elements of the Old Regime that controlled France, and that they must be given a blow. To get rid of slavery and the slave trade and to reform France were aspects of the same ideal. Such was the situation in 1789.

CHAPTER FIVE

Exit Slavery
and the Slave Trade

THE YEAR 1789 marked a new era in the campaign to terminate slavery and the slave trade in that it was thenceforth a
political issue and not a matter of propaganda alone. The propaganda, far from being abated, made the slave question one of the
burning issues of the day.

The action that precipitated the political aspect was the call
for cahiers of grievances by the royal government at the outset
of 1789. Every little hamlet in France hastened to draw up its
list of complaints and suggestions for the country, and from the
thousands of these local cahiers some six hundred general cahiers
were shortly formulated. The slave question was far from being
one of the major demands; nevertheless, Miss Beatrice Hyslop,
in her study of the general cahiers, found that forty-nine called
for the abolition of slavery or the slave trade. Illustrative of the
fact that the desire for reform was not present in the middle class
alone, it is noted that only twenty of these forty-nine were of the
third estate, seventeen were of the clergy, eleven were of the
nobility, and one was made jointly by the third estate and the
nobility.[1] The demands came not from some one localized region
but from all parts of France, from little towns as well as the larger
cities. Paris and its neighborhood, however, sent more than did
any other generality.

To influence those drawing up the cahier, or cahiers, for the
city of Paris, Condorcet early in 1789 wrote a letter asking that
they include a demand for the cessation of the slave trade and
of slavery. He mentioned his membership in the Amis des Noirs

and stated that he wrote at their request. He demanded liberty
for 400,000 slaves, who with their families were "exposed to the
arbitrary rigor of their masters, deprived of all the rights of nature and of society, and reduced to the condition of domestic
animals." He called attention to the example of the United States
Senate, which had gone on record as saying that justice and
humanity demanded the freeing of the slaves. He was under the
delusion that slavery in the United States would quickly be terminated.[2] He was not the only member of the Amis des Noirs to
exert influence on the cahier from Paris. Jean Claude Antoine de
Bourge, another member, later asserted that he was responsible
as an elector for the inclusion of the clause in the cahier from
Paris asking for amelioration of conditions for the slaves, adding
that it was only an oversight that he did not also ask civil liberty
for the Jews.[3]

When the king sent out his order for the election of representatives to the Estates General, the colonies were not included. The
colonials, however, did not care to be excluded from a political
assemblage of such importance, and early in 1789 the three divisions of Santo Domingo duly selected representatives, all large
landowners, some already resident in France, and drew up a
cahier. Mlle. Muriel, editor of this cahier, says that "for a long
time the great planters of Santo Domingo had requested reforms,"
but they had more to do with economic and political matters than
humanitarian considerations.[4] When the Estates General assembled in May, the colonial delegation from Santo Domingo presented their credentials and request for admittance. Their right
to sit as representatives of the colony, however, was challenged
by representatives of a group of mulattoes from the colony who
also were resident in France and wished admittance.

The whites were seated, but only after a battle with the mu-

[1] *French Nationalism in 1789 according to the General Cahiers* (New York,
1934), 276-77. Cf. Gaston Martin, *Histoire de l'esclavage et les colonies françaises* (Paris, 1948), 171.

[2] *Oeuvres de Condorcet*, IX, 471-75. Necker in 1785 had estimated the slaves
in the French colonies at approximately 500,000. *Administration des finances*, I,
332.

[3] J. C. A. de Bourge, *Discours prononcé, le 30 janvier, dans l'assemblée générale
des représentants de la commune* (n.p. n.d.), 8-9.

[4] *Cahiers de doléances de la colonie de Saint-Domingue pour les Etats Généraux de 1789*, ed. by Blanche Muriel (Paris, 1933), 52-53. Cf. Léon Deschamps,
"La colonial représentation à la Constituante," *RF*, XXXVII (1903), 135-37.

lattoes outside the Estates General and friends of the Amis des Noirs within it. The first skirmish therefore was fought in the summer of 1789 and was won by the whites. The mulattoes, or more properly *gens du couleur,* since some were quadroons and octoroons, were not inclined to give up, even though the battle went against them. They were aware that in Santo Domingo were more than 30,000 of their number, and that there were 450,000 or more blacks, most of the latter being slaves, in contrast to a bare 30,000 or more whites.[5] Many of the mulattoes were free. Some had been recognized by their fathers, had been trained abroad, and had been left money. They stood on an intermediary level in the colonies between the whites and the slaves. In the colonies, some of the mulattoes, as indeed some of the Negroes, were slaveowners, but they possessed no political and social privileges. They might marry the whites in the colonies, but oddly as it might seem in France, where no other restrictions bore on them, they might not legally (after 1778) intermarry with whites.[6] Numerous mulattoes, possibly several hundred, were resident at this time in France, and in Paris their leaders constituted an ardent group within the Amis des Noirs. Their two most active members were Ogé, later leader of an insurrection in Santo Domingo, and Julien Raimond (or Raymond), author of many political brochures.

In September, 1789, the mulattoes drew up a cahier of thirty articles for presentation to the National Assembly, and on October 18 published it, more as propaganda than from hope for immediate success. They requested the right to sit in the assembly. They asked that civil rights be accorded all men of color and free Negroes. They did not ask that freedom be granted Negro slaves, save in instances when Negresses became pregnant by their master. In this case, they asked that the mother as well as the child become free, unless the master were insolvent. In the latter event, the mother would continue a slave. Fundamentally the mulattoes thought only of their own class in formulating the cahier. They

[5] Detailed estimates for the several French West Indian colonies are given by Herbert Ingram Priestley in *France Overseas Through the Old Regime* (New York, 1939), 267 n11. Necker in his *Administration des finances* (I, 330) reckoned the number of mulattoes on Santo Domingo at 7,055 and the Negroes there at 249,098.

[6] Isambert, *Recueil général des anciennes lois françaises,* XXV, 257-58; Muriel, *Cahiers de Saint-Domingue,* 84 n4.

were interested in raising their status to that of the whites, but for the slaves they were little concerned. This same outlook displayed itself subsequently in their pamphlets and other activities.[7]

Santo Domingo was not the only colony to select representatives for the Estates General. It was followed by Guadeloupe and Martinique in 1789, and by Isle de France and Pondichéry in 1790. The Isle of Bourbon, or Réunion, in 1790 expressed the wish for representation but did not name representatives. Martinique left the matter of selecting delegates to her citizens resident in Paris.[8] The mulattoes from these colonies in France, however, were either too few or too lacking in aggressiveness to enter battle with the whites for representation in the Estates General.

The National Assembly voted to accept the white delegations from the colonies.[9] No mulattoes were admitted. The opening battle accordingly was won by the whites. The action was protested by Condorcet, who denounced the right of the planters to represent their slaves. The colonial delegates, moreover, he declared, had been elected by only a portion of the inhabitants, and were not legal representatives. The free Negroes had had no part in their election. Therefore they should not be seated.[10]

The action seemed only to arouse the Amis des Noirs and the mulattoes to more determined effort. They published brochures as never before in the century; they entered the political clubs that came to be formed, above all the Jacobin; they made speeches whenever possible; and they sent delegations to present their cause to the National Assembly. In every way conceivable they brought their issue before the public by agitation. The drawing up of the Declaration of the Rights of Man and the Citizen, in August, 1789, gave them ground to hope for eventual victory. In September several mulatto leaders called on the planters at the Hôtel Massiac, the latters' headquarters in Paris,

---

[7] Julien Raimond was the author of ten or twelve pamphlets published at Paris on the matter between 1789 and 1795.

[8] A. Brette, "Les gens de couleur libres et leurs députés en 1789," RF, XXIX (1895), 330-32.

[9] The white delegates from Santo Domingo were seated in June and were limited to six; the two white delegates from Martinique were seated October 14, 1789. Réimpression de l'ancien Moniteur, I, 63; Georges Lefebvre, La Révolution française (rev. ed., Paris, 1951), 184.

[10] Oeuvres de Condorcet, IX, 479-85.

and strove for a compromise. Any compromise would have been a gain for them. None, however, was forthcoming.[11]

The white colonists on their part also were active. They and their friends likewise resorted to pamphlets, letters, delegations, speeches. On their behalf two delegations appeared before the National Assembly February 25, 1790, pleading for continuation of the slave trade lest the colonies be lost. Rumors had been going about Paris that Martinique was on the point of declaring her independence, and Santo Domingo, of opening trade with other nations. One of the deputations appearing on February 25 represented the National Guards of Bordeaux, the other the Chamber of Commerce of France. Talleyrand, presiding, replied that the National Assembly would investigate the matter "in its wisdom and justice."[12]

The developments were too slow for one of the mulattoes in Paris. Vincent Ogé, a quadroon from Santo Domingo, left France in the spring of 1790 to return and stir up insurrection in the colony. Before going he discussed his plans with Grégoire, who advised him strongly against the action, and with Clarkson in England, who urged caution. But he would not listen. He returned home by way of the United States, where he procured arms, and landing near Le Cap, Santo Domingo, on October 23, 1790, he began his insurrection the next day. With a force of two hundred to three hundred men, he made certain demands on the colonial assembly, and when they were not forthcoming, administered a defeat to colonial troops sent against him. Thereupon a larger force was sent and he was defeated. He and some of his subordinates succeeded in escaping to the Spanish part of the island, but because of a treaty between the Spanish and the French providing for the mutual return of fugitives, he and his confederates were turned over to the French. After a lengthy trial Ogé and three others were executed by breaking on the wheel, fourteen were hanged, and seventeen were sent to the galleys. Their goods were confiscated.[13] So terminated, in late

[11] Lucien Leclerc, "La politique et l'influence du Club de l'Hôtel Massiac," *Annales historiques de la Révolution française* (hereafter *AHRF*), n.s. XIV (1937), 344.

[12] *Journal de Paris*, Feb. 26, 27, 1790, pp. 225, 229-30.

[13] Brette, "Les gens de couleur," XXIX, 335; Brissot, *Mémoires*, II, 93-100; *Mémoires de Grégoire*, I, 396; *NBG*, XXXVIII, 550.

February, 1791, the unfortunate enterprise. It was unfortunate not only for Ogé and his followers, but also for the whites. From that event onward bloodshed became the order of the day on the island. Instead of suppressing insurrection, the brutal execution served but to fan it.

In Santo Domingo strife arose between the whites on the one side and the mulattoes on the other, but in Martinique the whites were divided among themselves, the merchants against the planters, the creditors against the debtors, and the mulattoes joined in the fray on the side of the merchants.[14] In the other colonies, too, dissension arose.

What complicated the situation was the development of political confusion in the colonies. The planter class in several of the colonies, Santo Domingo, Martinique, and Isle de France, took advantage of the confused political conditions in the spring of 1789 to set up colonial assemblies and draw up constitutions which would give the islands greater self-government and place them more under the king's immediate control than under the military governors and intendants that he sent out. The National Assembly for a time tolerated these assemblies but in the autumn of 1790 declared them dissolved, not, however, before a feud had developed between the assembly of Saint-Marc in Santo Domingo and the governor of that colony. The governor had dissolved the assembly by force. The National Assembly instituted the practice of governing the colonies by commissioners sent out from Paris. This provoked even more confusion.[15] All might have gone well had law and order prevailed, but the same spirit that agitated the underprivileged classes in France spread to those in the colonies. First the mulattoes and then the Negroes arose in revolt.

Even then all might have gone well for the colonial whites had they been willing to recognize a decree of May 15, 1791, by the National Assembly providing for the granting of civil rights to the mulattoes; but this they refused to do. In consequence the whites won the enmity of the mulattoes, who hitherto had more or less been allied to them in the islands, where they formed the

---

[14] *La vie et les mémoires du général Dumouriez* (Paris, 1822-1823), II, 73-75.
[15] Lefebvre, *La Révolution française*, 184-85.

militia under white officers. The stubborn attitude of the whites led the mulattoes to shift their support to the Negroes.[16]

The National Assembly did not go farther than to endow the mulattoes with civil rights. Neither slavery nor the slave trade was abolished, and of the mulattoes only those that already enjoyed freedom were given civil rights. Professor Lefebvre considers that it was granted as a concession to the mulattoes after the assembly had agreed, that same day, that henceforth it would legislate for the colonies only on colonial request.[17] The assembly was dominated by the planter group, called the Club Massiac. The subsequent Legislative Assembly went no further. It is quite likely that this condition of things would have continued, and that neither slavery nor the slave trade would have been abolished in the 1790's had not France become engaged in war in the spring of 1792 and the king removed from office after the events of August 9-10 of that year. Oddly as it may seem, the destiny of slavery and the slave trade was tied up with the fortunes of Louis XVI. When he went, they, too, were destined to go.

In the meanwhile the propaganda of the abolitionists, in pamphlets, speeches, letters, plays, novels, and even stamps,[18] brought the colonial question more than ever to the attention of the public. The abolitionists emphasized the inhumanitarian aspects of slavery and the slave trade. They kept hammering away at the same arguments they had been presenting for two or three decades, but in addition they pointed out that the ideals of the Revolution, more especially as set forth in the Declaration of the Rights of Man and the Citizen, were being ignored so far as the Negro was concerned. To the slaveholders and their party, the slave had no claim to citizenship inasmuch as he was a chattel. The abolitionists recognized that legally this was correct, but insisted that slavery must end, as inconsistent with the new era.

[16] As early as March 8, 1790, the assembly had decreed that mulattoes should be eligible to all ranks in the militia forces in the colonies. This earlier decree was vaguely worded, and the mulattoes had considered that it gave them full civil rights but the colonists did not so interpret it. This had incensed Ogé. *Réimpression de l'ancien Moniteur,* VII, 404; Brissot, *Mémoires,* II, 97; Brette, "Les gens de couleur," XXIX, 335; Lefebvre, *La Révolution française,* 184.

[17] Lefebvre, *La Révolution française,* 185.

[18] Ducasse, *Les négriers,* 185.

The slaveowners, large wholesale merchants, shipowners, and their class whose fortunes were tied to maintenance of the status quo had a tendency to ignore the humanitarian arguments of their adversaries and to emphasize the economic aspects of the situation. It was a period of economic crisis for France, and this crisis would be enormously accentuated were the colonies lost. For they insisted that the colonies would be lost, or at least that the colonial trade would be dealt a death blow, if either slavery or the slave trade were abolished. This trade, declared Roussillon, deputy from Toulouse and a wholesale merchant, had an annual value of 200,000,000 livres, while the total of French trade abroad, with her colonies and foreign countries, was only 512,-000,000 livres, based on average figures for the years 1786-1789. If the colonies should secede (evidently Roussillon conceived of the French colonies taking a cue from the recent action of the English in North America), the action would be catastrophic. He quoted many figures on the extent of French economic activity resting upon the colonial trade. Six hundred ships, he mentioned, with a tonnage of 200,000 were engaged in this trade. He advocated that the race question should be left to the colonies for solution.[19]

This same theme was followed by Malouet, Moreau de Saint-Méry, Gouy d'Arcy, and other leaders of the planter faction in the assembly. Malouet placed the trade with the colonies at "more than 200 millions." In one way or another it involved "more than twelve hundred ships, twenty thousand sailors, and more than four hundred thousand national workers or artisans." He did not deny that there were those who profited from the slave trade and slavery. They might be called brigands, but, he asked, did not all countries have such men? Instead of resort to abolition of slavery and the slave trade, even gradually, an action that would seriously damage the mechanism of the colonial trade, he advocated removal of the abuses in them.[20]

Mirabeau, who emerged during the period of the National Assembly, until his death in early 1791, as one of the leading abolitionists, scoffed at all this economic argument. He challenged the figures, in the first place. The merchants of Bordeaux

[19] *Réimpression de l'ancien Moniteur,* IX, 767.
[20] Malouet, *Collection de mémoires,* IV, 64, 86-87.

in 1790 sent a deputation to the assembly in behalf of maintaining the current situation, asserting that the colonial trade amounted to 250,000,000 livres annually, but Mirabeau pointed out that government statistics revealed that in 1787 total exports to the colonies amounted only to 74,000,000 livres, of which 24,000,000 represented goods having their origin in other countries than France. Adding to this 20,000,000 livres for imports from the colonies, the colonial trade in 1787 totaled only 94,000,000 livres. According to the same government figures, he declared, 47,000,-000 livres annually went into "the useless and fatal expense of Negroes furnished by the treaty," and he concluded that the balance sheet would reveal that actually only 39,000,000 livres came from colonial productions and might be called revenue.[21]

These variations revealed that the two sides could not agree even on statistics. In an endeavor to impress the assembly with their viewpoint, one or both sides distorted the figures to accommodate their propaganda.

Whereas Malouet declared that European workers could not endure the work demanded in the torrid French colonies, and cited his personal experience and observations, Mirabeau denounced such an idea. It was ridiculous to think that one people should exist merely to serve another, and should be transported across the seas, subjected to lash and the gallows, and then not be allowed to share in the fruits of their labors.[22] Mirabeau's ideas, as is well known, were presented to a broader public in his *Journal de Provence,* much of which he wrote himself.

An army officer, the Chevalier de Laborie, wrote a letter to the editor of the *Moniteur universel,* published in the issue of March 7, 1790, asserting that the freeing of the slaves in the colonies would result in a doubling of colonial production. He would employ Europeans on the sugar plantations.[23]

In a debate on the colonial question on May 7, 1791, Malouet and Moreau de Saint-Méry, the latter a deputy from Martinique, declared that propaganda from France was being disseminated in the colonies urging mulatto and Negro slaves to arise and

[21] *Mémoires,* VII, 187-88.

[22] *Ibid.,* 163-64; Malouet, *Collection de mémoires,* IV, 109, 110-11. It appears that Mirabeau's speech was not actually delivered, although he wrote it and attempted to deliver it.

[23] *Réimpression de l'ancien Moniteur,* III, 539.

strike off their shackles. They charged the Amis des Noirs with the responsibility for this action. Malouet declared that the *Chronique de Paris*, "a celebrated gazette," had been sent encouraging "soldiers and sailors of the fleet to scatter out over the plantations (*habitations*), and invite the Negroes to declare themselves free." The charge was denied by several members, but Malouet insisted upon its accuracy. He and Moreau declared that in consequence of this propaganda trouble was apt to break out in the colonies at any time and that France ran the risk of losing her colonial commerce. Conditions in the colonies, said Moreau, were different from those in France. They should be so recognized.[24]

A factor that gave encouragement to the abolitionists was the success of their movement in several other countries to abolish the slave trade. A fraternal tie, particularly existing among the abolitionists of France, Britain, and the United States, resulted in exchanges of visits and correspondence. In 1788 Brissot had visited the United States to study the conditions of slavery there; in 1789-1790 Thomas Clarkson, the noted British abolitionist, visited France and for several months lobbied against the slave trade with the delegates to the National Assembly without success. Throughout 1788-1789 the *Mercure de France* carried accounts, often lengthy, from its London correspondent concerning the activities of the antislavery society of that city.[25]

News came at the beginning of 1789 that the slave trade in Negroes had been abolished in Bengal by a proclamation of Lord Cornwallis on the previous August 2. Maret, editor of the *Moniteur*, asked why if Britain could afford to do this in the East Indies, France could not do it in the West Indies?[26] This was but one of several occasions where Maret revealed his sentiments.

The United States was reported to be moving in the same direction. A correspondent in New York wrote back to the *Moniteur* in July, 1794, that slavery had been abolished in all the states save Maryland, Virginia, the Carolinas, and Georgia, and stated that Congress had passed an act by which it should cease

---

[24] *Ibid.*, VIII, 333-34, 335.
[25] Issues of Jan. 5, 1788, pp. 21-23; Jan. 12, 1788, pp. 75-82; Feb. 16, 1788, pp. 107-108; Feb. 23, 1788, pp. 177-81; and May 30, 1789, pp. 205-13.
[26] *Réimpression de l'ancien Moniteur*, III, 1; XII, 66, 89, 206-207.

in them too by November 1, 1795.[27] Little did it matter, apparently, whether the news was always accurate. It was important that the impression get abroad that it was the correct thing for civilized countries to do.

In early 1792 the Danish government, by royal ordinance, abolished the slave trade in its possessions, to take effect after 1802. Until 1795 importers might bring in as many Negroes as they wished, and after that date any number of male Negroes, until 1802, the government offering subsidies in raw sugar. The details of this action were spread in two issues of the *Moniteur*.[28]

A novel feature in propaganda during the Revolution was the appearance of deputations before the legislative body, the commune of Paris, and even the political clubs. There were deputations of many types. On the question of slavery both sides sent deputations. On December 1, 1791, a deputation from Saint-Malo appeared before the Legislative Assembly to demand that the fire and bloodshed then raging in Santo Domingo be brought to an end, charging that six million French lived on trade with the colonies and that their fortunes were jeopardized.[29]

More impressive perhaps were the mulatto delegations. The mulattoes of Paris asked in March, 1791, to send a delegation before the National Assembly, but Arthur Dillon, deputy from Martinique, spoke sharply against allowing this, saying that this would lead to wholesale uprising in the colonies on the part of the mulattoes and Negroes. The request was accordingly refused.[30] The assembly had already agreed to let the colonies handle their own internal affairs. The Legislative Assembly, however, did receive a delegation of eight mulatto leaders on March 30, 1792. Raimond spoke for the group, pledging the loyalty of all the mulattoes in the colonies and vowing their readiness to serve France in any capacity at any time.[31] France

[27] *Ibid.*, XXII, 313. The editor of *Révolutions de Paris* (Prudhomme) declared that the United States in declaring independence freed the slaves (issue of Oct. 9-16, 1790, p. 15).

[28] Issues of March 28, April 12, 1792, pp. 97, 737. Fuller details may be found in the London *Universal Magazine* for April 1792, p. 313.

[29] *Réimpression de l'ancien Moniteur*, X, 517-21.

[30] *Annales politiques et littéraires de la France, et affaires de l'Europe*, March 5, 19, 1791, pp. 1129, 1190; Lokke, *France and the Colonial Question*, 131-32. Carra, editor of the *Annales*, reported Dillon's speech and took sharp exception to it. He was a member of the Amis des Noirs.

[31] *Réimpression de l'ancien Moniteur*, XII, 3.

at that moment was on the verge of war with Austria and an expression of loyalty was not unwelcome. Under the Convention, visits of mulatto delegations became frequent, and their influence significant.

Numerous letters by supporters of both sides were written to journals, and even to the president of the assembly. Some were read before that body. Apparently all were published. The journals, too, were made vehicles of the two parties, with the greater number supporting the abolitionists. In this group, among others, were the *Patriote française* of Brissot, the *Annales politiques* of Mercier and Carra, the *Journal de Provence* and the *Analyse des papiers anglais* of Mirabeau, the *Journal de Paris, Le lendemain,* the *Révolutions de Paris* of Prudhomme, the *Révolutions de France et de Brabant* of Desmoulins, the *Chronique de Paris* of Condorcet, and for a time the *Moniteur universel* of Maret.[32] On the side of the colonists were the *Journal du cour et de la ville,* the *Ami du roi* of the Abbé Royou, the *Actes des Apôtres,* and for the period of 1790-1792 the *Mercure de France,* whose political section was written by Mallet du Pan. The influence of the press during the Revolution was considerable. After the flight of the king in June, 1791, however, the royalist journals suffered loss of prestige, and after the removal of the king from active duties on August 10, 1792, they were forced out of existence. Royalist supporters found it expedient to leave France. Thus the linking of the slave party with the king led toward eventual victory for the abolitionists.

So bitter became the attitude of each party toward the other after 1789 that it is difficult for the historian to determine whether the abolitionists, for example, were more actuated by love of the Negro or hatred of the aristocrat. Caustic language was used by each side in speech, pamphlet, and journal. Each group blamed the other for the outbreaks in the colonies.[33] Grégoire charged that the government in Martinique condemned a certain Nadan to five years' servitude in the galleys for introducing into that

[32] The issue of the *Moniteur* for Jan. 21, 1790, p. 168, carried a letter from an irate colonist advising it to take no stand on the matter of slavery, pro or con. The action was evidently provoked by a highly favorable review of Frossard's two-volume work against slavery in the issue of Dec. 8, 1790. Thenceforth the *Moniteur* pursued a neutral course.

[33] See, e.g., *Mémoires de Grégoire,* I, 395-96; Malouet, *Collection de mémoires,* IV, 204-207.

colony copies of one of his writings addressed to the mulattoes and Negroes. This servitude Grégoire boasted of having broken when he became a member of the National Convention.

It is not surprising that in such a charged atmosphere violence broke out in the colonies. In Santo Domingo in August, 1791, the inflamed slaves sacked plantations, plundering, burning, raping, slaying.[34] Le Cap, the city where Ogé was executed, was burned. By the end of October, according to H. I. Priestley, "more than a thousand whites had been killed, while two hundred sugar plantations and twelve hundred coffee plantations had been burned." The slaves captured with arms were "hanged, burned, or broken at the wheel."[35] Mallet du Pan, in the *Mercure de France*, charged in reports from the colonies that the Negroes "had slain around 400 hundred whites, violated and killed the wives and daughters, sawed the inhabitants between two planks, and massacred even infants at the breast." Yet he added that a large number of the slaves had remained faithful.[36] About four thousand Negroes were reported killed. The uprising lasted several months, and led to the sending of three commissioners with supreme powers to the island in late 1791 by the National Assembly. The Legislative Assembly in 1792 replaced these by three of their own choice, all Jacobins—Santhonax, Polverel, and Ailhaud. Ailhaud soon returned to France, and the others ruled the island to the extent that the subsequent troubles there came to be laid to them, at least by the planter class.[37] To a certain degree this was true. They sent Blanchelande, governor of the colony, back to France. He was replaced after some months by General Galbaud, but the commissioners refused to recognize him and he found it advisable to return to France. Ere he sailed, however, fierce fighting developed at Le Cap between sailors of the fleet and the mulatto soldiers of the commissioners. For a time the sailors supporting Galbaud had the advantage, but the commissioners opened the city gates to Negroes and retreat was necessary. Galbaud and some ten thousand whites managed to

[34] Even in the autumn of 1789 the Negroes of Martinique were reported to be getting out of hand and killing a planter. Six were condemned to death at the wheel, and one to the gallows. So a colonist on November 18, 1789, wrote Moreau de Saint-Méry, in a letter printed in the *Journal de Paris*, Feb. 1, 1790, p. 128.

[35] Priestley, *France Overseas*, 331.   [36] Issue of Nov. 26, 1791, pp. 297-98.

[37] Lokke, *France and the Colonial Question*, 140; Priestley, *France Overseas*, 331-32; *Réimpression de l'ancien Moniteur*, XIX, 105-106.

pile on the fleet in the harbor and sail to the United States.[38] The incident led to a new outburst of insurrection by the mulattoes and slaves, and the new commissioners stood by with sympathy for the insurrectionists. After all, did they not represent the oppressed classes in France that had now removed the king? A holocaust resulted, greater than that of 1791. All save the poorest whites fled the island, some to France, but most to the United States to become recipients of government charity. T. Lothrop Stoddard has graphically described the insurrection,[39] and Miss Frances Childs the emigration.

The government had sent twenty-four hundred troops at the close of 1791, but they were too late, too few, and too mismanaged. The whole story of the Revolution, in the colonies as in France, was one of stupid bungling, and nowhere more so than in Santo Domingo.[40]

With all seemingly lost, the self-exiled planters, in a secret meeting in London, empowered Malouet to represent them in negotiations and offer the colony of Santo Domingo to the British government in return for a promise to subdue the insurrection. Malouet assured them that the cession would not be permanent. He has left a short account of his negotiations with the British Foreign Office, of the agreement reached, of the British expedition of ten thousand men to the island, of the heavy mortality and expenditure suffered by them during the next three years, and, the British tiring, of their return of the colony into his hands and those of Bouillé, with a heavy subsidy to engage Spanish mulattoes inured to the climate to carry on the fight. It all ended in failure. Malouet detailed his difficulties. He and Bouillé were delighted to see the Directory come into being and to turn over to it whatever power they possessed.[41]

Already the slaves had gained their freedom. The story of the treason of the planters had become known and was shouted from the housetops. Brissot, who had an uncanny way of learning the secrets of the planters, had long revealed that they were nego-

[38] Frances Sargeant Childs, *French Refugee Life in the United States, 1790-1800: An American Chapter in the French Revolution* (Baltimore, 1940), 14-15.

[39] *The French Revolution in Santo Domingo* (Boston, 1914).

[40] *Mercure de France*, Nov. 5, 1791; Lokke, *France and the Colonial Question*, 120-21.

[41] *Mémoires de Malouet*, II, 264-65, 277-79, 280-84.

tiating with the British.[42] The Negroes and mulattoes insisted that they were loyal to France and were fighting to preserve the colony. News to this effect was brought before the National Convention in dramatic manner February 4, 1794. Three deputies from the colony had just arrived in Paris the previous day—a Negro, a mulatto, and a white—and were received with honor. One of the trio was asked to report on conditions in the colony, which he did in superb manner, showing that while the planter class had made common cause with the enemy (the British), the mulattoes and Negroes were fighting desperately to hold the colony for France. He ended by calling upon the body to remember its promises to give the colonies "the benefits of liberty and equality."

The effect upon the audience was terrific. Danton made a short speech in favor of Negro freedom. A Negro delegation was introduced, and an old ex-slave woman, allegedly one hundred and one years of age, was helped down the aisle to the front, where the president of the Convention welcomed her with a kiss on each cheek. In this charged atmosphere Levasseur de la Sarte proposed a motion that slavery be ended in the colonies. He called for an immediate vote. In the French legislative bodies of the Revolution it was customary for all bills to be examined and reported back to it after study by a committee. In almost unprecedented fashion it was decided to take a vote on the spot, and in the vote that followed there was a unanimous decision in favor of the motion. In this theatrical manner the French abolished Negro slavery in their colonies. It had long been abolished in France proper, and in 1793 the slave trade had been abolished. The excitement continued after the vote, and there was much milling about and fraternization on the floor.[43]

The ironical feature about this action of liberation was that it was not what the Amis des Noirs wanted. Bishop Grégoire, who along with Brissot and Condorcet had for some years been one of the leaders of the movement, has informed us in his *Mémoires* that, to a man, all the Amis des Noirs hoped and worked for gradual emancipation, fearing the consequences that might fol-

[42] *Ibid.*, 200-203; *Réimpression de l'ancien Moniteur*, X, 520-21.
[43] *Mercure français, historique, politique et littéraire* (the transformed *Mercure de France*), Feb. 8, 15, 1794, pp. 292, 297-300; *Réimpression de l'ancien Moniteur*, XIX, 387-88 and n., 389-95.

low from an act of instant emancipation. But when the situation made total emancipation possible, they decided that they could not refuse it.[44] Unhappily, few of those who had fought during the century for the success of that hour had lived to see it. Brissot had been guillotined, Clavière had committed suicide, Condorcet was a refugee in hiding, Bernardin de Saint-Pierre was living in recluse, Lafayette was behind the bars of a German military prison, the Duc de la Rochefoucauld had been killed, Liancourt was a refugee, and similar fates had come to many others.

Clearly, political motivation had more to do with the decree of emancipation than did humanitarian consideration. But for the treason of the planters and their alignment with the aristocrats in the terrible struggle that France was going through, settlement would probably have been postponed. The National Convention had already been seated for a year and a half and had been little concerned with the matter. Actually the Girondins, who had fallen from power and been expelled from the body in 1793, had furnished more antislavery leaders than had the Jacobins. Even Raimond, the mulatto pamphleteer who had been imprisoned by the Jacobins along with Brissot, was in prison at this time. One cannot argue that the Jacobins, because they represented the petit bourgeoisie, were more kindly disposed toward the Negroes than the Girondins, who represented the upper bourgeoisie: the facts do not support it. Indeed, many aristocrats and some clerics had been active members of the Amis des Noirs. The movement against slavery and the slave trade had elicited the interest and support of all classes, and it was much more the intelligentsia than the masses that had sponsored the movement throughout. Levasseur, Danton, and their clique who seized the opportunity on February 2, 1794, to make capital of the situation simply reaped the fruits of other men's toil. The politicians were responsible for the decree, but it is very unlikely that they could ever have succeeded had it not been for the intellectual preparation that the humanitarians had made.

The question may be raised whether the action on the part of the National Convention was anything more than a recognition

[44] *Mémoires de Grégoire*, I, 390-91; *Annales politiques et littéraires*, May 10, 1791, p. 1395.

of what had already taken place. Of course it was the events in Santo Domingo that had precipitated the action. The other colonies, although they had experienced turmoil, were not in the hands of the mulattoes and slaves, as was Santo Domingo. Their slaves, however, were included in the emancipation decree of February 4. Even in Santo Domingo the colored elements, though they had revolted against planter rule and slavery, paid deference to the ties with France and continued "loyal" until Napoleon in late 1801 sent the Leclerc expedition to subordinate the island and restore slavery. In the meanwhile the island continued to send representatives to the Convention and, subsequently, to the two councils of the Directory, until the end of the century. Apparently France, during this period, drew few if any economic benefits from the island. The colony to be sure, did render very useful military aid against the British and the counterrevolutionaries during much of the time. The colony thus was not lost to the French in 1794, and it was a strategic move for the Jacobin government to take the action that it did.

The fears of both the Amis des Noirs and the planters that immediate emancipation would bring catastrophe were in large part realized. Particularly in Santo Domingo, and in a lesser degree elsewhere, confusion followed abolition. The Negroes and the mulattoes having gained their day against the whites came in time to fall out with one another and civil war between them resulted, with Toussaint Louverture, Jessalines, and other Negro leaders exterminating almost the entire body of mulattoes in the colony of Santo Domingo. Those escaping did so by flight. For a time General Lavaux was in charge, but the mantle of authority came to rest in 1796 on the shoulders of a former slave from Martinique, the Negro Toussaint Louverture, a leader of great capacity, not only an astute general but a cautious and clever administrator. He sent his two sons to France for education,[45] and his policy was to recognize French rule but to govern the colony as he saw fit. He was a man of great ambition, and soon rumor had it that he intended to make the colony independent.[46] The

[45] The Directory in 1796 had set up a special school in Paris for colonials, of whatever color, entitled Institution Nationale des Colonies. Paul Roussier, "L'application des lois de la Révolution aux colonies," Cahiers de la Révolution française, III (1935), 66.

[46] Priestley, France Overseas, 333-35; Lefebvre, La Révolution française, 414.

government in France entertained fear of his policy, but not until after Napoleon had come to power was action taken to arrest it.

The colonists had warned that if freedom were given, the colonies would be lost. As events turned out, they were only partially right, for Santo Domingo alone came to break away. Terrific economic loss also followed, as they predicted. Perhaps in large part it would have come anyhow inasmuch as war with Britain during the eighteenth century had invariably been accompanied by economic blockade. As it was, the city of Bordeaux suffered disastrously from cessation of the colonial trade, reportedly as a result of the events in Santo Domingo. Trade was so stagnant that thousands were compelled to seek employment elsewhere, and the city's population fell from 110,000 in 1789 to 87,000 in 1797. Only with the Consulate was its commerce reactivated.[47]

The planters of course lost heavily. Malouet's case was perhaps typical. He lived in England on the generosity of friends, his chief benefactor being a certain D'Albiac, descendant of a Huguenot family that had left France after the revocation of the Edict of Nantes.[48] The desperate situation of the thousands that came to the United States and were fed by Congress may be read in Miss Frances Childs' *French Refugee Life in the United States, 1790-1800.*

The French lapsed into apathy concerning the colonies after the emancipation decree of February 4, 1794. Little mention of them was made in the legislative proceedings. Occasionally a colonial delegate would make a sarcastic remark or express some criticism of the Negroes and their rule.[49] The French merely shrugged their shoulders. The planter class for the most part was living in self-imposed exile, in Britain and the United States. The planters were ruined, the mulattoes were well-nigh exterminated, the colony of Santo Domingo came shortly to be lost, and current conditions on the island were scathingly condemned by a deputy before the Council of the Five Hundred on May 27, 1797, as em-

[47] G. Caudrillier, "Bordeaux sous le Directoire," *RF*, LXX (1917), 24-25; G. Renard and G. Weulersse, *Life and Work in Modern Europe (Fifteenth to Eighteenth Centuries)* (New York, 1926), 186-87; Martin, *Nantes au XVIIIe siècle*, II, 174. According to Renard and Weulersse, Santo Domingo on the eve of the Revolution provided two-thirds of the French trade with the West Indies.

[48] *Mémoires de Malouet*, II, 277, 494.

[49] *Réimpression de l'ancien Moniteur*, XXV, 103, 319-20, 323; XXVIII, 718.

bodying military and economic anarchy.[50] The whole affair was strangely a foretaste of what the United States was to experience in the next century in her Civil War and Reconstruction. Humanitarian consideration demanded the abolition of slavery, but the way in which it was accomplished was tragic.

[50] *Ibid.*, XXVIII, 718-19. The criticism drew Toussaint's ire, and he sent the Directory a letter repudiating the charges. *Ibid.*, XXIX, 133-34. In the meanwhile Tarbé demanded the recall of Santhonax, who was still commissioner on the island. *Ibid.*, XXVIII, 119.

CHAPTER SIX

Prison Amelioration
Before 1789

IMPRISONMENT in eighteenth-century France, aside from cases of indebtedness, sentence to the galleys, or confinement in certain instances in convents, was not a form of penalty for legal infraction; rather, it was a means of securing the person of an accused while he awaited trial. Theoretically all prisoners, except those noted above, were potentially innocent, since they had not been convicted in court. Yet though not sentenced by court, they were often subjected to prison confinement by official decree emanating from the king's own authority or more commonly from one of his ministers acting in his name. In no other matter was the arbitrary royal power in France more conspicuously seen than in imprisonment, and in no other matter perhaps did cruelty make itself more evident.

It is fitting at the outset to depict the types of prisons and their conditions.[1] First of all there were the state prisons, about twenty in number, scattered here and there over France, comparable to American federal prisons of today, in which supposedly only prisoners charged with offenses against the king or state were confined. In this category fell the Bastille and Vincennes at Paris; the Pierre en Cise at Lyons; Mont-Saint-Michel in Normandy; the Château de Taureau in Brittany; and the Château d'If near Marseilles.[2] More grim than the other prisons because of their fortresslike character, their deep dungeons, and their atmosphere of silence, they were actually not at all crowded and their living conditions more endurable than the local prisons.

The local or municipal prisons were vastly more numerous, of course. Paris had six or eight prior to the Revolution, such as the Grand and the Petit Châtelet, the Fort-l'Evêque, the Conciergerie, and the Force. Affiliated with them and indeed hardly distinguishable were certain *maisons d'arrêt* (detention houses), such as the Bicêtre, the Salpêtrière, and Charenton, at Paris, where persons were held on light charges like prostitution, vagrancy, knavery, and insanity. At Charenton the insane were confined; at the Bicêtre, men and boys accused of vagrancy or other petty legal infractions; and at the Salpêtrière, prostitutes were incarcerated, treated medically, and attempts made toward their reformation. These last three prisons were gigantic, they were maintained by monks or nuns, and their conditions far from wretched. In fact one writer has observed that conditions at the Bicêtre were doubtless better than most French peasants enjoyed.

In the latter half of the century fifteen or twenty *dépôts de mendicité* (detention camps for beggars and vagabonds) existed throughout France. French economic conditions during most of the century were far from happy, and one reads continually in the records of the 1700's of famine, beggars, and riots. The beggar was regarded as a potential rioter and criminal. Efforts were made for each city and province to provide for its own needy poor, but the beggar did not care to conform to regulations for getting charitable aid; he hoped to do better by wandering. The scores, in fact the hundreds, of riots during the century, more especially for bread, made the authorities aware that beggars and vagabonds should be put in concentration camps and forced to work. Such were the *dépôts de mendicité*. Their regimen was not severe, and it appears that confinement was usually for a brief period. Had they been operated with the efficiency desired by the government, the multitudinous riots of 1789 and later years would possibly not have taken place.

Another form of prison were the convents in which hundreds of women and girls, and in some instances even boys, were confined on *lettres de cachet*, more commonly for grounds of religion or family. The incarcerated were treated as the nuns themselves,

---

[1] The best general study of prisons of the Old Regime is Frantz Funck-Brentano's *Prisons d'autrefois* (Paris, 1935).

[2] S. N. H. Linguet, *Mémoires sur la Bastille, et sur la détention de M. Linguet, écrits par lui-même* (London, 1783), 107.

and could move rather freely within the institution, and in some instances even outside of it.

There were also the military prisons in which deserters and prisoners of war were kept. During each war a large number of prison camps came into existence for the custody of military and naval captives. While conditions in them might in some respects resemble those of the common prisons, in others they were markedly different and in general they appear to have been much more desirable places of incarceration.

The larger prisons were commonly of stone and had dungeons which, in many instances, were still used on the eve of the Revolution for the confinement of prisoners. John Howard, visiting the prisons of Paris in 1783, found six small dungeons at the Abbaye, a prison for debtors and military personnel, and was informed by its jailor that as many as fifty prisoners were sometimes confined in them. Howard told of the "dark and offensive" dungeons at the Conciergerie being in use. He found twenty-five men in them in 1776, sixteen in 1783.[3] Around 1770 the celebrated prisoner Latude, after one of his escapes, was imprisoned in irons in a dungeon of the Bastille, with only a little straw on which to sleep.[4] At Lyons, in 1776, Howard found "four horrid" dungeons in use at the Prison of Saint-Joseph, occupied by twenty-nine prisoners sweltering in the summer heat to such a degree "that few of them had any other garment on than their shirts." He added that "some of them were sick, and [none] looked healthy." At Châlons and other provincial cities he likewise found dungeons in use.[5] In the second half of the century the dungeons received much criticism in prisoners' memoirs, from Howard, and from various advocates of reform. The result was that on the eve of the Revolution in some instances dungeons were no longer used. New prisons constructed after 1770 did not have them.

In some cases the prisoners confined in dungeons were exercised in the court during the day, but it appears that in most instances they were denied this privilege. As a result they were pallid and

[3] *The State of the Prisons in England and Wales, with Preliminary Observations, and an Account of Some Foreign Prisons and Hospitals* (4th ed., London, 1792), 171. He also found dungeons in Portman Castle, off Toulon. *An Account of the Principal Lazarettos in Europe* (Warrington, 1789), 56n.

[4] *Mémoires de Henri Masers de Latude* (Paris, 1793), I, 81.

[5] *The State of the Prisons*, 179.

unhealthy. Latude claimed to have been bitten by rats in his dungeon until he made friends of them. He related the bizarre (and doubtful) tale of having tamed a dozen or more until they would eat from his hand, and stated that this helped to while away his loneliness.[6]

The prisoners slept on straw that was replaced only once or twice a month. In the damp cells it quickly became unfit for comfort or health, and it was often infested with vermin. A stench commonly pervaded the prison. Toilet facilities were of the rudest sort, consisting frequently of a trench at one side of the cell which served as a latrine for those in dungeons or on the ground floor. These offensive health conditions were condemned increasingly as the century advanced. Even in 1702 the physician who treated the prisoner David Serres, sick in his dungeon cell, was horrified at the conditions and commented that they were bad enough to drive one insane.[7]

The jail fever (typhus), so prevalent in English prisons of the eighteenth century, was rarely reported as occurring in the French prisons, but there were other epidemics, especially of scurvy. Some of the epidemics were undiagnosed, however, and could indeed have been jail fever. Writers of the day, not conversant with the discoveries of Lind and Cook, attributed the scurvy outbreaks to the foul conditions prevailing within the prisons.[8]

All the larger prisons had either hospital wards of their own or the privilege of sending their patients to a prison ward in the local Hôtel-Dieu (city hospital). Howard reported that the newly built Hôtel de la Force in Paris had both a "general infirmary" and "an infirmary for the *scorbut*" (scurvy). In the latter he found sixty-three patients. He called the disease "a distemper very common and fatal," and stated that in cases where it was not fatal it frequently ended in the loss of the limbs.[9] Mirabeau in a pamphlet of 1782 reporting his unhappy experience with the prison of Vincennes commented that that prison had a physician,

[6] *Mémoires de Latude*, I, 83-86. It is difficult to know how much of prisoners' reports can be believed. They usually wrote for the motive of establishing their innocence or of damning the government that put them there.

[7] Etienne Creissel, *Pierre, David et Jean Serres, 1685-1714* (Cahors, 1900), 97.

[8] Howard, *The State of the Prisons*, 164, 167, 173; Jean Baptiste Le Roy, *Précis d'un ouvrage sur les hôpitaux* (n.p., n.d.), 5; *Mémoires biographiques, littéraires et politiques de Mirabeau*, II, 379.

[9] Howard, *The State of the Prisons*, 173.

a surgeon, a dentist, and an oculist on its staff.[10] In the prison hospital were beds. Howard found iron bedsteads in use at the large hospital in Marseilles in 1786. It had walks and terraces and a new staircase with some remarkable features designed to serve convalescent patients.[11] These features, of course, were extraordinary, and had been urged by reformers; nevertheless it was common for each prison to have at its service a physician and a surgeon, and possibly a dentist.

In a few prisons male and female prisoners were thrown together, even in the years prior to the Revolution. This condition was reported at Ploërmel and Quimper, in Brittany, late in the century, and also at Rabastens in the Pyrenees.[12] At Ploërmel the intendant protested, and at Péronne, the curé, each hoping that the controller general of finances of Paris might be able to alleviate the situation.

More commonly debtors and criminals, young offenders and hardened ones were thrown together. Howard protested against this, both in regard to Britain and France; yet he did find at some French prisons care taken to keep these classes separate.[13] For example, regulations of 1782 for the new prison La Force in Paris strictly forbade mingling of the two sexes either within the prison proper or in its court.

Already prior to Howard's visits, in the 1770's and 1780's, the French had come to a realization of the evils in their prison system and were making efforts to remedy them. He and other writers of the two decades prior to the Revolution mentioned the fact that many of the prisons, both in the provinces and in Paris, enjoyed the attentions of some charitable organization interested in the sanitary conditions and the comfort of the prisoners. They concentrated their attentions principally, it appears, on the pro-

[10] *Des lettres de cachet et des prisons d'état. Ouvrage posthume, composé en 1718* (Hamburg, 1782), 20 nl. The title page carried the name of Mirabaud, but this was for deception and the work has commonly been attributed to Mirabeau.

[11] *Principal Lazarettos*, 54.

[12] *Inventaire sommaire des archives départementales . . . Ille-et-Vilaine,* I, 31; Département des Hautes Pyrenées, *Cahiers de doléances de la sénéchaussée de Bigorre pour les Etats Généraux de 1789,* publiés par Gaston Balencie (Tarbes, 1925), 509.

[13] *The State of the Prisons,* 166, 171. Cf. Guillaume François Le Trosne, *Vues sur le justice criminelle* (Paris, 1777), 41n; Charles Eléanor Dufriche de Valezé, *Lois pénales* (Alençon, 1784), 299-320; J. E. D. de Bernardi, *Discours sur les loix pénales* (Châlons-sur-Marne, 1781), 32; J. P. Brissot, *Les moyens d'adoucir la rigueur des lois pénales* (Châlons-sur-Marne, 1781), 88-89.

vision of the prisoners with fresh bed linen. Sometimes, too, they brought food. At Avignon and Marseilles the Frères de la Miséricorde brought fresh sheets once every week in summer and once every two weeks in winter. Twice weekly at Avignon they brought a loaf of wheat bread, soup, and wine; at Marseilles they brought soup daily. In Paris, according to Howard, "there is scarce a prison in the city that has not a patroness; a lady of character, who voluntarily takes care that those in the infirmaries be properly attended; supplies them with fuel and linen; does many kind offices to the prisoners in general; and by soliciting the charity of others, procures not only the relief and comforts mentioned already, but soup twice a week, and meat once a fortnight." At Christmas they supplied the prisoners with fresh clothes. At Troyes aid was rendered by a patroness who used charity funds contributed locally.[14]

As regards food, the state allotted a certain sum for bread per day for each inmate of a prison, state or local, if he was unable to pay. Three sous per day were given him for his food, and an additional sou went to the jailor for his service. The state required that the prisoner be given a pound and a half of bread daily. He was also given soup or meat and vegetables. Latude received enough food in the Bastille to share it voluntarily with the rats. While he complained about other aspects of his prison existence, he apparently had nothing to complain of in regard to his meals. The same was true of Linguet, who was imprisoned at the Bastille, of the Marquis de Mirabeau, at Vincennes, and of the Abbé Morellet, at the Bastille in 1760. The last reported receiving daily a bottle of good wine and a pound of excellent bread. For lunch he had "soup, beef, an *entrée*, and dessert"; for supper, "some roast meat and salad."[15] Prisoners in hospitals were cared for by the government at the rate of twelve sous a day. If soldiers, the expense came from the military budget. All in all, the food for prisoners, though by no means what these would have desired, was far from being their worst grievance.

14 Howard, *Principal Lazarettos*, 53-54; *The State of the Prisons*, 168; *Inventaire sommaire des archives départementales . . . Département de l'Aube*, C 1838.

15 *Mémoires inédits de l'Abbé Morellet*, I, 97; Mirabeau, *Des lettres de cachet*, II, 21; Jean Lorédan, *La grande misère et les voleurs au dix-huitième siècle* (Paris, 1910), 217; Latude, *Mémoires*, I, 83-86; *Inventaire sommaire . . . Ille-et-Vilaine*, C 106, 108, 115.

In reality conditions were far from bad in many prisons. It would appear that the greater number were not crowded. The Bastille when seized by the crowd in 1789 had only seven prisoners. The number at Vincennes varied from twelve to thirty. Some of the newer prisons, with more sanitary conditions, were those at Lyons and Toulouse, and the Force at Paris. The Conciergerie, at Paris, had a new infirmary in 1783, equipped with single beds.[16] In response to a government investigation in 1788, the aldermen (*capitouls*) of Toulouse replied that their city prisons were "in very good condition" and on occasion accommodated also prisoners from other towns and cities. Marseilles was busy with plans to build a larger and more sanitary prison when the Revolution occurred.[17]

In some prisons, as at the Châtelet, the prisoners were allowed access to the courts much at will throughout the day, save that women and men were segregated. At other places, as the Bastille, prisoners were allowed access to the courts for one or two hours daily but were not permitted to talk with one another, lest they plot escapes or mutinies. Latude reported his experience in such a prison, and how he took advantage of two indulgent guards to escape.[18]

Marion Faouët, female member of a robber band in Brittany, during two months' imprisonment at Quimper in 1752 was allowed to wander much at will over the prison, and from time to time in the court. She cooked her own meals, spent her time knitting, and conversed with the jailor's family and friends. Among those visiting her was a member of her band named Olivier, who had escaped from the jail at Carlaix and at that moment was being sought by the police, even at Quimper! Marion seemed to have experienced a rather pleasant stay in the jail. It was old and flimsy, and she realized that she could escape more or less at will. At length she did.[19]

The Abbé Morellet while in the Bastille was permitted to receive his friends, to read such books as he requested, to write

[16] Howard, *The State of the Prisons*, 171; *Principal Lazarettos*, 52; Tuetey, *Répertoire générale*, II, nos. 3300-3301.

[17] *Histoire générale de Languedoc*, XIV, 2461; Augustin Fabre, *Histoire des hôpitaux et des institutions de bienfaisance de Marseille* (Paris, 1856), II, 270-71.

[18] Robert Anchel, *Crimes et châtiments au XVIIIe siècle* (Paris, 1933), 95-96.

[19] Lorédan, *La grande misère*, 211-23.

essays and verses, to walk in the court, and all in all he had a very agreeable six weeks' rest there. His imprisonment increased his reputation, for he came to be regarded as a martyr for the *philosophic* cause, and he emerged with a popularity that he did not deserve.[20] Diderot at Vincennes found very much the same sort of treatment as Morellet experienced. He was even allowed to leave the prison walls one night to check on the fidelity of his mistress, Madame de Puisieux, and found her, as he anticipated, in the arms of another lover. Breaking with her, he went back to incarcerate himself again at Vincennes.[21]

More interesting than these accounts of prison entertainment is that related in regard to the celebrated actress Mademoiselle Clairon, imprisoned for refusal to perform at the Comédie Française after some government restrictions were placed on her profession. The performance at the Comédie was not the same without her. Imprisoned at the Fort l'Evêque, she became the heroine of the day, and swarms of prominent persons drove out in their carriages to call on her. In her cell "she gave a series of dinners and suppers, served with great splendor and patronized by illustrious guests." Saint-Florentin, grim minister of the Maison du Roi with jurisdiction over the lettres de cachet, was perplexed at what to do. Mademoiselle Clairon soon emerged the winner.[22]

One can say that these persons were celebrities and that they enjoyed special attention, which of course is true. Yet one can relate instances of obscure individuals that also were well treated in the prisons and had little complaint to make. According to Funck-Brentano, authority on the history of French prisons, many indigents sought admission to the Bicêtre, "because of the good treatment."[23] Similarly women often requested admission to the Salpêtrière, to be cured of venereal disease at state expense or to attempt reform of their errant life.

There were so many divergent and bizarre aspects of eighteenth-century French prisons that nearly all generalizations meet flat contradictions in specific instances. Thus almost universally the prisoners were lonely, and in some instances spent wearisome

[20] *Mémoires inédits de l'Abbé Morellet*, I, 95-99.

[21] Quoted, *Oeuvres complètes de Diderot*, I, xliv-xlv; II, 440; Louis Ducros, *Diderot, l'homme et l'écrivain* (Paris, 1894), 18-20; Funck-Brentano, *Prisons d'autrefois*, 6.

[22] J. B. Perkins, *France Under Louis XV* (Boston, 1897), II, 414.

[23] *Prisons d'autrefois*, 64.

decades in cells incommunicado. One prisoner reportedly spent thirty-five years in such confinement. He had lost his mind, the prison and even the government had no record of his name, and in his late years no one even knew why he was in prison. The story is not incredible, for there were other cases almost as fantastic.[24] Most prisoners complained of the solitude of the Bastille. Linguet charged that all prisoners on being released from it were forced to take an oath of secrecy on its conditions, but he fled to England and there published a book on the subject, entitled *Mémoires sur la Bastille,* still read, with a remarkable drawing opposite the frontispiece showing the towers of the mighty fortress being rent asunder by a bolt of lightning. This was in 1783, six years before the Bastille was actually taken by the revolutionary mob. The copy in the Bibliothèque Nationale is leather bound and bears on it the arms of the king of France, the personal copy of Louis XVI.[25]

One of the reforms sought by Howard and others late in the century was the opportunity for prison inmates to work and thereby to keep their minds occupied. Yet this need had already been anticipated and work had been introduced in an occasional French prison. Prisoners at the Bicêtre as early as 1770, on the occasion of a visit by the Dauphin, later Louis XVI, had the privilege of working if they chose to do so at polishing glass, making straw boxes, etc. They could buy from and sell to venders. They might write books. Some drew water for the hospital needs. From time to time, when the number of prisoners grew large, some were released, some were allowed to join the army, and others were sent to the Indies by arrangements with the Compagnie des Indes. The Salpêtrière, too, offered work to its inmates.[26]

---

[24] E. J. F. Barbier, *Chronique de la régence et du règne de Louis XV (1718-1763); ou, Journal de Barbier* (Paris, 1857), I, 247; *Réimpression de l'ancien Moniteur,* XIX, 636; Arthur Young, *Travels in France During the Years 1787, 1788, 1789, with an Introduction, Biographical Sketch, and Notes by M. Betham-Edwards* (2d ed., London, 1889), 313n.

[25] Linguet, *Mémoires sur la Bastille,* 5-6. Latude (*Mémoires,* I, 10) charged that prisoners at the Bastille were often kept incommunicado from their own families. Mercier (*Tableau de Paris,* IX, 128) about the same time as Linguet told of a bolt of lightning in 1562 striking one of the towers of the Bastille and shattering it. He predicted that the whole fortress would one day be destroyed in like fashion.

[26] Funck-Brentano, *Prisons d'autrefois,* 66-68; Jacques Tenon, *Mémoires sur les hôpitaux de Paris* (Paris, 1788), 88.

The French prisons seemingly were not so troubled as the English with *garnish,* that notorious practice whereby a newcomer to a prison was forced to treat at drink the fellow prisoners of his cell, or indeed all in the prison, or else to be stripped of his clothing. Neither were exactions by the jailors as common. Colbert in August, 1670, had forbidden these practices, and by ordinances of June 18 and September 1, 1717, the parlement of Paris renewed the act for the prisons within its jurisdiction, showing that the practices had not disappeared. Even as late as 1744, however, according to one writer, they had not ended.[27] Moreover, by a royal declaration of June 11, 1724, the French government strictly forbade *garnish* or any collection of fees by the jailor at any time. It specified that the jailor was to be appointed and paid for his service, and that the jails were not to be farmed out to the highest bidder—as in Britain. Even near the end of the century the Duc de La Rochefoucauld Liancourt referred to exactions as a practice, though banned, still existent in Europe, baffling efforts at suppression.[28]

From time to time inspections of the prisons were made by the minister. Both Latude and Mirabeau refer to them. The prisoners were asked if they had any complaints. Mirabeau sneered at these investigations as a farce, saying that the prisoners knew better than to complain, as they would suffer from the prison governor and turnkeys in consequence.[29] Yet the inspections doubtless protected the prisoners in many respects and prevented conditions that would have been much worse.

It is to be observed that while Latude was vitriolic in hatred of the lieutenants general of police De Sartine and Lenoir, considering them as in league with Madame de Pompadour in refusal to free him, Mirabeau, on the other hand, spoke highly of Lenoir and dedicated to him volume II of his pamphlet on the prisons. All with one accord admired Malesherbes, who when he was made minister of the prisons in 1775 visited each prisoner in his cell and talked with him on the cause of his imprisonment and

[27] Darcy, *Les prisons en Picardie. Etude historique sur la détention préventive et pénale et sur les prisons anciennes* (extract from *Mémoires de la Société des Antiquaires de Picardie,* 3d ser., VI [1880], 356-57).

[28] *Travels through the United States of North America* (London, 1799), II, 340-41; Isambert, *Recueil des anciennes lois françaises,* XXVII, 151-52.

[29] *Des lettres de cachet,* II, 28-29.

his treatment, with the design of seeing that justice was done. Even Latude, who suffered from a persecution complex and was almost certainly paranoiac, admired Malesherbes, but explained to his readers the reason for his nonrelease by saying that Malesherbes listened to his underlings in office who were prejudiced against him. It so happens that a letter from Malesherbes to the governor of Vincennes has been preserved, in which he discussed the case of each prisoner there incarcerated, including *Danry*, under which name Latude was imprisoned. Malesherbes there stated that during the conversation *Danry* had given clear evidence of being insane. It was thus to protect the public against a paranoiac that Latude's confinement was continued. Le Prévôt de Beaumont, another prisoner of Vincennes, confined for a trifling offense over a long period of years, was visited in 1777 by Malesherbes, but not released for similar reason. It seems almost unbelievable today that men like Latude and De Beaumont could be thrust into prison for thirty-nine years or twenty-two years, without trial, for such trivial grounds as attempting a hoax on Madame de Pompadour or attempting to call for an investigation of an alleged plot whereby the king's ministry and Louis XV himself would profit from cornering the grain market under famine conditions.[30]

Perhaps the most common type of imprisonment under the Old Regime came under the lettres de cachet, a form of arbitrary arrest, in which the cause of imprisonment was not set forth. It was on a lettre de cachet that Voltaire was imprisoned in 1726 for challenging the Duc de Rohan to a duel, after lackeys of His Grace had caned him in return for some mocking verses. On a lettre de cachet the Genevan Pelesseri was imprisoned late in the century for criticizing Necker's financial policy.[31] By this means, too, Nicolas Fréret, brilliant young member of the Académie des Belles-Lettres et Inscriptions, was imprisoned in 1714 for Jansenism.[32] Forty thousand lettres de cachet, most of them for the

---

[30] Letter of September 11, 1775, quoted in Gustave Bord, *Histoire du blé en France: le Pacte de Famine. Histoire–légende* (Paris, 1887), Pièces justicatives, 36-39; Latude, *Mémoires*, I, 220-32; E. Le Mercier, *Le Prévôt de Beaumont, prisonnier d'état, détenu pendant vingt-deux ans et deux mois à la Bastille et dans différentes prisons pour avoir dénoncé le Pacte de Famine* (Bernay, 1883), 305.

[31] Linguet, *Mémoires sur la Bastille*, 61-62.

[32] J. Delort, *Histoire de la détention des philosophes et des gens de lettres à la Bastille et à Vincennes* (Paris, 1829), II, 9-10, 17.

Jansenists, are reported to have been issued during the ministry of Cardinal Fleury alone (1726-1743). In fact, the greater number of lettres de cachets during the century were issued in the name of religion, either against Jansenists or Protestants, according to Sénac de Meilhan, one of the more enlightened provincial intendants on the eve of the Revolution.[33] Several hundred or more Protestant children were so imprisoned during the century in convents or the general hospitals for subjection to Catholic training.

Next to religion the most common cause for issuance of lettres de cachet was family demand. Sons and daughters not amenable to parental will were imprisoned by the hundreds. Usually the imprisonment was to protect the family honor, lest the daughter marry the coachman or the son ruin himself in dissipation. It is reported that Mirabeau was sent to prison twenty-two times on lettres de cachet by his father. In this case the son was wayward and the father churlish, even though the latter arrogated to himself the title of *Ami des Hommes.* Not a few indifferent or runaway apprentices were so imprisoned, here and there an unfaithful priest, and various writers whose publication offended some person of rank or challenged public opinion. No one was safe. Members of the parlements indeed were "exiled" to the provinces on lettres de cachet; twelve members of the Estates of Brittany were imprisoned in this manner in 1788; Madame du Barry was relegated to prison on a lettre de cachet in 1774; and in 1725 the Duke de Bourbon, the regent, was thus dismissed from his high office and exiled to Chantilly.[34]

In the great majority of cases the lettres de cachet no doubt served a useful purpose. The insane were sent to asylum or prison in this fashion; family honor was thus protected; and wayward members of society were thus handled. They nevertheless violated justice, inasmuch as the imprisoned was seldom brought to trial and had no way to defend himself. There were indeed

[33] *Le gouvernement, les moeurs et les conditions en France avant la Révolution* (Paris, n.d.), 151.

[34] Hundreds of lettres de cachet are described in detail in the *Inventaire sommaire des archives départementales . . . Ille-et-Vilaine,* C 158-231, and in the *Inventaire sommaire . . . Calvados,* C 315-450. See also Frantz Funck-Brentano, *Les lettres de cachet* (Paris, 1926), *passim;* Perkins, *France Under Louis XV,* I, 85; M. F. Buchalet, *L'assistance publique à Toulouse au dix-huitième siècle* (Toulouse, 1904), 51.

not a few cases of flagrant injustice, in which the imprisoned spent decades in prison for some trivial offense or in fact for no offense at all. Yet in general, according to a defender of the Old Regime, those imprisoned on lettres de cachet were not subjected to the worst prisons.[35] Moreover it is said that steadily during the reigns of Louis XV and Louis XVI the number of lettres de cachet decreased. Nor was this entirely a concession to public opinion, for Louis XVI and certain of his ministers, notably Malesherbes, were much opposed to them.[36] Indeed it is well to guard against the conclusion that the lettres de cachet had long been as unpopular as they were on the eve of the Revolution, when they figured in almost every cahier among the most flagrant abuses needing abolition.

It is safer to conclude that throughout most of the century they had been popular throughout France, as is attested by the abundant demands for them, especially by the clergy, the nobility, and the bourgeoisie. Even some victims of lettres de cachet were desirous of seeing them used against others. Voltaire, incarcerated on one in the 1720's, went to no end of trouble in 1730 to have the police issue one for a woman in his neighborhood (of the rue de Vaugiraud) who was a public nuisance. His efforts at last met success, but only for a few weeks, when she was set at large.[37] Occasionally a person asked for his own imprisonment. This happened in regard to various Protestant youths wishing an education or training as Catholics; sometimes it happened in regard to Protestant women with small financial resources. Not a few women, moreover, asked for their own incarceration at the Salpêtrière, and even attested to an immoral life, in some instances falsely, in order to receive free treatment for venereal disease. Some society women in Paris asked for their own imprisonment on lettres de cachet at the Convent of Nôtre-Dame-des-Près to get away from their husbands or the bustle of the world. Two husbands were imprisoned at the Bicêtre by their wives, and when one of them at length was offered freedom, he

---

35 Funck-Brentano, *Prisons d'autrefois*, 42-43.

36 Sénac de Meilhan, *Le gouvernement, les moeurs et les conditions en France avant la Révolution*, 154.

37 Frantz Funck-Brentano and Paul d'Estrée, *Voltaire, Beaumarchais et les lettres de cachet* (Paris, n.d.) (extract from the *Nouvelle revue rétrospective*, September 10, 1896, pp. 3-15).

preferred to remain on. One father had his son confined to prison in order that the latter might pass his examinations for admission to the engineering corps. Another had his pregnant daughter confined in a convent until she had made her accouchement.[38] There were no doubt many cases like this where the lettre de cachet served to protect the family honor. In other cases it protected the family pocketbook, for while in some instances the family requesting incarceration of a member was required to provide financal support of the member imprisoned, there were others in which they were not. The lettres de cachet were thus by no means an unmitigated curse; frequently they had a contribution to make.

Regarding the matter from another angle, government demand for the underwriting of expenses of the person incarcerated in a large percentage of the cases operated in all likelihood as a curb on them. In the same manner, demand by the government that the expense of maintaining debtors in prison be met by their creditors a month in advance operated in the same direction.[39]

Several of those imprisoned left records of their imprisonment, but most of them did not appear until 1780 or later. The most extended were written by Mirabeau, Linguet, Latude, and Beaumont. They appeared either on the eve of the Revolution or during its early stages, and were distinctly propagandistic in flavor. Also radical if not revolutionary in tendency were the denunciations of prison conditions in a large number of the pamphlets and books of the 1780's demanding judicial reform. Especially to be mentioned in this connection were Mercier's writings, *L'an 2440* and *Le tableau de Paris*, which are permeated with criticism of French prison conditions and demand for their amelioration. Also important in this connection was the denunciation of French prisons in Brissot's prize essay of 1780, published the next year.

The works of the English prison reformer John Howard, *The State of the Prisons* (1777) and *An Account of the Principal Lazarettos in Europe* (1789), were translated and published at Paris in 1788 and 1799 respectively and were much read in French cultured circles. A limited number of French readers

[38] Funck-Brentano, *Prisons d'autrefois*, 35, 65-66, 68-69, 116; *Inventaire sommaire . . . Ille-et-Vilaine*, C 170.

[39] Commandant Herlaut, *La disette de pain à Paris en 1709* (Paris, 1918), 96 n4. The sum fluctuated with living costs.

read the works in English prior to their translation. In his *Lazarettos* Howard gave a candid discussion of the conditions in dozens of French prisons that he visited in person, and suggested the improvements that he considered were needed. All readers of both works know that he advocated sanitary prisons, with fresh air, sunlight, clean linen, decent food, satisfactory toilet facilities, beds, and uniforms, and the absence of dungeons. He urged the abolition of torture, the separation of the sexes, of young offenders, and of debtors and criminals. He advocated the prisoner's need of daily exercise, the need of work to occupy his mind, and the need of religious instruction to reform him. He would attempt if possible to salvage the offender and return him from prison a useful member of society.

It is difficult to appraise his influence on the movement for betterment of French prisons. Few of his demands were original in France. Demands for prison betterment were not new, but they had not been made in Howard's thoroughgoing fashion. Prior to the Revolution his influence does not appear to have been outstanding.

In the late seventeenth century De Sacy, a Jansenist leader imprisoned more than two years for his convictions, had called upon the government to better conditions at the Bastille.[40] In 1706 another priest, Mignon, curé at Péronne, wrote to Controller General of Finances Chamillart complaining of local prison conditions. He asserted that persons of all ages and of both sexes were thrown together indiscriminately, sometimes for the most trivial causes, and were often held in prison "a very long time." He told of two women who had been there for six months, one "a poor widow of sixty," whose blind son was imprisoned also. Most of the prisoners were tobacco or salt smugglers, and the greater number were sick, due to the lack of sanitation. He wrote: "They almost all become sick there, because the prison is very obscure, as there is no court and no air. When they leave, at the end of five or six months, they fall sick at their homes and are reduced to extremity. What is more vexing is that neither the officers nor the tax agents (*commis*) wish to permit one to carry them to the Hôtel-Dieu." He had written earlier to the intendant of Picardy describing these conditions and asking betterment,

---

[40] Delort, *Histoire de la détention des philosophes*, I, 116.

but considered it well to write this letter in addition. He continued: "I consider myself further obligated, for the clearing of my conscience, to beg you very humbly, in favor of these poor men, to the end that it will please you to order a trial for them in a brief time, that they be punished or set free after a month or so in prison, as formerly, or at least that, if any of these prisoners falls dangerously sick, it will be possible, on a physician's certificate, to have him carried promptly to the Hôtel-Dieu."[41] Here we see a curé of high type taking an interest in the welfare of his flock. Unhappily his letter to the controller general made no greater appeal than that to the intendant, for Chamillart's cynical reply is also recorded. He said: "If you could see as I do the disorder created by most of those engaged in the contraband traffic of salt and tobacco in various provinces of the kingdom, far from requesting charity in their favor you would work by exhortations to prevent the abuses that they commit." There was no one higher than the controller general of finances to whom the good curé could go, except the king himself, and this he apparently did not attempt. The time was not ready for a man to make the crusade that Howard did, nor had the curé, apparently, the necessary monetary resources or the ardor.

In 1725 the Abbé de Saint-Pierre suggested that France follow the action of Britain, whose parliament the previous year enabled about twelve thousand debtors to leave prison. Those debtors owing less than £100 were accorded their freedom on making over voluntarily their possessions, in good faith, to their creditors; if they acted in bad faith, they were to be subject to death. On the basis of the population of the two countries, he estimated that eighteen thousand debtors in France would thus gain freedom and that number of families would be blessed. He estimated that the imprisonment of these debtors cost France annually 4,927,500 livres. Thus the country, too, would profit by such action. But of prison conditions otherwise the Abbé did not complain.[42]

Decades passed in silence, with no one espousing the cause of prison betterment. Then in 1767, Servan in his *Discours sur l'administration de la justice criminelle* attacked the prison con-

---

[41] Boislisle, *Correspondance des contrôleurs généraux*, II, 336, no. 1061.
[42] *Mémoire pour diminuer le nombre des procès* (Paris, 1725), 298-305.

ditions as frightful and wholly inconsistent with ideas of humanity. He portrayed innocent persons as thrown sometimes with criminals and as subjected to the most horrible tortures. He alluded to the "black dungeons where the light of day never penetrates," and to the pathetic beings "bruised from their irons, half-covered with rags, infected with an air that never renews itself . . . [and] gnawed alive by the same insects which devour cadavres in their tombs." In oratorical rhetoric he continued on the pathetic conditions and called upon the magistrates to alter them.[43] This was a decade prior to the publication of Howard's first book.

In 1776, still a year before the appearance in England of *The State of the Prisons,* an unknown French magistrate wrote at some length appealing to the king and queen to act in behalf of the poor prisoners. He appealed on humanitarian grounds for more sanitary conditions in the prisons in order that the prisoners, whether guilty or not, might emerge from prison in good health and with respect for authority. He asked for cleaner, better aired, roomier prisons. He described the horrible conditions prevailing at certain Parisian prisons—Fort-l'Evêque, the Grand and Petit Châtelet, and the Conciergerie; and he added that the provincial prisons were no better. He ended saying that any person might by chance one day find himself in prison.[44] Within less than two decades both Louis XVI and Marie Antoinette did find themselves in prison. That the manuscript was actually sent to the king probably explains its presence in government archives, and possibly it had some influence in paving the way for reforms undertaken by the king and Necker in 1780.

Voltaire, who died in 1778, had expressed himself in favor of work to occupy the minds of the prisoners. He criticized the sanitary condition of the prisons and the placing of debtors in the same cells with criminals. He criticized also the imprisonment of men without just cause and cited the means whereby those in England so imprisoned could get financial redress. He commended Louis XVI for making a start at prison reform and indicated that vastly more was needed.[45] However, he wrote re-

43 Pp. 38-45.
44 Reproduced by C. A. Dauban, *Les prisons de Paris sous la Révolution, d'après les relations des contemporains* (Paris, 1870), 2-6.
45 *Oeuvres,* XXX, 583-84.

markably little on the topic. His sole espousal of it was in a work of 1777 entitled *Prix de la justice et de l'humanité*. One may find no article either on the prisons or the galleys in his *Dictionnaire philosophique*.

Le Trosne, a distinguished lawyer of Orléans, in his *Vues sur la justice criminelle* in 1777 advocated the rendering of prisons sanitary and the separation of debtors and criminals. In fact he advocated two types of prisons, one for those charged with criminal offenses and another for those charged with civil offenses.[46] He made no reference either to Howard or to Beccaria.

Various other writers between this date and the early period of the Revolution called for prison betterment. Most of them shared Howard's views, some without mentioning him, and it is doubtful whether these last had read him. Almost without exception they called for clean, airy prisons, in order to guard the prisoner's health, and for abolition of dungeons and cruelty. The prison must be regarded not as a place of punishment but a spot where the accused was to be safeguarded until trial, and his innocence assumed until convicted. The segregation of debtors from the prisoners accused of crime, and also the segregation of first offenders from those previously convicted, was rather generally demanded. More than one advocate wanted two types of prisons. Brissot would not even imprison the debtor, taking the view that whoever had advanced him the money or goods could well afford to lose it.[47] Boucher d'Argis denounced the prisoner's solitude and inaccessibility to his family or friends.[48] Here and there one recommended that the prisoner be permitted to work, to occupy his mind.[49] Not one, however, appeared to have shared Howard's interest in the religious training of the prisoner or in his moral reformation. They did display interest in checking the young offender, and thus in his reform.

Several of these writers expressed admiration of the humanitarian concern of Louis XVI and of the reforms that he had already made, both in regard to the prisons and other matters. Nor were they insincere, as certain of them later were to suffer imprisonment, death, or emigration during the Revolution as

[46] P. 41n.   [47] *Les moyens d'adoucir la rigueur des lois pénales*, 92.
[48] *Observations sur les loix criminelles de France* (Brussels, 1781), 6.
[49] *Extraits de différens autres mémoires* (Châlons-sur-Seine, 1781), 11-12.

royalists. Two of the most ardent in referring to the king's humanity were Linguet, who contrasted Louis XVI in this respect to Louis XI, and Mercier, who prayed that he might be blessed for his "paternal regard" and his various acts of mercy. He added that Louis "will not need any other trophies around his statue than the title of these edicts published under his rule." He asserted that the nation awaited other such edicts, and that men would come to say: "Oh, how beautiful to see a man present (*enchassé*) in a king!"[50]

Fate was capricious in its treatment of Louis XVI, a king of good intentions shared also by certain of his ministers and intendants. Mention has already been made of the appointment of Lamoignon de Malesherbes in 1775 as minister with jurisdiction over the prisons, and of his solicitude for the welfare of the prisoners. To the Chevalier de Rougement, governor of the prison at Vincennes, he wrote on September 11, 1775, bidding him to make the prisoners there as content with their lot as possible, letting them walk in the courts and permitting them to write to their relatives and friends and even to officials if they chose. He directed, however, that officials read the letters, and not to let any be sent that were injudicious. The king's letter breathed sympathy for the unfortunates.[51]

Jacques Necker, director general of finance from 1776 to 1781, shared this concern for the prisoners, and gave some attention to prison betterment and the erection of new prisons and hospitals. In his *Compte rendu au roi* of 1781 he told of having made some grants to French cities for the rendering of prisons both more sanitary and spacious, to guard health of prisoners and permit the separation of debtors from criminals. Actually, however, he remarked that the grants were smaller than the sums needed, due partly to the American war.[52] He hoped to build some model

50 Linguet, *Mémoires sur la Bastille*, 58; Mercier, *Tableau de Paris*.

51 Bord, *Histoire du blé en France*, Pièces justicatives, 36-39. In a letter to Louis XV around 1770 Malesherbes severely criticized the usage of prison dungeons as cruel and unhealthy. *Oeuvres inédites de Chrétien-Guillaume Lamoignon de Malesherbes* (Paris, 1823), 53-56.

52 *Comte rendu*, 101-102. Madame Necker assisted him in establishing an infirmary at the Conciergerie in 1781, and also in other charitable enterprises. Edouard Chapuiset, *Necker (1732-1804)* (Paris, 1938), 247. Necker's own eulogy on his wife's charitable works may be read in his *Sur l'administration de M. Necker, par-lui-même* (Paris, 1791), 396-98.

prisons and hospitals at Paris, and in this aspiration he constructed the prison La Force, which won the plaudits of contemporaries, tore down the Petit Châtelet, sold the Fort l'Evêque, and ordered the improvement of the Grand Châtelet and the Conciergerie. The Grand Châtelet was to be used only for criminals, and the Force only for debtors.[53] Shortly later, in his *Administration des finances* (1785), he had much more to say on the prisons. He reported that already "the principal prisons of Paris have been absolutely changed." The conditions for prisoners had been "sensibly bettered." It was far, however, from being what he wished. Without mentioning Howard, whom apparently he had read, he espoused most of the features for prison improvement that Howard had urged in England. He discussed cleanliness, sanitation, food, clothing (uniforms), and bedding, physical exercise, prison administration, and prison inspection. He recommended that the economic administration of the prisons should be entrusted to the Sisters of Charity, as was commonly the case in the hospitals. Undoubtedly this was a good suggestion. He also urged that the government make some recompense to those who had suffered long imprisonment unjustly. He was able to rejoice that the efforts to improve the prisons had improved at Paris and that some of the provinces were emulating the example of Paris.[54]

Malouet, intendant of Toulon, and Thiroux de Crosne, intendant of Rouen, both displayed the enlightened spirit of the age by interest in the lot of the prisoner. De Crosne, made lieutenant general of police in 1785, "rendered the dungeons of the Bastille almost deserted, thanks to his mildness."[55]

In August, 1780, Louis XVI issued a declaration ordering betterment of conditions in several Parisian prisons. He also issued the royal ordinance of December 12, 1775, granting amnesty to all French soldiers who had deserted and were refugees either at home or abroad, and he stipulated that thenceforth only soldiers deserting in time of war would be executed.[56] "Indul-

[53] Marion, *Dictionnaire des institutions*, 457; Isambert, *Recueil des anciennes lois françaises*, XXVII, 149-55.

[54] *Administration des finances*, III, 141-58.

[55] E. Le Mercier, *Le Prévôt dit De Beaumont* (Bernay, 1883), 232-33; *Mémoires de Malouet*, I, 48-50, 207-13.

[56] *Oeuvres de Turgot*, ed. Daire, II, 449-50; Mirabeau, *Mémoires biographiques*, II, 379.

gence characterized his reign," according to Sénac de Meilhan, one of his liberal intendants. His weakness was not that he did not welcome reform but that he moved too slowly and grudgingly for the time.

The year 1789 came and the cahiers from all parts of France demanded prison amelioration. The sentiment was shared by all classes, but it was expressed especially by the third estate. The cahiers voiced the same sentiments as the pamphleteers of the two previous decades. Perhaps the most ringing demand was that for the abolition of lettres de cachet. It was almost universal. There was also a demand for sanitary prisons. Many localities requested new ones, others that their prisons be reconstructed. The third estate of Paris asked, among other things, for the abolition of the Bastille, the suppression of underground dungeons, and for the means of giving prisoners work to do.[57] From a community in Normandy came the demand for a cot, straw mattress, and sufficient cover to protect the prisoner from rigorous weather. It also asked that two pounds of bread, rather than one pound and a half be given.[58] Several cahiers called for the suppression of state prisons.[59] One or more asked that debtors and criminals not be imprisoned together. All in all the requests were many, but most of them were in line with those of the pamphleteers.

It is remarkable how widespread the demand for prison reform had come to be. It is noteworthy, too, that this demand for reform had emanated little from the *philosophes* themselves, but rather from pupils of the *philosophes* and others. In 1789 the problem was presented in all its facets to the Estates General and to the king as a matter of urgency demanding solution.

[57] *Réimpression de l'ancien Moniteur,* Introduction, 572-73.
[58] Département de la Manche, *Cahiers de doléances du bailliage de Cotentin,* ed. by Emile Bridrey (Paris, 1907-1912), I, 721, 771.
[59] Seligman, *La justice en France pendant la Révolution,* 177.

CHAPTER SEVEN

Prison Reform
During the Revolution

FEW MATTERS could have faced so auspicious an outlook early in the Revolution as prison reform; the surprise is that so much more was not accomplished. Not only had public interest in it been awakened by the brochures and books and cahiers on the eve of the Revolution but also by two prison episodes in Paris in 1789. On June 30 a mob had released sixty soldiers of the regiment of French Guards incarcerated on minor charges in L'Abbaye. Then on July 14 came the incident of the capture of the Bastille, again by a mob in which members of the French Guards had a part. The king on both occasions granted his pardon to those who had participated, perhaps against his will. The two incidents attracted widespread attention, and everyone in France if not indeed in Europe knew that the Revolution had begun.

Prison interest early in the Revolution was also whetted by the publication of some animated prison memoirs and studies. Howard's second volume, *An Account of the Principal Lazarettos of Europe*, had appeared in England in 1789, and a second edition in 1791. Though a French edition did not appear until 1799, the English version was read by many in France. Much more sensational for the French reader, however, were the prison memoirs of Le Prévôt and Latude, published at Paris in 1789 and 1790 respectively. Le Prévôt, who assumed the title "De Beaumont," was a prisoner in the Bastille at the time of its capture and indeed did not gain his freedom until several months afterward. Trained as a lawyer, he became a secretary to the French clergy, and was imprisoned on a lettre de cachet in 1768 for accusing, on flimsy evidence, the king of France and sundry of his high officials of having entered into a plot (which came to be designated Pacte de Famine) to profit from a grain monopoly at the expense of the French people in time of famine. It has subsequently been shown by Gustave Bord and others that there never existed such a plot, but it was easy to persuade credulous persons that one did exist, and Le Prévôt spent twenty-two years and two months in five prisons in consequence. His stay would have been much briefer had he been tractable or reasonable. Malesherbes made a call on him in his cell on July 22, 1772, and discussed his case. He became convinced that the man was insane, and Le Prévôt did not gain his freedom. Release from the Bastille attracted attention to him, and it was suggested that he write his prison experiences, which were published on the last day in 1789 under the title *Le prisonnier de l'état*. A second edition appeared in 1791, and in 1790 it was published serially in the prominent *Révolutions de Paris*.

At the same time this journal published, or rather republished, portions of the *Mémoires* of Latude which had just appeared in book form in three volumes, composed for him by the lawyer Thiery. Thiery had already published two shorter sketches of him, and in 1787 the Marquis de Beaupoil Saint-Aulaire had published a story of his imprisonment. Probably most persons in France had already heard of his thirty-five-year imprisonment in three Parisian prisons for attempting a hoax on Madame de Pompadour in 1749 and of his remarkable escape from the Bastille in 1756 by means of a rope nearly two hundred feet long that he had woven in his prison cell. His memoirs were exceedingly well written and even today fascinate a reader. His readers of that day did not know, as it has later been shown (1889) in a remarkable study by Frantz Funck-Brentano, that his *Mémoires* were "a tissue of lies": that he was not a marquis, that his name was not Latude, that he was of illegitimate birth and his father unknown, that he was never an engineering student but a surgeon's apprentice, that he assumed the name of "Danry" when he entered the army and not when he was taken to prison, that he attempted to wheedle money out of the war department before attempting to wheedle some from Madame de Pompadour, and that he was not the "brains" who conceived and executed the brilliant escape from the Bastille but rather it was his companion in that escape, Allègre, a former engineering student who was very clever with his hands and able to make almost anything he wanted. Fortunately for Latude, Allègre had gone insane and could not deny his story. Fortunate for him also was the Revolution; in fact, as Funck-Brentano says, it seemed made for him. He became a great hero, a victim of despotism and not a rascal. The Legislative Assembly gave him a pension of three thousand livres, which he enjoyed until his death in 1805. The American Ambassador Jefferson invited him to a meal; a French duchess similarly had him as her guest; and he was the recipient of other marks of honor and distinction.[1]

Such was the atmosphere early in the Revolution favorable to prison reform. In such an atmosphere and with a request in almost every cahier of 1789 calling for abolition of lettres de cachet, it is surprising that these were not abolished until March 13, 1790. Action leading to their abolition developed somewhat strangely in October, 1789, not by premeditation and planning but by a request to the assembly by a monk imprisoned on a lettre de cachet proposing that he be released from prison provided he make a certain monetary contribution to the state. In short, he proposed to pay a fine without having been condemned. The assembly at once saw that it would create a scandal; on the other hand, it feared that the liberation of all persons in prison on lettres de cachet without trial might do the same. After a lively discussion it was decided to request the king to revoke the lettre de cachet in this instance and to decline the monetary offer. Thereupon the Comte de Montmorency, member of one of France's great families, proposed that all lettres de cachet be revoked, and not this one alone. The proposal was greeted with applause, but the assembly postponed action. This was on October 9.

A few days subsequently the matter came up again. On October 12 the Comte de Castellane moved that the usage of lettres de cachet for the future be abolished and that all persons

---

[1] Frantz Funck-Brentano, "Latude," *Revue des deux mondes*, XCV (1889), 638-76. See also the article on Latude by Funck-Brentano in *La grande encyclopédie*, ed. by André Berthelot *et al.* (Paris, 1886-1902) (hereafter *GE*) XXI, 1024.

at that moment incarcerated on them be released. This he declared to be only a logical sequel to Article VII of the Declaration of the Rights of Man and the Citizen. The proposal, however, met opposition, Deschamps pointing out that some of those imprisoned on lettres de cachet were being detained on criminal charges, and that while all would agree that innocents held in prison should be released, no prisoner charged with crime should be. Then he commented sarcastically upon the thoughtless humanitarian sentiment which would dump upon society the refuse elements from which it ought to be protected. Deschamps carried the day and the motion was adjourned. It was considered again on October 22 and decision was made to appoint a committee of four to compile a list of prisoners confined on lettres de cachet, with reasons for their confinement, and submit it to the assembly.[2]

Fear lest all persons detained on lettres de cachet might be released impelled the learned and cautious Bailly, mayor of Paris, to write to the president of the assembly, "setting forth the danger that would come from liberating at once all the prisoners of the Bicêtre, in a moment of trouble at the beginning of winter, and asking that none of the detained be allowed to depart without a statement of the reasons for his detention being set forth." Subsequently (November 29) he wrote again expressing his fear and remarking that it was to the vagabonds like those incarcerated at the Bicêtre that "one attributes most of the robberies and disorders committed in Paris." Meanwhile he worked away at compiling the information desired by the assembly on prisoners at the Bicêtre, and transmitted it on February 20, 1790, in eleven memoirs.[3]

The prisoners at the Bicêtre, on their part, wrote Bailly in February and March, 1790, demanding their release and threatening revolt. Bailly in turn sent a large detachment of troops to prevent their rioting. Action of the assembly on March 13 ordering that within six weeks all persons in France confined on lettres de cachet be set at large, unless detained for insanity or for legal infraction, however, solved the problem, and on April 30 Bailly was able to announce that calm had been restored. Among those

2 *Réimpression de l'ancien Moniteur,* II, 30, 52, 83.
3 Tuetey, *Répertoire générale,* II, 343-44.

ardent for the passage of the motion of March 13 was Maximilian Robespierre, who thought it a shame that so much time had elapsed without action being taken to release those imprisoned who were not charged with crime.

The wheels of administrative machinery nevertheless did not turn with more speed and effectiveness under the Revolution than under the Old Regime, for by no means were all those detained on lettres de cachet released at once, as later reports made clear. On November 23, 1792, Tallien declared before the Convention that a multitude of prisoners on lettres de cachet were still held in jails and private institutions. Thereupon Barère, who had been a member of the Committee on Lettres de Cachet under the National Assembly, informed the Convention that a vast collection of information assembled by his committee had been deposed in the archives, and suggested that the minister of justice be directed to examine this material and collect information relative to those still imprisoned. A decree to this effect was adopted.

Even this did not terminate the matter, for a decree of December 31, 1793, indicated that there were still persons in the prisons on lettres de cachet issued prior to July 14, 1789, and provided that they might request trial before the Court of Cassation within three months.[4]

Then in March, 1794, came a nasty exposé. It was revealed that in the prisons of Lille was confined a Swedish officer, under the name of François Decosse, who had been there under arbitrary arrest since 1749, a period of forty-five years. At that moment he was confined in an insanitary dungeon. He had lost both his sanity and his health and was blind. Until four years previously his family in Stockholm had sent him an annual subsidy of four hundred livres to make him comfortable. The case was brought to light by Florent Guyot, a local official of Lille who discovered him and set forth his findings in a letter to the Convention. On the reading of the letter Deputy Duhem arose to express his amazement at the case, asserting that he and others of the Convention had "repeatedly visited the prisons of Lille, interrogated the prisoners, and on different occasions had put at

---

[4] *Réimpression de l'ancien Moniteur,* XIV, 557-58; XIX, 105.

liberty those who had appeared to be the victims of arbitrary orders." Yet "this Swedish officer," he asserted, "has constantly escaped our view." He expressed a fear that perhaps the one who handled the funds from Sweden for the prisoner had purposely hidden him and pocketed the money. In consequence he suggested that an inquiry be made by Guyot. A decree to this effect was passed, and another providing the Swedish prisoner with an annual pension of two thousand livres, to be paid six months in advance.[5] What came of the inquiry is not revealed.

Ironically enough, the Revolutionary assemblies while they did away with lettres de cachet resorted to the same practice without employing the term, and during the Reign of Terror, when from ninety thousand to five hundred thousand persons were imprisoned in France as suspects (estimates by scholars), incarcerated more in this manner than were ever incarcerated at any given time during the Old Regime. Actually the arbitrary arrests of the Revolutionary period long antedated the Terror, going back to 1789, and there is reason for believing that there was no period when they were not made. Delaunay, deputy for Angers, made the charge in November, 1792, and gave figures to support it.[6] Despite all this, the condemnation of the lettres de cachet in 1790 did operate for the abolition of arbitrary arrest after a few years.

A second aspiration of the prison reformers was achieved on February 7, 1791, when the National Assembly decreed that thenceforth there would be a distinction between the prisons for those awaiting trial and the prisons for those convicted. Within the area of these two general types of prison there were to be subdivisions or special prisons, each to accommodate a particular class of the accused or convicted. Thenceforth there were to be no state prisons, but all prisons were to be local and controlled by the municipal administrations, with the departmental administrations exercising supervisory powers and the prerogative of appointing the jailors. To avoid arbitrary arrests, it was stipulated that no jailor might receive or hold any man without a specific order. Neither might a prisoner awaiting trial be placed in a

[5] *Ibid.*, XIX, 636; *Journal des débats et des decrets*, no. 530, pp. 185-86.

[6] See accounts of the arrest of Augéard and Granet in the *Mercure de France*, March 20, 1790, pp. 272-73; January 29, 1791, pp. 361-62; also *Réimpression de l'ancien Moniteur*, XIV, 481.

prison for those already convicted, or vice versa. The assembly in the same decree took care to stipulate that prisoners were to be treated humanely, with good food, clean quarters, courteous treatment (unless unruly, in which case they might be placed in solitary confinement or irons), and their health watched. Any mistreatment of a prisoner was to render the jailor liable to fine. And to see that all went properly within the prisons, inspection was to be made twice a week by one of the municipal officers. This was a far-reaching measure, and had circumstances permitted its proper execution, many of the hopes of the reformers would have been achieved. Unfortunately that was not to be; yet it may be remarked that throughout the Revolutionary era prison inspections appear to have been made regularly as ordered. This law was incorporated bodily in the penal code of September 25, 1791.[7] The French in 1791 ended their practice of sending prisoners convicted of crime to the galleys, ordering that thenceforth they be put in irons (i.e., loaded with a ball and chain) and employed at works useful to society. September, 1792, the galleys were abolished, only to be reestablished on a temporary basis the next month and to continue as such throughout the 1790's.[8] They rapidly came to be known as hulks (*pontons or bagnes*) rather than galleys (*galères*), but actually they had been hulks since the reign of Louis XIV.

Prisoners for debt also were slow in obtaining release, despite the fact that before the Revolution, Howard and others had called attention to their plight and many of the cahiers had asked for their liberation. The debtors that drew public sympathy most were the fathers imprisoned for inability or refusal to pay for the "month of nursing"—the expense of caring for the illegitimate children of which they were allegedly the fathers. Not until

[7] *Réimpression de l'ancien Moniteur*, VII, 327; *Mercure de France*, Feb. 19, 1791, pp. 188-90; J. B. Duvergier, *Collection complète des lois, décrets, ordonnances, réglemens* (2nd ed., Paris, 1834-1906), III, 346-47, 403-404.

[8] Duvergier, *Collection complète des lois*, III, 403-404; IV, 475-76; V, 20; *Réimpression de l'ancien Moniteur*, s.v. "galérien" in Table des matières. On April 4, 1793, the Convention freed deserters that had been placed in the galleys, since it needed them for army service again, and on September 21 of that year it prohibited galley slaves to wear longer their time-honored caps, now become the bonnet of liberty. *Réimpression de l'ancien Moniteur*, XVI, 58, 717. Certain galley centers had been suppressed in 1789—at Nice, Le Havre, Lorient, and Cherbourg. *GE*, IV, 1154, s.v. "bagne."

September 15, 1791, and August 25, 1792, were laws made terminating the practice, the prisoners freed, and the public treasury assumed their debts.[9] Other debtors continued to languish in prison until 1793 with little interest manifested in their plight. At length on March 3, 1793, Danton, minister of war, spoke before the Convention in their behalf, eulogizing liberty and urging the immediate release of all imprisoned debtors. A decree to this effect was passed by acclamation. Jeanbon Saint-André declared that this was not enough and called for another decree which would prohibit for the future arrest for debt. This too was enacted. But lest the first decree bring the release of some receivers general then in prison for bankruptcy toward the state, it was ordered that the Committee on Legislation present a bill dealing with exceptions. This of course served as a staying order, and by April 8 nothing had been done to release the debtors. On that day Robespierre sharply complained at the slowness and demanded immediate action in releasing the imprisoned debtors, declaring that they should be freed to provide for their families. A decree adopted ordering the immediate release of all debtors throughout the republic, and directing the minister of justice to report within two days on its execution, remitting the names of those released. How such a report could be made within two days is inconceivable.[10]

This did not complete legislation on prisons during the Revolution. On October 18, 1794, the Committee of Public Works made a report to the Convention bitterly indicting existing conditions and calling for better sanitation and better treatment in general in the prisons. In consequence, the Convention decreed the next day that prisons of all types should at once be made more sanitary and habitable, and that those needing to be abandoned should be replaced by new ones having these qualities. The Committee of Public Works was ordered to have this in charge. It was also directed to see that all prisoners, more especially the old and sick, were well fed and clothed. Two other committees were directed to take steps immediately to see that all prisoners of

[9] Duvergier, *Collection complète des lois*, 415; Tuetey, *Répertoire générale*, II, no. 3118. The law was not amended exempting debtors for the *mois de nourrice* from imprisonment until August 25, 1792.

[10] *Réimpression de l'ancien Moniteur*, XV, 666; XVI, 125.

both sexes were given work which would occupy them throughout each day.[11] Already the penal code of September 25, 1791, had ordered that convicts should be employed at work, and this provision had been renewed in the act of September, 1792, abolishing the galleys, but apparently it had met negligent compliance, even as other matters had. Emphasis on work to occupy the prisoner's mind had been stressed by Howard as a means of combating boredom, one of the worst features of the prison regime.

The Revolutionary governments set out to build new prisons, with attention given to better light and sanitation. In 1791-1792 they engaged the architect Giraud to draw up a set of plans for making the prisons of Paris more sanitary, but for lack of money and other reasons the plans were not carried out. A unique feature in them was that of a circular hallway (*chemins de ronde*), evidently at Bentham's suggestion. He also proposed more windows, more grills, thicker walls, and more courts for exercise than hitherto.[12] At Marseille plans for building a new hospital were adopted in 1790, only to be dropped shortly later. It appears that actually few if any new hospitals were constructed in the 1790's, save for the makeshift reconstruction of other buildings to serve as prisons. Of these there were many. Paris at one time during the Terror had thirty-four prisons, most of them makeshifts, but by December, 1794, they had been reduced to fourteen. These newer prisons are reported to have been better on the whole than some of the older ones and the treatment in them more humane.[13]

Had there been no Reign of Terror in the 1790's, the story of the prison regime of that period might have been entirely different. The reform of the prisons as set forth on paper by the Revolutionary bodies was extensive, possibly all that should have been needed for a complete transformation; but one who reads the records of the actual conditions prevailing in the prisons is unable to see that much change for the better was inaugurated.

[11] *Ibid.*, XXII, 291, 397.

[12] For a discussion of Giraud's plans, which were submitted in 1793 but not adopted, see Charles du Bus, "La Révolution à l'exposition du Cabinet des Cartes," *RF*, LXII (1912), 519-29.

[13] Dauban, *Les prisons de Paris sous la Révolution*, 141-42; *Réimpression de l'ancien Moniteur*, XXII, 769-70.

Indeed in some prisons the conditions were worse. This was due to crowding, brought about by the chaotic state of the times.

The crowding, at least in the prisons of Paris, began very early in the Revolution. Bailly, mayor of Paris, complained of it in a speech before the National Assembly on November 18, 1789. His complaint, he stated, was made at the direction of the municipal corps and the commune of Paris. The prison sanitary conditions had become alarming. The cause of the congestion he attributed to the slowness of the courts in handling the cases awaiting trial. More than a month had elapsed since the new judicial system had been inaugurated, but the new system was inadequate to meet the needs, and he urged the establishment of some temporary courts to assist in meeting the acute situation.[14] He did not add, as he might have done, that many of those in the prisons were unemployed workers from Paris and other cities who had been arrested in Paris for rioting and for other forms of lawlessness with which all France was afflicted throughout 1789 and 1790. It is doubtful if any period of the century had witnessed as much legal disorder, and in reality only a fraction of the legal violators had been arrested or could be arrested, for enforcement of law and order had come well-nigh near collapse.

At length on December 1, 1790, the assembly, acting on the recommendation of its Committee of Criminal Jurisprudence, decreed the establishment of a special court of ten judges to help relieve the congestion and called upon the city of Paris to furnish a place for the court to sit.[15]

The royalist journal *L'Ami du roi of* December 3, 1790, charged, erroneously, that the prisons were being filled with political opponents of the Revolution, while debtors and criminals were being released, and that laws were being enacted to benefit these classes. More serious was the complaint of debtors imprisoned at La Force, in Paris, made in a letter to the National Assembly under date of September 4, 1791, stating that they were being placed with prisoners charged with crime and that they were receiving an allowance inadequate to meet the cost of living.[16]

[14] *AP*, XX, 521-22; XXI, 171.
[15] *Réimpression de l'ancien Moniteur*, VI, 525.
[16] Tuetey, *Répertoire générale*, II, no. 3315.

Sanitary conditions in the Paris prisons were bad at that period, as was attested not only by Bailly but also by François Doublet, who was well informed on the prisons both there and in the provinces and in 1791 published a brochure, after the manner of Howard, with the objective of prison amelioration.[17]

The reform measures of February 7, 1791, had been carried out with partial success. Inspections were made regularly and the food appears to have been ample in quantity, but sanitation and civility varied widely from prison to prison. At least complaints continued in such numbers that in May, 1792, the minister of the interior called upon the mayor of Paris for an investigation and a report on the city's prison conditions. The investigation revealed that the conditions were as charged. The air was foul and the straw on which most of the prisoners slept was alive with vermin. The worst conditions were found at the Conciergerie.[18]

Nor was Paris alone in this respect. The surgeon Héraut of Grenoble wrote to the departmental council of Isère on December 15, 1792, stating that sick prisoners were "piled one on top of another," and asking aid.[19]

Little improvement took place in the prisons during the Revolution; in fact, from the summer of 1793 until the death of Robespierre on July 28, 1794, the prisons became progressively worse, especially in the larger cities, as they were filled with an ever-increasing horde of "suspects"—political prisoners drawn from every walk of life whose views ran counter to those of the Jacobins. While the greater number of the prisoners were royalists, many were Girondins, and as time passed even Jacobins whose views or actions did not meet the approval of Robespierre found themselves imprisoned. The greatest congestion came in 1794.

Prison sanitary conditions grew noxious in almost direct proportion to the crowding. The greatest source of trouble was the lack of adequate toilet facilities. The result was that the larger

17 *Mémoire sur la nécessité d'établir une réforme dans les prisons et sur les moyens de l'opérer. Suivi de la conclusion d'un rapport sur l'état actuel des prisons de Paris, lue à la séance publique de la Société Royale de Médicine, le 28 août 1791* (Paris, 1791), "Conclusion d'un rapport sur l'état actuel des prisons de Paris," 1-16.

18 Tuetey, *Répertoire générale*, VII, nos. 1869, 1873, 1876, 1888, 1889, 1891.

19 *Inventaire sommaire des archives départementales . . . Isère*, sér. L, I, 232.

number of prisons were pervaded from one end to the other
with a disgusting odor, of which memoirists of the time commonly
complained. Failure to open the prison windows to their full
extent often was a contributing factor. The smell moreover was
disseminated by the use of buckets for toilet purposes at night.
The prisoners nightly were locked in their cells, often many together, with one bucket for the cell.

The next greatest source of prison discomfort was the straw on
which most of the prisoners slept, or rather the vermin that infested the straw.[20] It was supposed to be changed twice a month,
but memoirists charged that this requirement was not followed.
This of course was for prisoners without means. Most of the
political prisoners of the era of the Revolution were people of
means, and it was possible for them to rent rooms with beds, and
indeed have bedding sent them from their homes. It was no
doubt due to inheritance from the royalists and Girondins during
the Terror that the prisons came to be much more provided with
beds.

Except at night the prisoners were permitted to move about
the prisons freely, and in most prisons were allowed to stroll in
the courts for fresh air and exercise. They suffered little from
the cold, for there was commonly at least one stove in the prison
for the men and another for the women; often there was a stove
on each floor. Around the stoves they gathered, save for prisoners
in the dungeons. Dungeons, unfortunately, still were in use in
the Revolutionary era, and many persons were placed in them,
generally for unruliness.[21]

In some prisons the political prisoners were confined in the
same quarters with those charged with crime, and they complained bitterly of this.[22] Some complained, too, that the food

[20] Albert Savine, *Les geôles de province sous le Terreur (récits de prisonniers)*
(Paris, 1911), 190; Pescayre, *Tableau des prisons de Toulouse* (Toulouse, 1794/
1795), 79, 95, 191; [Sir William Codrington] "An English Prisoner in Paris During
the Terror (1793-1794)," ed. by V. T. Harlow, *Camden Miscellany*, XV, 6.

[21] Pescayre, *Tableau des prisons de Toulouse*, 154, 194, 198, 226, 321; *Almanach
des prisons* (Paris, 1794/1795), 18; Savine, *Les geôles de province*, 179-80; Eugene
Saulnier, "Une prison revolutionnaire: les otages et prisonniers de guerre à l'Hôtel
du Dreneuc en 1795," *RF*, LXVI (1914), 213.

[22] Dauban, *Les prisons de Paris*, 173-75; Savine, *Les geôles de province*, 36.
Debtors, too, complained of being imprisoned with those charged with crime.
Tuetey, *Répertoire générale*, II, no. 3315.

was insufficient and poorly prepared, and certain prison inspectors made reports to the same effect. Nevertheless the larger number of writers indicate that the food was satisfactory up until the spring of 1794, when public attention was called to their good lot (for France was undergoing a severe food shortage) and the Convention ordered the fare reduced. The reason for this was that many of the prisoners, with money at their disposal, had been ordering fancy meals for their tables, either prepared in the prison kitchen or by an outside caterer and served in their cells. Due to the war and the military draft food was scarce and the government had resorted to price ceilings (Law of the Maximum) in an endeavor to keep prices within range of the poor. It was natural that complaint should be made that in the prisons the hated aristocrats were basking in sumptuous fashion while loyal republicans outside were supporting the government and fighting the war on scarce rations. Thenceforth the government ordered that all prisoners were to eat the same diet and at common tables. At the same time money and all metallic possessions were taken from the prisoners to meet war needs.[23]   These confiscations quite naturally evoked great complaint from the "suspects," but what else could they have expected? Aside from these confiscations, there were a few charges of monetary exactions by the jailors and of garnish by the prisoners charged with crime.

Many of the prisoners, as already intimated, had fared all along better than the others. It was possible for those with money to obtain special accommodations, both as to room and food, which made their lot enviable in comparison to that of the common prisoner. They could have their beds with linen, servants to attend them, and frequently were allowed to keep their wives and children in prison with them if they chose. Mistresses and friends, too, might come and go freely in most prisons, at least until 1794, when restrictions in all respects were tightened. This looseness of association led toward the accusation that the prisons had become brothels.

Contributing in the same direction was the not infrequent confinement overnight of male and female prisoners in the same

[23] Poirier and Montgey, *Les angoisses de la mort, ou idées des horreurs des prisons d'Arras* [1794], 19, 21-22; Dauban, *Les prisons de Paris*, 347-48; Pescayre, *Tableau des prisons de Toulouse*, 204-209.

quarters.[24] In the prisons generally male and female prisoners were allowed to mingle rather freely. Helen Maria Williams, who with her sister was placed at the Luxembourg in an "apartment" adjacent to that of two Girondist members of the Convention, reported that the four of them frequently assembled at night.[25] There must have been some instances of impropriety, but in general the relationship of the two sexes was held on a high plane. In some prisons the prisoners powdered their hair and assembled with all the show of civility and dignity portrayed in Taine's famous description of them, but in other prisons they were dejected, dressed shabbily, and cringed for fear of the outcome.

In the spring of 1794 the social conditions in the prisons were changed. Wives, children, and servants were removed. No guests were allowed, and no letters might be received or sent. The government feared that the prisons were the centers of hostile plotting and it moved in self-defense. The confiscation of metal objects in the possession of the prisoners, mentioned above, was due in part to the many suicides and in part to the many evasions. The prisoners, on their part, not knowing or not believing the true reason, ascribed the action to various conjectured reasons and complained bitterly at the action. Many hid their possessions in the chimneys or elsewhere.

The prisoners often charged their keepers with brutality. Some of the jailors, turnkeys, physicians, and surgeons no doubt were cruel as charged; but the majority were considerate and kind. Kindness toward the prisoners even caused certain of the prison keepers to become suspect and lose their jobs.[26]

[24] Jean Edmond Weelen, *Rochambeau, Father and Son,* tr. by Lawrence Lee (New York, 1936), 158-59, 162-67, 185-86; Etienne Charavay, "Le Conventionnel Gardien," *RF,* VIII (1885), 723; Savine, *Les geôles de province,* 7, 20-23, 28-29, 40, 183; *Journal des prisons de mon père, de ma mère et des miennes,* par Mme la Duchess de Duras, née Noailles (Paris, 1888), 41; Poirier and Montgey, *Les angoisses de la mort,* 17, 60.

[25] *Letters Containing a Sketch of the Politics of France. From the Thirty-first of May 1793 till the Twenty-eighth of July 1794 and of the Scenes which have Passed in the Prisons of Paris* (Philadelphia, 1796), 22-23.

[26] Dauban, *Les prisons de Paris,* 143, 271, 279, 283, 285-86, 289, 291, 309; Williams, *Letters,* 8-10, 30, 97; A. F. Delandine, *Tableau des prisons de Lyon, pour servir à l'histoire de la tyrannie de 1792 et 1793* (3d ed., Lyon, 1797), 158-59; Joseph Paris de l'Epinard, "L'humanité méconnue," *Mémoires sur les prisons* (in *Collection des mémoires relatifs à la Révolution française,* ed. by Berville and Barrière [Paris, 1823], I, 163-72); Poirier and Montgey, *Les angoisses de la mort,* 51, 57-58.

Certain memoirists complained of the fierce dogs used for policing the prison yards to prevent escapes. No instance has come to my attention of a dog attacking a prisoner. On the other hand the dogs were sometimes friendly and abetted the escapers.

In the provincial prisons during the Terror conditions varied even as they did in Paris. Professor Sirich, who has made the best study of the provincial prisons, has reported that while conditions varied from prison to prison, they were on the whole not bad.[27] It appears that the larger places experienced the worst conditions, due to the great congestion of prisoners.

The Thermidorian Reaction that set in with the execution of Robespierre on July 28, 1794, effected a reduction in the number of prisoners and thereby an improvement in prison conditions. Several dozen imprisoned deputies were permitted to go to their homes for the alleged purpose of regaining their health. This action was taken in response to letters of request they made to that end.

The charge was made by some memoirists that the sick were not properly cared for in the prisons, but other memoirs and letters make it clear that serious effort was taken to give proper medical attention to those needing it. Each prison had its own physician or surgeon or both. In general those imprisoned probably got better medical and surgical treatment than most of the French outside the prisons. Some epidemics did occur in the prisons, especially in scurvy and smallpox, but the authorities were solicitous to prevent them.

Such were the conditions that prevailed in the French prisons from 1789 to 1795. It was a time of great national crisis and civil war. Perhaps more surprising than the fact that the prisons were crowded and insanitary was the fact that so much consideration for the lot of the prisoners was shown. It is remarkable that in the prisons so many beds had been introduced, that heat was provided rather generally, that medical and surgical care on the whole was laudable, and that so many of the prison keepers and turnkeys were considerate. It would have been too much to expect that all conditions would have been ideal in a period of storm and stress when class hatred ran high. Nor should it be

---

[27] John Black Sirich, *The Revolutionary Committees in the Departments of France, 1793-1794* (Cambridge, 1943), 74-81.

forgotten that during this period no torture was applied, a radical change in itself.

The era was marked by much solicitude for the improvement of the prisons. Not all who wrote on the prisons were interested in this. Several score memoirs came to be written during the 1790's by political prisoners recording their experiences. Most of them appear to have been actuated by the political motive of damning their captors, and comparatively few were concerned with influencing future prison construction or administration. Nevertheless some treatises and speeches and reports of this period did have that end in view. In fact one finds in this period more interest in prison improvement than in the 1770's and 1780's.

Among the expressions of concern over prison conditions was that of the Committee of Mendicity of the National Assembly in its report of December 5, 1790. The whole question of human detention and its ends was discussed. The committee, headed by the Duc de La Rochefoucauld-Liancourt, took roughly the position of Howard in all matters.

The report or letter was written more particularly to Adrien Duport, minister of justice, by the Committee of Mendicity preparatory to its examination of conditions prevalent at the Bicêtre and the Salpêtrière, in response to numerous letters of complaint from the prisoners. The committee considered that it should acquaint the minister with its attitude as to what it would consider desirable in prison conditions. Duport, it happened, had been deputy for the nobility of Paris and one of the leaders in the assembly on the matter of reform of the criminal law. There was therefore no occasion for surprise that he wrote back on December 14 saying that he strongly shared the committee's sentiments.

These humanitarian sentiments were shared by Mirabeau, who in early 1790 drew up for the Committee on Lettres de Cachet a report in which he criticized the system of imprisonment and servitude then prevalent in France. He attacked especially arbitrary imprisonment on lettres de cachet, servitude in the galleys, and branding, and recommended a system whereby prisoners might be reclaimed for society. He advocated the establishment of a penitentiary system, with a "house of betterment" and about twelve acres of land set apart in each department, whereby prisoners might work in the fields or at manufactures from one to seven years, and at length leave the institution better fitted to reenter civil life. The chief note of his report was the desire for the reformation of the criminal. Prisoners who had shed blood should be left in prison, but their prison should be one where the air was pure and the food sufficient. Prisoners until proven guilty should be regarded as innocent and treated as such. Finally, prisoners for debt should be freed.[28] The report marked an advance in Mirabeau's thinking since he had published in 1782 his *Des lettres de cachet et des prisons d'état*. His ideas had crystallized and coincided with those of Howard.

Another supporter of Howard's ideas was one Reynier, a deputy who in 1790 published three or four articles on penal matters in the *Moniteur universel,* evidently to influence the assembly in its revision of the criminal law and in penal reform. In his article of February 26 he advocated a system of penal institutions such as existed in Amsterdam. Howard had praised the Dutch prisons and Reynier, long a resident at Amsterdam, had visited them and was familiar with them. The whole design of the Dutch prisons was to bring about the prisoner's reformation.[29]

From another quarter the prison of Philadelphia was extolled as ideal. In 1788 Brissot de Warville, organizer and the most ardent member of the Amis des Noirs, had made a voyage to the United States of America to get information useful in that cause. While in America he was greatly impressed with the prison near Philadelphia. It was a penitentiary for convicts rather than an institution for prisoners awaiting trial. Its purpose was the reform of the prisoners. They were all obliged to work. The place was sanitary. He particularly praised the light and cleanliness prevailing in the prison hospital. He claimed to have visited hospitals in various parts of France but nowhere save at Besançon had he seen a hospital whose sanitary conditions could be compared with those at this hospital.

The Administrative Assembly of the department of Isère was also among the advocates of prison reform at that period. On November 30, 1791, after hearing a report from one of its committees sharply criticizing the conditions in the prisons of Gre-

28 Vicomte H. Begouen, "Un rapport inédit sur le régime des prisons," *Revue d'économie politique,* I (1887), 504-12.
29 *Réimpression de l'ancien Moniteur,* III, 460-61.

noble, it adopted recommendations for "healthy, well-ventilated, and safe lodgings," where the straw would be changed once a month rather than once every four months, to the end that vermin and sickness might be eradicated. It ordered that some architects be engaged to draw up plans for giving the prisoners better quarters. At the same time praise was given the prison concierge, Bigillion, for his "kindness and humanity" to prisoners.[30]

More elaborate than any of the other proposals of reform was a pamphlet published in 1791 by François Doublet, a physician of Paris.[31] Member of the Royal Society of Medicine, he had been sent by the government in 1787 with another physician, Delaporte, to investigate an epidemic of jail fever at Lorient, Brittany. There his interest in prison conditions was awakened, and in the succeeding years he investigated prison conditions elsewhere, especially in Paris. He read Howard's books and became his disciple in opinion. Sharing also his zeal, he sent his brochure in manuscript form to the chairman of the Committee of Mendicity in 1791, and later read it before the Royal Society of Medicine. Commenting that very little legislation on the prisons had been rendered by the National Assembly, he proceeded to publish the work.

At the outset he presented pictures of the prisons in Paris, Melun, Provins, Dôle, Vesoul, and Strasbourg. All were insanitary, foul, and their food poor. Immorality abounded, and the jailors and their subordinates were little tyrants and exploited the prisoners. As for the Parisian prisons, only one, the Force, recently built, was desirable, and even there the smell of urine prevailed throughout. All of the other sixteen prisons were badly placed and badly constructed, dark, damp, and foul. All the prisons had good quarters reserved for those able to pay, but accommodations for others were uncomfortable and unhealthy. This state of things he resented as an affront toward the poor.

He would introduce radical reforms. He suggested the establishment of two *maisons de force* in each of the eighty-three French departments, one for beggars and vagabonds, the other

[30] *Inventaire sommaire des archives départementales postérieures à 1790. Isère,* L 55. Dungeons were still in use in the prison at Grenoble.

[31] *Mémoire sur la nécessité d'établir une réforme dans les prisons et sur les moyens de l'opérer* (Paris, 1791), 92, 116.

for prisoners charged with crime. All state prisons he would sup-
press entirely. The women and the men should be kept strictly
separate. In each prison there should be assembly halls where
the prisoners might gather, also an infirmary and individual cells.
There should be no dungeons. Each prison moreover should have
its courtyard for men and another for women, where the prisoners
might take daily walks.

He made detailed recommendations about the prison fare, its
content and how it should be subsidized, and similarly regarding
the clothing and bedding of the prisoners. He drafted a proposed
law for assuring the health, comfort, and care of the prisoners.
Though never adopted, it presented clearly his ideas and revealed
how he was influenced by Howard.

Above all, he was solicitous to provide for the sanitation and
comfort of the prisoners. The floors should be swept daily, and
the walls scraped and whitewashed every two years. He did not
even forget the latrines and night vessels, which he insisted
should be cleaned daily.

He was interested in the religious and moral life of the prisoners
and specified that each prison should have its chapel and religious
services. Endeavor should be made to reform the prisoner; in
fact this was the chief end of imprisonment. He even went so
far as to denounce as "barbarous" the sentencing of prisoners for
life terms, when a few years might expiate the wrong done to
society.

There is no evidence that he exerted any perceptible influence.
His brochure was not printed a second time, he was not called
before the National Assembly for a report, and there is no record
of his making further efforts for the cause.

In 1791 a more famous plan for prison construction and administration was brought to the attention of the French government
and by it published, drawn up by the English philosopher Jeremy
Bentham. The scheme known as the Panopticon had first occurred
to his brother, Samuel Bentham, when in Russia in the 1780's, and
Jeremy got the idea from him on a visit there in 1787. In 1791
he sent a copy of his project to Garran de Coulon, a member of
the Legislative Assembly's Committee on the Reform of the
Criminal Law. Perhaps it was in recognition of this act that in
1792 the assembly incorporated Bentham's name as one of fifteen

prominent foreigners on whom it conferred honorary citizenship. The assembly did not adopt the scheme, however, perhaps because it lacked the money.

The chief feature of Bentham's proposed prison was conveyed by its designation Panopticon (all-seeing), since the jailor was to have an elevated central office from which he could see with the aid of mirrors what was happening in every cell in the building. The structure would be circular or polygonal and the hallway circular, with the cells opening on it. This arrangement was designed to prevent disorders or attempts at evasion. The building would also be equipped with running water and central heating. All these were new features.

Not less interesting was the contract-management mode of administration under which it would operate. The prisoners would be leased out to the jailor, who would contract for them at a specified sum for each prisoner. Whatever he might make above that would be his rightful profit. However, he would promise to care for all the needs of the prisoners adequately, and the prisons were to be open at all time to inspection from any who wished to make it. The jailor would be required to teach the prisoners trades, and to let them share in the profits. This would encourage them in their labor. The jailor moreover would be required to take out group life insurance on the prisoners, partly as a protection to himself, partly to them.

The prisoners would wear a uniform and be compelled to work. He would not permit alcoholic drink of any type to be brought into the prisons, considering that temperance was essential to good prison conditions. He would permit the prisoners to associate with one another in small bands, believing that they would gain from it in knowledge and morale. He would permit unmarried prisoners to marry, provided that their conduct was good. He considered that it might prove an incentive toward good conduct. Further, he would see that the prisoners received instruction, partly to occupy their time, partly to inform them better on useful and wholesome matters. Ignorance he regarded as conducive to crime; education would help them to make their way in the world. Moreover, like Howard he believed that religion should be emphasized in the prisons, as it was important in the reformation of prisoners. He would have a chaplain in each prison to hold public services and to act as a friend and counselor to the prisoners.

At length in 1796 the Duc de La Rochefoucauld-Liancourt published anonymously at Philadelphia, in both French and English, a pamphlet *Des prisons de Philadelphie,* in which like Brissot before him he extolled the prisons of that Quaker city.

Three years later he praised further the Philadelphia prisons, rather penitentiary, in his *Travels Through the United States of North America.*[32] At some length he set forth its commendable features. Those convicted for more serious crimes were given solitary confinement for a portion of their sentence; petty offenders, however, were not confined. The cells were eight by six by nine, well lighted and heated. The prison was equipped with water closets, one in each cell. The cells moreover were whitewashed twice a year.

Prisoners not in solitary confinement wore a uniform and were put in wards with other prisoners. No exactions were made of them, by the jailor or other prisoners. They were well fed, having three meals a day. The women worked at washing and nursing. The men were put at various tasks according to their ability— carpentry, shoemaking, tailoring, weaving, marble polishing, combing wool, beating hemp, etc. Payment was made each prisoner four times a year, and when he left the prison walls a general settlement was made with him.

The Duc was impressed that the state of New York had set out to emulate the Philadelphia system with a prison that would cost $900,000.[33] His *Travels* as well as his brochure on the prisons were designed for French readers primarily, and in France nothing like the Philadelphia system had yet been inaugurated. Once again, as so often before, French advocates of reform drew on their travels and reading of other countries for ideas. The Philadelphia system, which was only the Dutch workhouse system more developed, embodied the best ideas for treatment of prisoners during the century.

Had it not been for war and the Terror, the French might have developed a prison system equally laudable as a result of the Revolution, but the internal strife was too disrupting. Yet, it is doubtful whether a wholesome prison system could have

[32] II, 336-48.   [33] *Ibid.,* 464-65.

been created without destroying the old prisons completely and building an entirely new set, with features needed to meet the new conditions and standards. The Legislative Assembly and certain departmental administrations realized this and made plans for elaborate prison construction, only to be obliged to lay them aside when war came. Even so, the Revolutionists inaugurated some remarkable changes in the prisons, though crowding and indifference on the part of the jailors and others in many instances prevented the proper execution of the changes. Here again, as in other fields, the thinkers paved the way for the legislator and administrator.

CHAPTER EIGHT

Criminal Law Reform
Prior to 1770

R EVISION of the criminal law was one of the most badly
needed and eagerly sought eighteenth-century reforms, and
probably no other factor had greater influence in provoking the
Revolution than the feeling of injustice that was rapidly disseminated among the masses in the three decades prior to 1789.
From the time of the Calas Case in 1762 a score or two of writers,
many of them jurists, set out to enlighten the public concerning
the cruelties and stupidities existing in the French laws and in
French legal procedure. Not uncommonly their writings were
provoked by cases of flagrant criminal injustice, and with one
accord they declared France to be a country where the innocent
suffered. So many illustrations did they give of innocents imprisoned for years or decades, tortured, and executed, that the
public came to regard it as difficult if not well-nigh impossible
to get justice in the courts, and to accept the conclusion that the
whole system needed revision. Happily both Louis XV and
Louis XVI showed themselves interested in rectifying injustice.
Louis XVI indeed undertook a number of reforms, so that the
populace did not lay their discontent at the royal door but at
that of the ministers and magistrates. It was not their monarch,
but the system that needed changing.

The French laws were a cumbersome accumulation that had
come into existence during hundreds of years. Some were national, others provincial. In the latter little uniformity prevailed.
Made by the provincial estates or by the parlements, some had
originated prior to the union of their province to the French

kingdom. Of the national laws, some were royal declarations or edicts, others orders of the royal councils. Ordinances of parlements affected only those provinces under their particular jurisdiction; those of the parlement of Paris affected between a third and a half of the kingdom. In this confused mass of laws there had never been a reform of large proportions nor any codification to make them available in clear form. Magistrates accordingly wasted much time in deciding the jurisdiction of questionable cases and lawyers labored away in the labyrinth of laws to find the statutes governing any case in question.

In the legislation many acts were treated as crimes that today would not be so regarded, or that would not have been so considered at that time in some other country. Thus it was a crime for anyone living along the seacoast in France to boil down sea water and make salt. It was a crime to hunt on the royal or noble estates, save for those enjoying the privilege. It was a crime to publish a book which had not received the imprimatur of the royal censor, or to sell a book that the parlements had condemned. It was a crime to treat in sacrilegious manner the ceremonies of the Roman Catholic Church or to steal the sacred vessels or vestments. It was a crime to disseminate or hold Jansenist opinions. It was a crime to commit suicide or even to attempt it. And so on. Many infractions of the law that today would be considered merely misdemeanors then were classed as crimes.

The penalties were harsh. Not only for murder and treason but also for a vast number of charges the convicted party was put to death. This, in turn, was inflicted in a variety of ways. Damiens, for attempting to assassinate the king in 1757, was drawn and quartered. His hands and feet were tied securely to four horses, which were lashed and driven in the direction of the four points of the compass; and when after several attempts of this his limbs had not been pulled asunder, an executioner used a butcher's cleaver to cut him apart and later burned the body.[1] For counterfeiters who tampered with the king's coinage, death in boiling water was the penalty. For those who committed sacrilege in a church and certain other offenses, the sentence was death by burning. D'Argenson reported two peasants burned

---

[1] Fernand Mitton, *Tortures et supplices en France* (Paris, 1909), 335. The execution took two hours.

for sodomy in 1750, and in 1768 three thieves were burned for stealing sacred vases in a church at Paris.[2] For highway robbery, housebreaking, murder, and other atrocious deeds, the penalty was either hanging or breaking on the wheel. This latter was a brutal mode of execution in which the victim was bound prostrate to a cross of Saint Andrew and struck by the executioner eleven times with an iron bar, each blow breaking a bone, until the legs had been broken below and above the knees, the arms below and above the elbows, the thighs crushed in, and finally the chest. The mangled body was then placed on a horizontal wagon wheel and raised aloft, before the gaping eyes of perhaps ten or twenty thousand spectators that had come from far and near to witness the brutal spectacle, many of them paying fancy prices for the vantage points of nearby windows and roofs. After the midcentury the victim was often smothered prior to this savage affair.[3] Nobles might claim exemption from execution on the wheel or by hanging and ask for decapitation. The Chevalier de la Barre was executed by strangling.

Punishments of lesser nature might include mangling by cutting off the hand, a penalty reserved for parricides which legally persisted until 1832 but was apparently not administered in the 1700's, and by cutting or piercing of the tongue. Branding on one of the shoulders was commonly administered to galley slaves, to robbers receiving lighter sentences than execution, and to beggars and vagabonds convicted more than once. The mark varied, "M" for beggars (*mendiants*), "V" for robbers (*voleurs*), "Gal" for galley slaves (*galériens*), and the fleur-de-lys for other grounds.[4]

Conviction to the galleys for a period of years or for life was

2 Département de la Seine, *Supplément à l'inventaire sommaire des archives hospitalières antérieures à 1790*, rédigé par M. Brièle (Paris, 1888), 313; *Journal et mémoires du Marquis D'Argenson*, ed. by E. J. B. Rathery (Paris, 1859-1867), VI, 227.

3 A. Chéruel, *Dictionnaire historique des institutions, moeurs et coutumes de la France* (4th ed., Paris, 1874), I, 1111-12. This mode of execution is called by S. Baring-Gould a relic of the ancient practice of human sacrifice to the sun god. *Strange Survivals: Some Chapters in the History of Man* (3d ed., London, 1905), 245.

4 Chéruel, *Dictionnaire historique*, I, 441; Robert Anchel, *Crimes et châtiments au XVIIIe siècle* (Paris, 1933), 116-17. While branding was abolished in 1791, it was revived for two types of legal violators in 1802 and continued until 1832. *GE*, s.v. "Marque," XXIII, 286-87.

meted for certain crimes, and compared to a penitentiary sentence of today. Its regime was rigorous but much to be preferred to the lot of "rotting" in the prisons on a lettre de cachet, without trial, as happened to many. Legal infractions of a degrading type were punished by scourging, the pillory, and public exhibition in the streets. Banishment was administered. Prostitutes and beggars at times were banished to the colonies, and members of the parlements were occasionally expelled from Paris, on royal order, to the provinces.

Not only were the punishments terrifying by their severity, the criminal procedure for settling the question of guilt or innocence was equally frightening. The accused was thrust into prison without the possibility of posting bond, and he might not obtain legal counsel until he had already deposed under oath all his testimony on the case. This examination was private, with no one present but one of the two or three judges who would sit on the case and render the decision. His secretary might also be present. The accused was forced to depose all that he knew, both concerning his own guilt and that of any accomplices. The judge obtaining the testimony was thus from the outset a sort of prosecuting attorney. If in any way he was dissatisfied with the testimony, he had but to issue the order and the accused was submitted to torture, of which various forms existed, such as the rack, the iron horse, heavy weights, the strappado, the forced drinking of water, roasting of the feet over a fire, the placing of peas in shoes, etc.[5] Marie Tromel, the moll of a notorious robber gang of the midcentury, was forced to sit on a ducking stool, clad only in a chemise, while her feet were brought five times over the flames of a fire. The object was to get information on her confederates. She "talked," but was careful to give information chiefly on members of the gang already dead and to shield those yet alive.[6] Similarly the young brother of Cartouche, notorious robber executed in the early 1720's, was tortured by suspension in the air with cords about his armpits for two hours, until he died. The object was to obtain information on accomplices of

[5] Paul M. Bondois, "La torture dans le ressort du Parlement de Paris au XVIIIe siècle," AHRF, n.s. V (1928), 322-35. The forms of torture varied somewhat in France according to locality.

[6] Lorédan, La grande misère, 295-97. For the use of burning sulphur in extracting information from her paramour, Henri Peyron, earlier, see ibid., 103-109.

his brother, but the lad would not talk.[7] Thus a person often was tortured even though he had confessed his guilt or was not even suspect of a crime, merely to force him to give information that would lead to the conviction of others who were guilty. The use of torture for the extraction of evidence continued in France down to the 1780's.

After the accused was interrogated, witnesses were called in by the judge and their information likewise was given in secret. Their testimony was delivered under oath, and they were not permitted later to alter it without being subject to prosecution for false witness. This sometimes worked to the disadvantage of the accused. Moreover the accused was not permitted to know prior to the trial the nature of the evidence against him. Nor was his counsel, if he was able to afford counsel, permitted to know the evidence; and if he was too poor to afford counsel, none was provided by the court.

Throughout the long period of waiting, for many months might elapse before he was called for trial, he remained in a filthy prison, without possibility of bail; and if more than one trial was necessary, he might be there for years.

At his trial he was forced to sit on a stool, called the *sellette*, in humiliating fashion. It was there for the first time that his accusers were brought before him. He was treated in all respects, from the moment of his arrest to the end of his trial, as if guilty. The burden of proving his innocence was upon him.

This briefly was the state of things in eighteenth-century France, and it is little wonder that it provoked increasing condemnation as the century advanced from a score or two of writers, who viewed their social institutions in the light of reason and humanity and considered reform imperative.

Some extenuation for this Draconian system of laws and punishments might possibly have been made had crime been rampant in France, but in truth it was not. She had her criminals indeed, but conditions were not exceptionally bad. Occasionally there were robbers on the highways, but on the whole the mounted police (*maréchaussée*), forerunners of the modern *gendarmerie*, kept the highways and the cities well protected. Travelers were never forced, as in Italy, Spain, and sometimes even in England,

---

[7] Barbier, *Chronique de la régence et du règne de Louis XV*, I, 226.

to go in convoys with armed guards. If crime was more prevalent in France than in Switzerland, Holland, and the Scandinavian regions, it appears to have been less prevalent than in most of southern Europe or in Britain.

Nor were the French necessarily intimidated by their severe laws and rigorous legal procedure. This was evidenced by the flouting of the religious curbs by the Protestants, by the wholesale disregard for local and governmental legislation during the Plague of Provence (1720-1722) and the cattle epizootics (1714-1715, 1744-1745, and 1775-1776), and by the multitude of riots that occurred in the periods of famine. The Frenchman of the eighteenth century was very much as he is today, an individualist doing as he wished. Criminals in our modern concept of the term were relatively few, and it is certainly doubtful that the harsh penal system was the factor responsible. Many of the advocates of legal reform, however, insisted that crime was great in France, and that harsh punishments did not lessen it.

The factor responsible for the preaching of legal reform was not the lessening or the accentuation of crime but rather the change that had come over men's minds as a result of the astounding developments in natural science and philosophy of the 1600's and 1700's. Contact with non-European peoples through travel and commerce, disgust with the wars of religion and religious persecution, and greater acquaintance with the writings and legal systems of the Greeks and the Romans had much to do with the developing social consciousness. The Age of Reason and Humanity had resulted. Its prophets were the French *philosophes,* and their pupils were the intellectually promising young men of Europe. Nearly all of the advocates of legal reform in France in the 1700's were either *philosophes* or their pupils, and many of the latter lived to take a part in bringing their dreams to pass in the period of the Revolution. Not a few, too, ironically enough, were executed as royalists during the Revolution or escaped this fate only by fleeing abroad as refugees until the Revolution had ended. In brief, most of them were moderates and not the extremists that they might have appeared in that day.

Prior to the 1760's the criticisms were few and mild.[8] In 1725 the Abbé de Saint-Pierre made a call for a wholesale revision of

---

[8] Bondois, "La torture dans le ressort du Parlement de Paris," V, 323-24.

the civil law. Yet beyond a simple statement that the criminal law also needed revision he had nothing to say. He observed that for 140 years no attempt had been made at revision of the civil law, which varied widely from province to province. The laws should be made both shorter and clearer, so that even the layman might consult the statutes and interpret them without difficulty. Moreover, they should be made uniform for all France. By making these reforms he thought that the expense of lawsuits could be reduced two-thirds, and the number of lawyers likewise reduced.[9] He called upon the king to be a modern Justinian, and assured him that mankind would long be grateful to him for it. He commented that he had spoken to various lawyers and found that they, too, had long realized the necessity of this reform. Needless to add, the reform did not come.

At the summit of the French legal profession sat the Chancellor D'Aguesseau, who in a tract dedicated to Cardinal Fleury suggested a mild legal reform—the abolition of "spices" and the establishment of gratuitous justice in the courts, through state subsidy. The "spices," it may be explained, were gifts or legal fees that had to be paid the magistrates by all those whose cases were heard in their courts, and were far from negligible. This situation had come about through the sale of magistral posts, started under Louis XII as a means of getting funds necessary for the French treasury. Legal posts thus continued to be bought and transmitted from father to son. Realizing that the situation needed relief, D'Aguesseau proposed that the government pay the magistrates and recorders and bring about some changes, suppressing many unnecessary posts. Among the beneficial results that he envisaged would be the speeding up of justice and aid to the poor against extortion from the rich. But D'Aguesseau did not press his recommendation of reform, and nothing resulted.[10]

The advocate Barbier, of the parlement of Paris, in his *Journal* in 1750 revealed his cynicism toward the employment of torture. He told of a poor tavern keeper of Charenton, near Paris, being tortured and condemned, unjustly, for highway robbery. The

[9] *Mémoire pour diminuer le nombre des procès,* 1-2, 5-9, 35-38, 137-38, 153, 167, 169, 440.

[10] François Monnier, *Le Chancelier d'Aguesseau: sa conduite et ses idées politiques et son influence sur le mouvement des esprits pendant la première moitié du XVIIIe siècle* (2d ed., Paris, 1763), 478-81.

real robber had later confessed and was broken at the wheel for it. Barbier, however, was no agitator of reform, and even his *Journal* was not published until decades later. His random remark does, nevertheless, permit us to see how some of the more intelligent magistrates were thinking.[11]

Meanwhile, more boldness was demonstrated by still another eminent magistrate. Charles de la Brède, baron de Montesquieu, president of the parlement of Bordeaux, in his *Lettres persanes* of the 1720's made some satirical remarks regarding French laws and customs that irritated the government and prevented his election to the French Academy for a number of years; later in 1748 in his *Esprit des lois* he set forth other criticisms and suggestions with both more deftness and far-reaching extent than in the former work. He hesitated to speak forth on the matter of torture, after "so many men of learning and genius" had opposed it in writing. He insisted that punishment should be proportional in gravity to the crime committed, and that this last should be judged by its effect on society. Therefore highway robbery should not carry the same punishment as murder. In the event that the same penalty be given for both, opportunity should be left for pardon. This, he declared, had its influence in England, where hope of transportation led robbers never to murder; but contrariwise in Russia, where the two crimes were punished alike, the robbers always murdered their victims.[12]

The spirit of moderation ever should guide the legislator, he asserted. Extremes should be avoided. Some laws were badly made. Indeed, legislators in ignorance sometimes made laws which opposed the very ends they wished to obtain.[13] Montesquieu's work clearly contributed toward a critical examination of eighteenth-century laws.

And yet in the *Esprit des lois* one does not find French laws and legal procedure singled out for attack. Too deft for this, Montesquieu made there a great analytical and comparative study of the laws of all countries, both ancient and contemporary, Asiatic as well as European, commenting on the merits of various forms of government, as Plato, Fénelon, and others before him had done. Censorious of despotism and arbitrary rule, he casti-

---

[11] Esmein, *Histoire de la procédure criminelle en France*, 357.
[12] *Esprit des lois*, book VI, chs. XVI-VII.   [13] *Ibid.*, book XXIX, ch. I.

gated brutal and capricious features of the European legal systems of his day. Over and over he remarked that harsh punishments did not really work for a diminution of crime. An Anglophile, he was one of the first *philosophes* to point to England as the land with institutions for France to copy. Not only the English system of limited monarchy but also the English system of trial by jury he idealized. It was fitting that a man should be tried by twelve of his peers. The judge or judges merely should deliver the verdict. Moreover he discredited the system of torture by questioning its value, and insisted, after the British, that a man should be considered innocent until proven guilty.[14] This method of citing English precedent was followed thenceforth by nearly every advocate of legal reform for the rest of the century. And not only did they point to England as a beacon light, they followed Montesquieu also in citing the legal conventions of Greece and Rome and of various contemporary European countries, more especially in regard to precedent they wished followed by France.

His most influential pupil, the Marquis de Beccaria, was not long thereafter in publishing his great work. A young Italian, resident of Milan, it is essential to consider him here because of his enormous influence in France. His treatise, the *Essay on Crimes and Punishments*, published in 1764 in Italian, at once caught the attention of the reading public, was translated into virtually every other European language, and went into almost countless editions before the end of the century, as all persons of aspiration to culture, including the crowned heads of Europe, read and admired the little work. Its reception was nothing less than astounding, and few books in modern times have so influenced the ideas of subsequent generations.

The greatest single feature of his work was his attack on the use of torture. He had little if anything more to say on the subject than what some predecessors, even in the late 1600's, had said, but he wrote in a clear, persuasive fashion that none before him had possessed. Bolder than any predecessor suggesting legal reform, he called the use of torture "a cruelty consecrated by custom in most nations" and added: "Either he [the accused] is

---

[14] See, e.g., his discussion of the cruel laws and harsh enforcement in Japan, *ibid.*, book VI, ch. XIII; also, book VI, ch. IV, book XIV, ch. XV, and book XXV, ch. XIV; Esmein, *Histoire de la procédure criminelle en France*, 369-70.

guilty or not guilty. If guilty, he should only suffer the punishment ordained by the laws, and torture becomes useless, as his
confession is unnecessary. If he be not guilty, you torture the
innocent." He stated that torture also "is used to make the
criminal reveal his accomplices," but he asked how could one
depend upon confession any more for accuracy in this instance
than the other? In unmistakable language he condemned torture
as unworthy of the age in which they lived.[15]

Torture was already on its way out. It no longer existed in
Britain, after some telling attacks had been made on it, by
Reginald Scott and others, in connection with witchcraft; and
inevitably it would have disappeared in time on the Continent
without Beccaria. But this little treatise rang its death knell,
and within the next half century torture was gradually abolished
from the courts of one European country after another. In France,
Louis XVI abolished its usage to make a man confess his own
guilt in 1780, and in 1788 its usage to discover accomplices in a
crime. The Revolutionists, to make certain of its termination,
abolished it again. The little book of Beccaria would rate as one
of the world's great treatises on human liberty had it espoused
nothing else; but it did.

Beccaria went further and questioned the whole system of
capital punishment. Had society through its courts the right to
take human life? Who gave it that right? No, he continued: "the
punishment of death is not authorized by any right; for I have
demonstrated that no such right exists. It is therefore a war of a
whole nation against a citizen, whose destruction they consider
as necessary or useful to the general good." He could justify it
only in case of treason or revolution, threatening overthrow of the
state.[16]

Beccaria noted that "the experience of all the ages" proved "that
the punishment of death has never prevented determined men
from injuring society." And he pointed to the twenty-year reign
of Elizabeth of Russia, who had abolished the death penalty in
her domains as an example worthy of emulation. The shedding of
blood, even in execution of a criminal, is a terrible thing. He

[15] *An Essay on Crimes and Punishments, translated from the Italian; with a
Commentary, attributed to Mons. de Voltaire, translated from the French* (3d ed.,
London, 1770), 62, 68.
[16] *Ibid.*, 103-104.

lamented the spectacle that had been made of executions. The cruelty suffered by the executed tended to defeat the purpose of the execution by exciting the sympathy of the crowd for the criminal. "A punishment to be just should have only that degree of severity which is sufficient to deter others."[17]

Then, strangely for a humanitarian, he argued that life punishment at useful work would be preferable to the death sentence, saying that it would be more severe and terrifying to the criminal. On the other hand it would be more beneficial to society. Of what value is it to the state to kill one of its citizens who can then perform no further service for it? He would sanction this "slavery" of criminals as altogether preferable.[18]

He was one of the first to attack the severe laws directed against suicides. The laws of France, as of other countries, ordered that the body of the suicide be dragged on a hurdle at a horse's tail about the streets and denied decent burial, and that the suicide's property be confiscated for the crown. Beccaria declared that suicide was a crime incapable of being punished, since the party committing it was already dead. To punish the suicide would be like scourging a statue. Discussing the propriety of punishment further, he commented that the suicide did his country less harm than did an emigrant, for whereas an emigrant might take money from the country with him, the suicide took nothing but himself. Moreover the suicide rendered no aid to a rival country, but an emigrant might by throwing in his lot with it. Since emigration was no crime, why should suicide be so considered?[19]

The laws of a country ought to be mild, and there should be little need of pardons; but if pardons are to be granted, he insisted, they should be given by the legislators rather than the executive. If given by the executive, he said, they tend to be in conflict with the laws and to undermine them.[20]

Shortly after the publication of Beccaria's work, Voltaire wrote a commentary on it, which subsequently was generally published with it, both in France and elsewhere. The *Commentaire* carried

---

[17] *Ibid.*, 104-107, 112-13.   [18] *Ibid.*, 105-107.

[19] *Ibid.*, 132-34. Mercier in his *Tableau de Paris* (III, 195) stated that in the 1780's the suicide's body was no longer treated with abuse, but was buried privately at police direction, with little noise.

[20] *Ibid.*, 175-77.

Voltaire's blessing. He was delighted with Beccaria's handling of the matter and proceeded throughout his seventy-nine pages to nod approval. Beccaria he called "that friend of humanity." As for torture, if a single country in the world were to abolish it with success, other countries would be justified in doing likewise. England was such a country. Moreover, other countries too, he declared, had abolished it with success. "The question therefore," he said, "is decided. Shall not a people who pique themselves on their politeness, pride themselves also on their humanity? Shall they obstinately persist in their inhumanity, merely because it is an ancient custom?"[21]

With regard to the death penalty, Voltaire remarked: "It hath long been observed, that a man after he is hanged is good for nothing, and that punishments invented for the good of society ought to be useful to it. It is evident that a score of stout robbers condemned for life to some public work would serve the state in their punishment, and that hanging them is a benefit to nobody but the executioner." The English, he observed, seldom executed thieves but transported them to their colonies; and in Russia, Elizabeth and Catherine II, in their respective reigns, had not executed a single criminal, nor had crime been increased thereby. He was of the opinion that crime developed from "too much holiday, and consequently too much idleness, and too much debauchery." "Oblige men to work, and you certainly make them honest." With this conclusion, of course, many will not agree. But he found more support in saying that the sword of justice "ought seldom to be drawn," and "that we ought rather to blunt than to sharpen its edge." He declared that for every guilty person who managed to escape penalty in the courts, a thousand who should be saved were convicted under the laws. Voltaire, however, did not go to the point of agreeing with Beccaria in denying that courts should have the right to take life, or of saying that the death penalty should be restricted to cases of danger to the existence of the state. He was mute on the subject.[22]

In regard to suicide, he asked where is it forbidden in Old or New Testament? The Romans did not forbid it, nor did they

[21] *Ibid.*, xlii-xliii.
[22] *Ibid.*, xxxvi-xxxvii. In Russia, he added, the criminals were commonly sent to Siberia, where in time they became "honest people."

seize a suicide's property. But what do we do? he asked. We drive a stake through the suicide's body, we render his memory infamous, we dishonor his family. "We even confiscate the effects of the deceased, and rob the living of that which is justly their due." He charged that the custom of confiscation was due to canon law, and he commented that the canon law through its harsh treatment of suicide rendered the action of Judas in killing himself more heinous than that of betraying Jesus.[23]

He agreed with Beccaria that light infractions of the law should not receive the same punishment as more serious violations. To inflict heavy sentences for light crimes caused the public to be reluctant to report violations and worked to defeat the very end for which the laws were directed. Thus he stood for a revision of the laws in regard to punishment. Moreover he advocated their revision so that uniformity would prevail throughout France. "Shall a man be right in Brittany, and wrong in Languedoc?" he asked.[24]

Criminal procedure too, he said, needed drastic revision. It operated from start to finish to the prejudice of the accused. By it the judge was rendered more or less an enemy, for he must question and grill the accused in private with only a secretary present. Afterward the accused might not change his evidence without liability to prosecution. He was denied legal counsel until after he had deposed all his evidence, and even then until he could pay for it. He had no recourse for damages if falsely imprisoned and accused. Though in England it was possible for one to collect damages for false imprisonment, it was not so in France. There one might emerge from prison, though innocent, with joints dislocated from torture, reputation damaged, and no hope of action against an accuser.

Whereas Beccaria wrote but a single treatise on the subject of criminal law reform, and Montesquieu set forth his ideas chiefly in his *L'Esprit des lois*, Voltaire contributed to the subject near a score of writings.[25] For the most part they were not written, as those of Beccaria and Montesquieu, in philosophic calm, dealing with general situations, but to meet particular situations, in which he considered that innocent people had been pronounced guilty

---

[23] *Ibid.*, xliv-xlv.   [24] *Ibid.*, lxi-lxii, lxxvii-lxxviii.
[25] Seligman, *La justice en France*, 94n, gives a list of these writings.

in the courts. The cases of Calas, Sirven, Montbailly and his wife, the Chevalier de la Barre,[26] and the Comte de Morangiès evoked his sympathy and some burning pamphlets in their behalf. Voltaire attacked injustice in the concrete and directed the attention of all cultured Frenchmen to the capricious character of French laws and criminal procedure.

After the members of this great triumvirate, the most influential person in the movement for reform of the original laws was a young lawyer of southeast France named Servan, who in 1764 at the age of twenty-four became advocate general to the parlement of Grenoble. In his initial address before that body in 1765, he made also his debut as an advocate of reform. He criticized both cruelty and archaism in the laws of the period in the light of the new philosophy. The address was published, widely read, and met a favorable reception. Voltaire, ever ready to confer his blessing on young men with liberal attitude, welcomed him to Fernay. Thenceforth Servan was a true disciple of Voltaire and the *philosophes*. The next year he made a yet bolder and more famous address. Published under the title of *Le discours sur l'administration de la justice criminelle*, it went into more than one reprinting. "This address," says his biographer, "established definitely his reputation and spread his name throughout all France. He was received with transport by the *philosophes* and their party, whose importance increased every day."[27] Choiseul offered him a position as master of requests in the royal council, but he declined it. Later, in 1772, Servan became disgusted at the servility of the parlement of Grenoble and resigned his position. The scholarly life appealed to him, and he preferred it to judicial or political posts. He continued from time to time to publish pamphlets dealing with legal cases of injustice and with the need for judicial reform. When the Revolution came, he was elected as a delegate from two constituencies but declined to serve. For a time in 1792 he served in the Girondist cabinet with Roland and Clavière, and as Girondist he bitterly attacked the

[26] Marc Chassaigne, *Le procès du Chevalier de La Barre* (Paris, 1920), 273. In this doctoral dissertation at the University of Paris the author sets forth the facts ferreted from the archival records of the courts and approves of the verdict rendered. Voltaire is condemned for his interference in the case.

[27] Charles Prud'homme, *Michel de Servan (1737-1807), un magistrat réformateur* (Paris, 1907), 7-8, 13, 16-17.

Jacobin Reign of Terror and had to flee to Switzerland. In fact, during the Revolution he appeared to have held back in horror from the reforms he had done so much to advocate. He considered the Revolution merely an upheaval in which those without property wished to plunder the rich, and those with little money wanted to rob those with more.[28]

As for Servan's ideas, he was an opponent of the use of torture; he advocated the abolition of the death penalty; he hoped that this reformation would come under Louis XV, whom he praised as a loving monarch; yet inconsistently in the same treatise he held that one execution may be needed to deter a thousand others from committing the same crime. In common with Beccaria, he thought that justice to be effective should be speedy. He criticized various features of criminal procedure, as also the system in France whereby men were condemned to death for crimes of varying magnitude.[29] Servan was admired by his contemporaries for being outspoken, but he lacked the challenge of Beccaria and Voltaire, and the modern reader is impressed rather by his conservatism than his radicalism.

Such was the situation in France in 1770. The agitation for criminal law reform had already reached an important stage and the minds of all cultured persons were directed to critical examination of the matter. The greatest of those who were to figure in legal reform movement in France had made their contributions; those that followed were to do little more than repeat their ideas and stir the country to action.

[28] Prud'homme, *Michel de Servan,* 22, 50-51.
[29] *Discours sur l'administration de la justice criminelle,* 32-34, 38, 129-31, 141-42; Esmein, *Histoire de la procédure criminelle en France,* 388.

CHAPTER NINE

Criminal Law Reform
After 1770

AFTER 1770 the advocates of legal reform were so numerous that only the general trends deserve consideration. Most of the advocates were young lawyers with philosophic leanings; certain of the others, as Brissot, Linguet, and Marat, were journalists. The best brochures, as those by Brissot and Lacretelle *fils,* were evoked by prizes offered by learned academies on the subject of judicial reform. For interestingly enough several of the learned societies in France, Italy, and Switzerland in the period of the 1780's offered prizes for the best essay on some aspect of legal reform, and the competition was keen. Twenty-two papers were submitted in the contest promoted by the Société Royale des Sciences et des Arts de Metz in 1784, in which Lacretelle *fils* won the first prize and Robespierre the second. The subject of all the papers was the prejudice carried by conviction for infamous crimes and the matter of reparation to those proved innocent. The money for the two gold medals awarded was given some years earlier to the society for a contest on the subject of canals, but no papers being submitted, the society asked Roederer for permission to change the subject and he assented, with the result that the competition was keen.[1] Not only did the society publish the winning paper but also excerpts from many of the others. Similarly the contest promoted by the Académie de Châlons-sur-Marne in 1780 on "The Means of Modifying the Severity of the French Penal Laws, Without Endangering Public Safety" evoked twenty or more papers. The winning paper, by Brissot, as also that by the accessit, Bernardi, advocate of the parlement of Aix, and in addition excerpts from other papers were published. The paper by Brissot was probably the best treatise after that of Beccaria to appear in France during the century on the reform of the criminal law. Well written, thoughtful throughout, and reflecting wide reading, it was trenchant in tone. That it did not have wider sale and influence is surprising.[2]

The academicians accordingly deserved no little credit for promoting the movement among the younger men, and so did the journals that carried the announcements and discussions of the contests. The *Mercure de France,* for example, carried a full account of the contest sponsored by the society of Metz, the article being written by Lacretelle *fils,* a member of the literary staff of that review as well as an advocate of the parlement of Paris.

It may be observed that after 1770 the tone of most of the pamphlets appearing on the subject of judicial reform became increasingly biting in tone, and that in the last years before the Revolution, those by Brissot, Boucher d'Argis, and Dupaty above all, became almost defiant. This last was a late eighteenth-century Voltaire, who had drunk from the same bottle, so to speak, and participated in several *causes célèbres,* defending his clients both in the courtroom and in a series of pamphlets written to incite public feeling and to influence the court decisions. This he did with amazing success. But his pamphlets asked more: they demanded wholesale reform both of the criminal law and of criminal procedure. It is well at this point to observe that despite their defiance all these writers were very deferential toward the king—even Mercier, Brissot, and Robespierre, who later, in the Revolution, were to change in this matter. With the utmost respect they looked to Louis XVI, and with reason, for the young king from the beginning of his reign showed himself deeply interested in the welfare of his people and from time to time granted reforms. He was slow by nature, however, and wanted to move slowly. Moreover he had deep loyalties, to the Catholic Church, to the aristocracy, to his Bourbon lineage, and to his wife—loyal-

---

[1] Lacretelle related these facts in the preface to his brochure, *Discours sur le préjugé des peines infamantes, couronnés à l'Académie de Metz. Lettre sur la réparation qui seroit due aux accusés jugés innocens. Dissertation sur le ministère public. Réflexions sur la réforme de la justice criminelle* (Paris, 1784), i-viii, xii.

[2] *Les moyens d'adoucir la rigueur des lois pénales en France.*

ties that made it difficult for him to be the reformer demanded by the pamphleteers.

The reforms advocated both in criminal law and in criminal procedure by the young radicals of the 1770's and 1780's had little in them that was original. The ideas were those of Montesquieu, Beccaria, and Voltaire. Over and over again in these later writers one encounters the ideas, and often the very illustrations and phraseology, of the three great *philosophes*.

The use of torture continued to be condemned, although after abolition of the *question préparatoire* in 1780 fewer references to it occurred. I have observed only one writer advocating its usage, Le Trosne, a lawyer of some prominence at Orleans and a member of certain academies, who while condemning the use of torture to extract information relative to the guilt of the accused considered that its usage was justified if the condemned would not divulge information concerning his accessories in the crime.[3] Le Trosne, while he began writing on the matter of legal reform in 1764, was one of the most conservative of those wishing it.

The question of capital punishment was discussed widely and vigorously. Nearly all the writers would greatly limit its use, and some would abolish it altogether. The influence of Beccaria on this matter is clear. Society may put one of its members to death by way of punishment only if it is "necessary to the welfare of the others," said Nicolas Bergasse, a lawyer of Paris and later a deputy to the National Assembly.[4] This roughly was the attitude of Rousseau, who devoted a chapter to the subject in his *Contrat social* (1762). The criminal by attacking society loses his rights as a citizen and his right to exist, and society is justified in executing him. But Rousseau proceeded to comment that "the frequency of executions is always a sign of feebleness or laziness in the government. There is not a scoundrel that is not able to render good [service] at something."[5] Boucher d'Argis, a young Parisian lawyer whose father had written articles for the *Encyclopédie* on judicial topics, asked if there was no other way of punishing crime than by death. Mere repentance of the criminal would, in his

---

[3] Le Trosne, *Vues sur la justice criminelle*, 83-89.

[4] *Discours sur l'humanité des juges dans l'administration de la justice criminelle* (Paris, 1788), 40 nl.

[5] Vaughan, *The Political Writings of Rousseau*, II, 47.

opinion, be of more value in expiating for his deed than execution, for no physical punishment could expiate for it. He was of the opinion that servitude to the state for a more or less extended period of time would be preferable to the death penalty, and he cited the example of Russia. Work on the roads would not only be useful to the state but also would lessen or relieve altogether the peasant from work on the *corvée*. France in her Age of Enlightenment made blood flow too freely, he asserted. He censured the cruelty attending executions, and declared that they only provoked sympathy for the executed. He castigated the role of the church in the executions. He considered the attendance of a priest on the condemned as indicative of ecclesiastical approval of the brutal executions in force, and as utterly inconsistent with the spirit of the Christian religion. The priest shared with the judge the muttered curses of the spectators at these scenes, while the condemned were exculpated.[6]

Robespierre leaned in the same direction, asserting "We repeat every day this equitable maxim that it is better to spare a thousand guilty persons than to sacrifice a single innocent."[7] Brissot de Warville considered that only the crimes of high treason and regicide were of sufficient gravity to warrant capital punishment. Strangely inconsistent with his otherwise humanitarian attitude, he referred to Châtel, Ravaillac, and Damiens as "these monsters vomited by hell," and asked who regretted what was done to them. Execution of counterfeiters by throwing them into boiling water, however, he regarded as "the height of inhumanity." The death penalty for counterfeiting should be abolished, and also for smuggling, espionage, rape, seduction, heresy, and other crimes. Instead of capital punishment he would substitute "slavery and perpetual works." He would replace the work of Negro slaves in the colonies by that of criminals.[8] Of course in all this he was but extending somewhat the ideas of Beccaria and the practice of indentured servants followed by Britain at that period.

[6] André Jean Baptiste Boucher d'Argis, *Observations sur les loix criminelles de France* (Brussels, 1781), 78-79, 86-89, 96-99.

[7] *Discours couronné par la Société Royale des Arts et des Sciences de Metz, sur les questions suivantes, proposées pour sujet du prix de l'année 1784* (Amsterdam, 1785), 26.

[8] *Les moyens d'adoucir la rigueur des lois pénales en France*, 54-55, 57, 61-75, 83-84.

Louis Sebastian Mercier and Dupaty likewise denounced the wholesale shedding of blood for crime, and also the brutal modes of execution. Mercier scoffed at the idea of paying an executioner only 200 or 250 francs annually (when the average priest got around 800), and at his mounting the scaffold "in lace sleeves and sword at his side, to break the members [bones] of a poor miserable." He dared to call the drawing and quartering of Damiens "the shame of the century."[9] Dupaty denounced the atrocious mode of execution by breaking on the wheel, and added that its employment had done nothing to lessen crime. "One has robbed and assassinated as before; proof that neither the rigor of executions *(supplices)* nor that of forms are always effective means for preventing crime." He too would substitute lighter punishments, and in particular would transport the guilty to the colonies for work.[10] Others who advocated abolition of capital punishment were Condorcet, Vasselin, Roederer, and Grégoire; but only Condorcet publicly expressed his views on the subject prior to the Revolution.[11]

Least humanitarian of the group, F. M. Vermeil, though desirous of a thorough reform of the French criminal laws and willing to remove heresy from the category of capital crimes, would still retain the death penalty for armed robbery, assassination, and false witness at court in capital cases. Not only would he retain execution on the wheel as the penalty for assassination, he would increase the cruelties at execution to such a degree that might have made many medieval executioners blush. As examples, he would have criminals convicted of arson "thrown alive in the flames," and said that parricides should have their eyes put out and then be placed nude in an iron cage except for an iron belt, and there they should be exposed to the rigor of the seasons, from

---

[9] *Tableau de Paris*, IX, 145; Béclard, *Sébastien Mercier*, 607. He agreed that attempt at royal assassination, since it represented the most severe form of attack on the government, should be punished by execution, but not by the form the French used.

[10] *Lettres sur la procédure criminelle de la France, dans lesquelles on montre sa conformité avec celle de l'Inquisition, et les abus qui en résultat* (En France, 1788), 165-68.

[11] *Oeuvres de Condorcet*, IV, 502-503; Vasselin, *Théorie des peines capitales, ou abus et dangers de la peine de mort et des tourments* (Paris, 1791?), 184; Eugène Hatin, *Histoire politique et littéraire de la presse en France* (Paris, 1859-1861), V, 193-94; *Mémoires de Grégoire*, I, 55.

summer heat to winter cold, with only bread and water for nourishment.[12]

With one accord these writers condemned the French laws regarding the punishment of suicides as barbarous and stupid. Boucher d'Argis pointed out that philosophers both of antiquity and of modern times had been divided on the question whether suicide should be condemned, described the brutal aspects of French law on the subject, and asked: "What advantage does society draw from a punishment of this sort?"[13] Mercier observed that no longer, in fact, did the Parisian police execute the provisions of the law on suicides, but when a suicide was reported, "a commissioner comes without his robe, draws up a report without the least noise, and obliges the curé of the parish to bury the dead without noise." He compared the number of suicides annually in London and Paris and remarked with questionable accuracy that whereas in London it was the rich afflicted with tuberculosis who killed themselves, in Paris it was the poor afflicted with poverty.[14] Even Vermeil, conservative that he was, deplored the ignominious treatment of the suicide's corpse and the confiscation of his property. According to his reasoning, life is the gift of God and punishment should be left to Him. Human punishment only strikes the suicide's children who are innocent.

Vermeil also complained of the severity of the French law against dueling. He decreed death even though no death resulted from the duel, and the property of the participants was to be confiscated. If the challenge had come from a bourgeois citizen to a noble, the challenger was to be executed by hanging. The intermediary carrying the invitation to the duel was to be scourged and branded for the first offense, and for the second sent to the galleys. "Spectators were to be deprived forever of all [government] positions, honors, and pensions; and if they held none, one was to pronounce against them either confiscation or the fine of a fourth of their property (biens)." Well did Vermeil refer to it as "this formidable law." But "the rigor of the law," he said, "has

---

12 *Essai sur les réformes à faire dans notre législation criminelle* (Paris, 1781), 127-29. Rousseau, although one might expect to find him among the opponents of capital punishment, advocated its retention in the case of treason or subversion of the government. See his *Contrat social*, ch. V.

13 *Observations sur les loix criminelles*, 131-39.

14 *Tableau de Paris*, III, 193-96.

had no effect in preventing duels, . . . it has [only] produced some very great inconveniences." These he discussed, and then suggested penalties that he thought would be more effective and just.[15] One today considers that his position was well founded. The provocation to dueling lay in the false sense of honor that was deeply rooted in French social prejudice, and it was to continue throughout the century, even after the legal reforms of 1791 and 1793.

Two of those contesting for the prize offered by the Académie de Châlons-sur-Marne in 1780 opposed vigorously the confiscation of the convicted's property in any case, suicide or not, since it was a penalty that fell on innocent members of the family. If the convicted were rich, it might be justified, but not for others.[16] Vermeil took virtually the same stand, citing the position of Beccaria. He recommended that the law be changed and that confiscation be permitted only after the welfare of the criminal's family had been secured. That some such steps should be taken was evidently the attitude of most of the reformers.

They considered moreover that recompense should be made to innocent parties who were convicted, or merely charged and imprisoned. The damage that they suffered, financial, physical, and in reputation, was great, and justice demanded that society reimburse them. Vermeil would use toward reimbursement of the innocent, funds confiscated from those that were guilty.[17] Lacretelle wrote at considerable length on this matter. Some have suffered imprisonment for years, some death under horrible forms, he said. They, or at least their families, should be financially reimbursed—the only way that society could reimburse them. How should the funds be raised? That was not his problem, he observed. He was only concerned that the innocent should be reimbursed for their sufferings and for their lost years and opportunities.[18] The state moreover should publish a report of their innocence. In the case of seven men falsely condemned by the parlement of Metz in 1769, Dupaty asked that the crown reimburse their families, painting at much length the sufferings these

---

[15] *Essai sur les réformes à faire*, 100-105, 119-23, 132-36.
[16] *Extraits de différens autres mémoires envoyés à l'Académie, sur la même question* (Châlons-sur-Marne, 1781), 26-27.
[17] *Essai sur les réformes à faire*, 59-62.
[18] *Essai sur le préjugé des peines infamantes*, 225, 229, 231-34.

men and their families had undergone.[19] Some of the men had been condemned to death and the rest to the galleys, because of an armed robbery of an elderly Jewish couple. Late in the 1780's the true robbers confessed, and the innocence of the previously condemned men was established. Apparently Dupaty was unsuccesful in getting them reimbursement, but he gained the attention of all France and persuaded the public that this condition was unjust.

A constant theme of the reformers of this period was that of the innocence of persons imprisoned and convicted. After Voltaire, who appears to have been the originator of this idea, no one did more than Dupaty to convince the public of this situation.[20] In several *causes célèbres* he was legal defender of the accused, and he did not limit his activities in their behalf to the courtroom but also resorted to the questionable means of writing heated pamphlets to persuade public opinion and put pressure on the courts. Success crowned his efforts in virtually every case, and he did more than anyone else in France to arouse public opinion in indignation against both the errors of the courts and the insufferable state of the laws and of French legal procedure. His denunciation of conditions was in staccato notes, with a tang to his remarks. Despite his reverence before the crown, he was a revolutionist in tone. Men like him and Mercier and Brissot were responsible for lashing the public into revolutionary fury. And it may not be inappropriate to observe that one of the three great "innocents" that Dupaty and others devoted so much printer's ink to defend in the 1780's—Bradier, Simare, and Lardoise—later came to impress the public as a doubtful "innocent." Lardoise was the party in question. Thanks to Dupaty he had been saved from death on the wheel. Released in 1788, he was even provided a home by Dupaty, but vagabond by nature he again took to the road with a wench. The two presented themselves at an inn in the village of Faremoutiers October 11, 1788. After some time

19 *Justification de sept hommes, condamnés par le parlement de Metz en 1769* (n.p., 1787), 28-29.
20 Voltaire in a short article on "Criminal Laws" in the *Dictionnaire philosophique* charged that every year "some innocent father of a family was condemned to a frightful death" by a callous-hearted judge who was no more concerned over the matter than he would be over the killing of a turkey in his backyard. This same attitude was expressed in various other writings by him.

the owner charged them with stealing a silver cup and three tin spoons. Indignantly denying the charge, Lardoise made off without paying his bill. The *maréchaussée* were notified and Lardoise was arrested. In his sack were found the three spoons, but not the silver cup, which possibly he disposed of before his arrest. He tried to browbeat the *maréchaussée* and prevent his arrest, by stating that they were going to needless trouble since he had the support of Dupaty; but they declined to be intimidated. This time Dupaty did not come to his assistance. Lardoise was whipped, branded with the letter "V," banned from the bailliage of Meaux, and convicted to a year in prison. The parlement of Paris retried the case and shortened the prison term to six months, but the affair very naturally cast doubt upon the earlier case of the three "innocents" who escaped the wheel.[21]

The inequality of justice was a matter bitterly criticized. The poor and the rich were not treated alike in the courts, and penalties were not apportioned to the crimes committed. Among those denouncing the distinction displayed between the rich and poor in the courts were Robespierre, Vermeil, Bergasse, and Boucher d'Argis. If the death penalty was to be imposed, it should be inflicted on men of the upper classes as well as those of the lower, in the opinion of Boucher d'Argis. If magistrates were to make any distinction at all, it should be in favor of the poor, Bergasse said. He insisted that the magistrate should be fundamentally a psychologist, considering on the one hand the public welfare and on the other the accused and his background. But the idea that all men were treated equally before the law, as claimed, was ridiculous. Vermeil shared this sentiment.[22]

With respect to the absence of any sense of proportion between the gravity of a crime and its punishment there was almost unanimous agreement. Here and there appeared a rare defender of cruel punishments, but they were lost in the pack that called for reform and, like Beccaria, denounced the imposition of severe penalties for light crimes. Valezé, a lawyer who in 1784 dedicated his pamphlet to Monsieur, brother of the king, insisted that men

21 Seligman, *La justice en France*, 204-207.

22 Robespierre, *Discours couronné par la Société Royale des Arts et des Sciences de Metz*, 16; Bergasse, *Discours sur l'humanité des juges*, 35-38; Vermeil, *Essai sur les réformes à faire*, 41-42; Boucher d'Argis, *Observations sur les loix criminelles*, 16-18, 36, 38, 85.

should be punished in proportion to the harm they had done. He would have the rich man receive a heavier punishment than the poor man, although this would run counter to the practice of the times, since everywhere the rich got lighter sentences than the poor.[23] Calling for radical reform, Brissot de Warville asserted that "no scale of proportion between crimes and punishments" existed. He likened the French criminal code to Oriental despotism, and commented that future generations judging the French of his day by their laws might well consider them to have been maneaters.[24] Blame for the continuance of these laws he attributed, interestingly enough, to militarism, which had kept men accustomed to combats and bloodshed.

Various writers attempted to set forth the causes of crime, and certain of their explanations were interesting. Brissot's were particularly so. Bitter against the rich, he repeatedly attributed robbery and other crimes against property to the misery existent among the masses. As a preventive of such crimes he urged the redistribution of wealth among men on an equitable basis. Thereby the breeding ground of crime would be dried up. For a long time, he said, the government had tried without success to get rid of mendicity by means of *maisons de force* (concentration camps) and other palliatives. Get rid of mendicity he urged, and the source of crime would be eradicated. To do this, men must be made happy. But this was not all. Ignorance too, he said, must be eradicated; and to achieve it, there must be a system of national education provided by the government.[25] Here, of course, we have a new idea. Brissot the socialist went much farther than Voltaire or Beccaria, royalists and liberals who stood neither for redistribution of property nor for mass education. Brissot's program was that of the modern socialist. Crime and all evil will vanish when governments have abolished warfare, inequality, misery, and ignorance.

Ideas strikingly similar were held by Lacretelle *fils*, who as early as 1774 wrote his first pamphlet on legal reform, in which he designated misery, oppression, ignorance, and intolerance as causes of crime. He distinguished between "good" and "bad"

23 Valezé, *Lois pénales*, 272-73.
24 *Les moyens d'adoucir la rigueur des lois pénales*, 51-53.
25 *Ibid.*, pp. xv-xvi, 35-39, 79n, 358-59.

education, the latter encouraging crime.[26] But he was not a socialist, saying nothing about the inequality of property and the need for its redistribution, or indeed about the need of a system of national education. A decade later in his prize essay of 1784, he did, however, advocate a system of national education, and stated that "the inequality of fortunes" must be corrected; yet he did not suggest a redistribution of wealth.[27]

The confusion of the French laws was attacked rather generally. According to Brissot, French law was a morass that had come down partly from Roman times, partly from the Middle Ages. He hoped for a drastic reform based "on reason and humanity."[28] Linguet, another ardent reformer, declared that they ought to be clear, simple, and uniform for all the kingdom. He related attempts of St. Louis, Philip the Fair, and Charles VII to reduce the mass of laws and bring some order in it, though without much success.[29] Bernardi shared this desire for uniformity and simplification. The ancients had clearer laws. In modern times jurisconsults had erred in following the philosophers, whose ideas were good but impractical. All save the Advocate General Louis Seguier were dismayed at the legal confusion; Seguier was of the opinion that the French laws had arrived at a state of near perfection. He was opposed to all reform.[30]

Not only did the reformers, apparently without exception, advocate a reduction and simplification of the laws, but also they wanted a complete transformation of judicial procedure. Dupaty was not the only one who likened the French court methods to those of the Inquisition. Secrecy must depart from French trials. Evidence must be obtained openly, and it should not be left to a single judge to acquire the evidence. The accused should have the right to legal counsel when he requested it, and "always should minors, women, [and] illiterates have it." Conviction,

[26] *Discours sur ce sujet: Assigner les causes des crimes, & donner les moyens de les rendre plus rares et moins funestes* (Nancy, 1774), 12-13, 18-20, 26-27, 29-31.

[27] *Discours sur le préjugé*, 358-59.

[28] *Les moyens d'adoucir la rigueur des lois pénales*, i-xvi.

[29] Simon Nicolas Henri Linguet, *Nécessité d'une réforme dans l'administration de la justice et dans les loix civiles en France, avec la réfutation de quelques passages de l'Esprit des Loix* (Amsterdam, 1764), 8, 100-101.

[30] Bernardi, *Discours sur les lois pénales*, xiii-xiv; Esmein, *Histoire de la procédure criminelle en France*, 376. (The treatise by Bernardi was printed by the Academy of Châlons-sur-Marne and bound with that by Brissot.)

moreover, should be by jury, as in England. The accuser should be brought before the accused, and the latter given a chance to question him and also the witnesses. Moreover, the accused should be furnished with a statement of the accusation. Dupaty attributed to the secrecy of French criminal procedure the conviction of a number of unfortunates, including Montbailly and Calas, and commented, "What an infinity of others am I not able to add?"[31]

Boucher d'Argis, while demanding drastic revision of legal procedure, differed from Dupaty on some points. He would retain certain aspects of secrecy; otherwise criminals would escape just punishment. He would continue to examine the accused and witnesses in secret. Moreover he was opposed to adoption of the English jury system. Anglomania had extended itself to dress, manners, laws, and other things, and he considered that it had gone too far. On the other hand, he objected to the practice of requiring the accused to sit in court on the *sellette* (wooden stool) while undergoing his last questioning by the judges; he objected to the French custom of refusing to accept evidence in court from a deaf-mute; he advocated the state's furnishing the accused with legal counsel, and its publication of the charges against him. He insisted that witnesses should be confronted by the accused and that they should be examined prior to the accused. He questioned moreover whether the accused should be retained in prison pending trial. Despite these many changes that he advocated, he spoke highly of the criminal code then in existence (the ordinance of 1670), calling it "some monuments of wisdom," but adding that "a century and more of its habitual usage has necessarily led one to discover in it some inconveniences [and] some omissions." One would judge him by language at this point as a moderate conservative, but considering his pamphlet as a whole he wanted rather thoroughgoing reform.[32] His deferential remarks would appeal more to the crown and to his compeers in the legal profession, and it was not without interest that in 1788 he was placed by Louis XVI in charge of the court of the Châtelet with direction to reform it. He was one of the

---

[31] Dupaty, *Lettres sur la procédure criminelle*, 1-3, 23, 25-29, 89, 94, 169-70, 172-74.

[32] *Observations sur les loix criminelles*, 21, 30-47, 54-55, 63-69.

young men of the legal profession on whom Louis XVI evidently would have leaned heavily in the future.

Boucher deserves some passing attention for his efforts in behalf of providing the poor with free legal advice. An Association of Judiciary Benevolence existed in Paris on the eve of the Revolution, and he appears to have been the leading figure in it. His speech at its first meeting on January 14, 1788, was afterward published.[33] In it he praised the free legal aid clinic set up in Lyons in 1711 by Archbishop de Rochebonne and also the still larger enterprise of this nature established at Nancy in 1750 by Stanislas, king of Lorraine. The establishment at Paris was modeled after them, with support from the Duc de Charost, members of the royal council, members of the parlement of Paris, and many other magistrates. He also advocated the reimbursement by his association of the poor who should be proven innocent in court. Evidently he did not envisage reimbursement on a large scale, as otherwise it would have been beyond the reach of a private charitable society.[34]

Other pamphleteers had their suggestions to offer toward the revision of criminal procedure. Linguet, for example, urged that cases be heard in courts close to the scene of the violation; otherwise in his opinion the poor would be discriminated against in favor of the rich. Moreover for the same reason cases should be heard speedily. Vermeil advocated that in sovereign courts of three judges at least two must agree for conviction. He was not, however, in favor of adoption of the English jury system, as he considered that the requirement of unanimity of decision by the jury for conviction provided a loophole for the accused to escape. Just here we may observe that during the Revolution the French refused to follow the English precedent in regard to jury conviction, and that even today a simple majority renders the decision in French courts. Bergasse and various others, however, advocated the British system without raising the question of jury unanimity.[35]

[33] De la bienfaisance dans l'ordre judiciaire: discours dans lequel on prouve la nécessité de donner aux pauvres des défenseurs gratuits, & l'obligation d'indemniser ceux qui, ayant été accusés, décrétés & imprisonnés à la requête du ministère public, ont ensuite obtenu des jugemens absolutoires (London, 1788), 71.

[34] Ibid., 19-21, 25-31, 32-53, 60 n8.

[35] Linguet, Nécessité d'une réforme, 9; Vermeil, Essai sur les réformes à faire, 174, 239-41; Bergasse, Discours sur l'humanité des juges, 48.

The hope of all reform as envisaged by these writers lay in the monarch, who after 1774 was Louis XVI. The first to address Louis XVI in this respect was Malesherbes, one of a delegation from the Court of Aides that called on the young monarch November 27, 1774, to thank him for recalling it from exile in the provinces, where it had been sent for "impertinence" by Louis XV. In a brief, deferential, and courteous address, Malesherbes urged the new ruler to a policy of peace and legal reform. Boucher also, in 1781, expressed the hope that Louis XVI would distinguish his reign by making the needed legal reforms that Montesquieu, Beccaria, Servan, Le Trosne, and others had advocated. Vermeil, publishing his pamphlet in the same year, referred in laudatory manner to the reforms that Louis XVI already had made of a humanitarian character and stated his hope that the criminal laws too would be reformed by him.[36]

The reforms already made to which Vermeil alluded were the abolition of serfdom on the royal estates, the abolition of the death penalty for army deserters, some prison reforms, and the abolition of preparatory torture (1780). The young king had commenced his reign with excellent intentions, and his controller general of finances Turgot had undertaken some sweeping financial reforms in the two years that he was able to hold office (1774-1776); but Louis wavered before the complaints that were hurled from all sides at his reforming minister and let Turgot go. Thenceforth with Necker, Calonne, Brienne, and others successively as finance minister, he showed himself greatly interested in humanitarian matters, as for instance in the lavish grants of government assistance to those in need, but he did not again attempt reform on so extensive a scale as in 1774-1776. And yet he did not cease in it. He continued to make reforms. Earlier I have described his reforms of 1787 with regard to the Protestants. In 1788 he abolished the second form of torture—the preliminary question, directed at the obtaining of evidence concerning accomplices in a crime. Indeed at the beginning of that year, on a suggestion from Malesherbes, he appointed a commission of six jurists to recommend legal reforms. On May 8 their six edicts were approved by the royal council but never actually went into effect,

[36] *Oeuvres inédites de Malesherbes,* 144; Boucher d'Argis, *Observations sur les loix criminelles,* 10-11; Vermeil, *Essai sur les réformes à faire,* 15-17.

since in July the Estates General was called and all matters of reform were shelved for consideration by it.

The legal reforms recommended and adopted in May, 1788, were not extensive but embodied a number of the changes that Dupaty and others had suggested. The *sellette* (culprit's stool) was abolished, and thenceforth the accused was to occupy an elevated position in full view of all the judges, sitting or standing as he chose. The second form of torture, the "preliminary question," was abolished. In cases of riot or sedition no execution might be made until a month had elapsed after pronouncement of guilt by a court. This was to facilitate reconsideration of the sentence by a court of appeal. In capital cases, moreover, a plurality of three votes rather than two was required for condemnation. The court in rendering sentence must designate the grounds for it. "Reparation of honor" must be made the accused in case he was found innocent. Instead of the parlements being courts of last resort in criminal cases, the courts of the large bailliages (lesser courts) were to have this jurisdiction. In fact, those drawing up the reforms set out purposely to cripple the parlements, and in particular the parlement of Paris, which had protested an action of the king and shortly later was exiled. Even Malesherbes, himself a former member of this parlement and a former exile because of offending the king, was opposed to the parlement at this time and wanted to clip its wing. The cases of Calas and of the three men Dupaty defended in 1785-1787 had done much to put the parlements of Toulouse and Rouen in disfavor. The prestige of the parlements was therefore weakened, and the membership of the parlement of Paris was drastically reduced in number.[37] The reforms were small in view of the task to be accomplished, but it would have required a remarkable personality on the part of the king or of his minister to have achieved more at one blow. Other reforms almost certainly would have followed, since the demand for them was great. But for the king and the Old Regime the opportunity was lost. The Estates General soon was summoned and the problem of reform passed to it.

[37] Esmein, *Histoire de la procédure criminelle en France*, 399-409; Seligman, *La justice en France*, 111-15, 174-82; Hyslop, *A Guide to the General Cahiers*, 223, 250, 253-54, *et passim.* Another of the requests was for speedy justice. The public was weary of the interminable delays of the courts, and regarded them as a trick of the lawyers and magistrates for enriching themselves.

Decision to call the Estates General was made in July, 1788, and thenceforward great excitement and discussion prevailed in France. Early in 1789 the king ordered the election of delegates and the submission of cahiers by the three estates. On May 5 the delegates assembled at Versailles for the opening session, the delegates bringing with them the cahiers of their bailliage, district, or order, as the case happened.

Most of the cahiers contained requests for reform in the laws, civil and criminal, and for reform in judicial procedure. Little if any distinction can be discerned in the requests in this matter between the three orders making them. All had come to accept rather generally the demands of the great *philosophes* and of their followers. The pamphlets of the 1760's, 1770's, and 1780's had done a remarkable job of provoking and formulating public opinion on a very needed matter.

Among the demands was that for the abolition of torture—of the "preliminary question" as well as "preparatory torture." The *sellette* should be replaced. Evidence should be obtained in open fashion, and oath by the accused should be omitted. Publicity should be given to the charges, and also to the verdict. The accused should be permitted to have counsel; if destitute, it should be furnished by the court. Witnesses should be permitted to change their testimony without incurring a penalty for falsehood. In all criminal cases trial should be by jury. "The severity of the penalties should be moderated," and capital punishment should be given only in the case of "atrocious crimes." The innocent members of the criminal's family should not suffer because of his misdeed. Here, then in the cahiers came a sort of Alpine echo to virtually every demand of the pamphleteers. The cahiers were designed by the king and his council to provide suggestions for work to be undertaken by the Estates General, and they did so to a degree little dreamed of. A remarkably large number of their requests came to be approved.

The reforms came piecemeal. Lettres de cachet and all modes of arbitrary arrest were rendered illegal by the Declaration of the Rights of Man and the Citizen, adopted in late August of 1789. Article 7 of that famous bill of rights provided that no man might be arrested or detained without just ground, prescribed by law, and Article 9 stated that every man was to be considered innocent until proven guilty. If arrest was warranted, the arrested should be spared any unneeded physical punishment. Article 8 protected the public against *ex post facto* laws, and declared that only "penalties strictly and evidently necessary" should be prescribed.[38] Without making much actual legal change, these broad principles paved the way for the great legislation that was to follow.

On September 10 the Committee on Reports presented before the National Assembly a request from the commune of Paris for immediate reform of some of the features of penal procedure. A committee of seven members was thereupon appointed and asked to report within three days on the commune's request. Its report was made as ordered, but discussion of it did not take place on the floor of the assembly until October 5, day of the march of the market women to Versailles. These last on their arrival sidetracked the discussion to that of provisioning, but the topic of judicial reform was later renewed and on October 8-9 a decree was passed abolishing several obnoxious features of the old system—the *sellette*, the "preliminary question," and "the oath required of the accused." It also specified that the accused was to have legal counsel "with whom he might communicate freely." If he were unable to provide counsel himself, the court was to provide it for him. All evidence henceforth must be obtained openly, and the accused might have his counsel to assist him. Finally the judges must render their decision openly and before adjournment.[39]

Later, on April 30, 1790, the assembly voted that for the future juries would be employed in criminal cases, but not in civil. Duport, deputy for the nobility of Paris, and Sieyès, deputy for the third estate of Paris, among others, advocated without success the employment of juries in civil cases also. Malouet would have juries sit in civil cases, oddly enough, but not in criminal! In general the radical wing of the assembly wanted the civil jury.[40]

At length, by a decree of September 7-11, 1790, the tribunals of the Old Regime were abolished and new ones set up in their place. "Spices" (gifts or bribes) and the *paulette* (inheritance of

---

[38] Seligman, *La justice en France*, 200-201.   [39] *Ibid.*, 201-203.

[40] *Ibid.*, 284-96. Robespierre, too, was outstanding in pressing for these reforms. See *Pages choisies des grands républicains, Robespierre* (Paris, 1907), 15-16.

magistral positions) were abolished, and judges thenceforth were to be paid by the state. Thus the demand for "free justice" came into being. Even the robes and wigs of former days disappeared, and the magistrates thenceforth were dressed as civilians, save for a plumed hat and a tricolored ribbon.[41] They were thenceforth to be elected to office. This decree, however, did not set up a sufficient number of criminal courts to handle the cases before them, and in March, 1791, additional courts were created to fill this deficiency.[42]

All these measures preceded the reform of the penal code proper, which was rendered by the decree of September 25–October 5, 1791. They constituted rather a reform in the criminal code itself than in criminal procedure. Earlier some animated and lengthy debate took place May 30-31 on the question of the retention of capital punishment. The speeches were published *en extenso* by the assembly and provide very interesting reading. On the one hand there was warm advocacy of its abolition by Robespierre, Duport, and Pétion, and on the opposing side, advocating its retention, at least for certain crimes, were Barère, Prugnon, and Mougins-Roquefort.[43]

Those advocating its abolition followed the line of argument presented by Beccaria and his supporters prior to the Revolution. They asked the question, "Has society the right to inflict the penalty of capital punishment?" Also, "Is the penalty useful and ought it to be pronounced by the legislator?" They pointed out that those countries that executed the most criminals, citing Japan, on which they had little information, were precisely those countries in which crime abounded most; and on the contrary, they asserted that those countries where capital punishment was

---

41 Seligman, *La justice en France*, 326, 400; Esmein, *Histoire de la procédure criminelle en France*, 66.

42 Decree of March 13-14. Seligman, *La justice en France*, 399-401.

43 M. Robespierre, *Peine de mort. Discours de Robespierre, prononcée à la tribune de l'Assemblée Nationale, le 30 mai 1791* (Paris, 1830), 14; *Opinion sur la peine de mort, par Adrien Duport, deputé de Paris, imprimée par ordre de l'Assemblée Nationale* (n.p., n.d.), 22; J. Pétion, *Discours sur la peine de mort* (n.p., n.d.), 12; Bertrand Barère de Vieuzac, *Opinion de M. Barère, deputé du département des Hautes-Pyrénées, sur la peine de mort* (n.p., n.d.), 15; Prugnon, *Opinion de M. Prugnon sur la peine de mort, prononcée le 31 mai 1791, imprimée de l'ordre de l'Assemblée Nationale* (n.p., n.d.), 15; Mougins-Roquefort, *Discours prononcé par M. Mougins-Roquefort, deputé du département du Var, à la séance du 31 mai 1791, sur la peine de mort, imprimée par ordre de l'Assemblée Nationale* (Paris, 1791), 16.

least used were those with the least crime. Here they cited the example of Russia, on which also they were poorly informed. Tuscany, Korea, and Egypt were other countries they cited as being virtually free of crime. If the purpose of executions is to prevent crime by fright, they stated, they do not succeed. Those willing to commit crime are ready to run the risk. In this connection they cited the remarks of the notorious Cartouche, that "death is only a bad quarter hour, soon passed." The real purpose of punishment in their view was the reform of the criminal. According to Duport, the criminal (or at least the assassin) is a sick man and should be treated as such. Such men when executed are simply "massacred." Their execution simply creates sentiment in their behalf among the spectators. The best way to prevent crime, Duport added, is to provide honest, just government; and the next best way is to furnish men with work. Robespierre, on his part, insisted that murder can never be painted as a frightful thing so long as the law itself condemns men to be put to death in spectacles. To make it horrible, the law must abolish it as punishment.[44]

Those who argued for the retention of the death penalty asserted that the legislator had to prevent crimes, and this could best be done through inducing fright. Before the death penalty should be removed, thought should be given to what would be adopted in its place. Caution advised that they move slowly. As for Tuscany and Russia, cited by their opponents as countries to be followed in abolishing the death penalty, they remarked that Tuscany was a small country and not in the same class as France, and as for Russia the question was asked why had Catherine the Great reestablished capital punishment if conditions were so favorable without it? They cited in favor of the death penalty, at least for certain crimes, such eminent thinkers as Montesquieu, Rousseau, Filangieri, and Mably. According to Barère, everyone would like to abolish the laws carrying "violence to man," but it was not possible. All agreed that the National Assembly should proceed slowly in this matter.[45] Nevertheless they wanted to see

[44] Robespierre, *Peine de mort*, 3, 10-11, 13; Pétion, *Discours sur la peine de mort*, 3, 5-9; Duport, *Opinion sur la peine de mort*, 4, 7-8, 10.

[45] Prugnon, *Opinion sur la peine de mort*, 2-7, 15; Barère, *Opinion sur la peine de mort*, 4-5, 11, 14-15; Mougins-Roquefort, *Discours sur la peine de mort*, 6-8, 11, 15-16.

the death penalty retained only for the most atrocious crimes such as murder, treason, arson, and counterfeiting; and even in these instances it should be inflicted without cruelty.

The desire to see the death penalty inflicted as painlessly as possible had found an ardent exponent in the assembly in Dr. Guillotin, who as early as 1789 had urged it to adopt the mode of execution by decapitation. At first he got no further than to provoke smiles and quips, but Dr. Guillotin was persistent and in January, 1790, succeeded in persuading the assembly to adopt this mode. The instrument that has later gone by his name, however, was not adopted until March, 1792, and even then for a time it went by the designation of *Louisette*, after the famous surgeon Marc Antoine Louis, who was asked by the Legislative Assembly to make a report on it.[46]

Not until the closing days of the National Assembly was its revised penal code reported, and the last reading was not made until October 6, when the Legislative Assembly had come into power. This celebrated law retained the death penalty for very few crimes—murder, treason, insurrection, counterfeiting, arson, castration, and venality by legislators. Death was to be rendered by decapitation, and executions were to continue open to witness by the public. Murderers and arsonists were to be clothed in red shirts for their execution. Parricides, on the other hand, were to wear a black veil.[47] The committee rendering the report recommended the abolition of the death penalty altogether, but this was overruled.

For lighter crimes there were other forms of punishment. For robbery, "induction of minors into prostitution," bigamy, attempt to overthrow the government, perjury, and "fraudulent bankruptcy," sentence of forced labor for a period of time, up to a maximum of twenty-five years, was to be given. Those condemned in this category were to carry an iron ball and chain attached to one of their legs. For certain violations of the common law and for political offenses of a lesser nature mere imprisonment for a period might be given.

Those convicted of several attempts to change the form of

[46] Seligman, *La justice en France*, 207-208, 464-65; Esmein, *Histoire de la procédure criminelle en France*, 448.
[47] Seligman, *La justice en France*, 448.

government by violence and also those convicted of violating the laws on censorship of the press were to lose their citizenship in a humiliating public ceremony. Women (who were not citizens) and foreigners so convicted, since they could not be degraded from citizenship, were to be humiliated by public exposure in the iron collar *(carcan)*, a holdover from the Old Regime. Later, by an act of August 31, 1792, the Legislative Assembly made an alteration for pregnant women, specifying for them a month's imprisonment rather than exposure in the *carcan*.

In all these forms of punishment carrying humiliation of the condemned by public exposure, the legislators considered that a public ceremony of rehabilitation was fitting for those who had undergone it. Accordingly it was ordered that they were to be conducted into court, where certain officials were to announce that they had satisfactorily expiated for their wrongs and that "the law and the tribunal removed the stigma *(trace)*" of their misdeeds.[48]

Through this great reform all of the worst features of criminal justice under the Old Regime were removed. Arbitrary imprisonment, torture, extraction of evidence by secret process, and obligation of the accused to prove his innocence were discarded. So, too, were the horrible modes of capital punishment, and the many lesser causes of capital punishment. Unfortunately executions still were left a public spectacle. Attempt was made at a fairer gradation of punishments than hitherto had existed. Certain humiliating sentences, such as banishment to the provinces, the *amende honorable,* the hurdle, and branding were abolished. Certain features of the new system did not please all the legislators. There had been sharp debate over the retention of capital punishment, and also over its mode, some advocating execution by strangling rather than by decapitation. Many argued for retention of branding. Nevertheless, the new changes marked a great advance.

Of course the Old Earth was not replaced instantly by a New Heaven. There were some among the lower classes of society or among the victims of injustice under the Old Regime who no doubt so regarded the justice of the Revolution. Sober reading of the history of the period however reveals that justice during the

[48] *Ibid.,* 449.

Revolution had its sad defects even as under the Old Regime, and perhaps that there were as many victims. More particularly was this true of multitudinous mob scenes, from early 1789 to late 1795, in which human life was snuffed out by infuriated *sans-culottes,* as bloody and cruel as any French tyrant that ruled the throne. Much of this injustice was the work of the courts themselves, more particularly during the Reign of Terror, when special courts acted as much on caprice as on evidence. Part was due to legislation. Confiscation of property abolished in January, 1790, was reinstated on September 3, 1792, and continued actively in force until the Restoration in 1814. The grounds for capital punishment, moreover, were extended after the events of August 10, 1792, one of the first being the refusal to serve in the army or attempt to desert to the enemy. This was passed on September 2, 1792. Despite all this, however, the historian must laud the legal transformation achieved by the Revolutionary legislators, even though to some extent it existed only on paper. The foundation was laid for a new day. It was solid, tested both by reason and humanity. Some subsequent changes affecting both the criminal courts and procedure were made in the final session of the National Convention (1795), but in general it left them as it found them.[49]

In closing it may not be inappropriate to reflect a moment on the lot of those who had advocated this transformation in justice. Several who had written in its behalf took part as deputy in the National Assembly in 1789-1791—Brissot, Robespierre, and Bergasse. Bergasse, however, retired from the assembly in October, 1789. Lacretelle was a deputy to the Legislative Assembly, and in the National Convention sat Valezé, Brissot, and Robespierre. None, however, had an outstanding role in the legislative reformation; that was primarily the work of others, notably Pelletier de Saint-Fargeau and Duport, members of the old parlement of Paris. Several who had advocated legal reform prior to the Revolution, liberals then, came to be regarded during the Revolution as royalists. Boucher d'Argis and Malesherbes were guillotined as royalists. Servan, Lacretelle, Bernardi, and Duport were suspected of royalist sympathies and were forced to flee the country

---

[49] Jean Bourdon, *La réforme judiciaire de l'an VIII* (Rodez, 1941), I, 187; Esmein, *Histoire de la procédure criminelle en France,* 439-40.

after the events of August 10, 1792. Brissot, Linguet, and Valezé were condemned to death as Girondins during the Reign of Terror; the first two were guillotined, and the last committed suicide by stabbing himself in open court when his sentence was given. Robespierre later was executed, and Pétion committed suicide while in flight near Bordeaux and his body was half-eaten by wolves. Dr. Guillotin was imprisoned. Barère narrowly escaped execution at the time of the fall of Robespierre. Later he was exiled both by the Thermidorians and by the Directory. A strange fatality seemed thus to overtake many of these humanitarians who were so solicitous for human betterment. Their lot seems incredible. But other humanitarians in history, Socrates, Jesus, and the Christian martyrs, ran into the same fate. Does the world ever want reformation?

CHAPTER TEN

Child and
Youth Welfare

THE EIGHTEENTH century was not altogether the first that gave attention to children's needs, but it far excelled its predecessors. There were three distinct aspects of the problem that drew the attention of thinkers in eighteenth-century France: first, the care that was needed by the child of normal parentage; second, the needs of orphans and abandoned children, maintained on charity funds and known as *enfants trouvées;* and thirdly, the most desirable form of education for the masses, as over against that for the youth who entered the professions. Each of these three matters received a great deal of consideration, and many writers did not limit their discussion to one or two of them.

The first aspect attracted public attention for what was perhaps the first time in history. Hitherto the matter of how parents cared for their children, other than making sure they did not kill them or expose them, drew little or no solicitude. In the second half of the eighteenth century parents came to be advised how they should rear their children. Pioneers in this criticism were two old bachelors, the Swiss-born Jean Jacques Rousseau and the Parisian philanthrope Claude Humbert Piarron de Chamousset (1717-1773), who censured the practice of the time whereby mothers of the aristocracy and the upper bourgeoisie farmed out their children to be suckled by needy wet nurses of the lower classes, more commonly of the peasantry. Rousseau complained of the callousness of heart thus shown by the wealthier women, and urged those with affection to nurse their children themselves, saying that even the animals did this for their young. Not only would the chance of survival for the child be increased, but also the likelihood of his being strong and sturdy.[1] Chamousset similarly criticized the farming-out practice, pointing out that the poor mothers who undertook to suckle the rich nurslings had often if not generally their own infants as well to nurse, and that in consequence it was likely that one or both children suffered neglect. Yet instead of urging the rich women to nurse their own children, he urged with even more reason than Rousseau that the milk of animals be employed for them, in like manner as did mothers in northern Europe. Hearing of a peasant woman in Burgundy who used animal milk for infants on a large scale and with much success, he visited her and brought her to Paris to head an institution for children that he set up with his own funds. Placed at Grenelle, near the Ecole Militaire, this institution reportedly acquired a great reputation and crowds visited it, until one night four children died and two others were taken violently ill. Poisoning was suspected, and thenceforth only individuals with satisfactory introductions were admitted. The record of success continued.[2]

Rousseau also denounced the current practice of enveloping children in swaddling clothes as though they were in danger of freezing. With epigrammatic terseness he charged that these were symbolic of the chains in which men everywhere found themselves. "Civilized man," he said, "is born, lives and dies in slavery; at birth, one sews him in swaddling clothes; at death, one nails him in a coffin; while he keeps the human figure, he is enchained by our institutions."[3] Rousseau would discard these fettering clothes and leave the child as nearly in the state of nature as possible.

He also would do away with all physical punishment for children as tyrannical and injurious to the personality. Animals, he pointed out, treat their young only with kindness; why should humans use cruelty? He would employ only reason and persuasion with children, and he would let them learn from unfortunate

[1] *Collection complète des oeuvres de J. J. Rousseau, citoyen de Genève* (Paris, 1791), V, 22, 25-30.

[2] Abbé Cotton des Houssayes, *Oeuvres complètes de M. de Chamousset, contenant ses projets d'humanité, de bienfaisance et de patriotisme* (Paris, 1783), I, xlii-xlviii.

[3] Rousseau, *Oeuvres,* V, 18-24.

consequences the unwisdom of their follies. In short, he would let nature correct them. Only if necessary would he use force.[4]

In these matters Rousseau was widely followed by later eighteenth-century reformers, nor were they necessarily of the philosophic band. The royal historiographer Duclos on his Italian tour of 1763-1764 advised a young couple on shipboard to remove the clothes from their screaming infant, with consequent peace.

This same enthusiasm for clothing children as lightly as possible was exhibited in a book on child welfare published in 1775 by a former army officer, J. L. de Fourcroy. He had read Rousseau and Locke. He had also observed with interest while serving in Santo Domingo how little clothing the slave children and others wore there and yet were more healthy than the children in France. He insisted that the wearing of tight clothing by infants, as in France, produced hernia, especially in males. It also tended, he charged, toward making children hunchbacked. The wearing of whalebone corsets by women, he asserted, led to the crippling of many children. He was an advocate of cold baths daily for children, in order to develop their physical resistance. His own two sons had been reared under the conditions he advocated, and he proudly described their physical vigor. He had inoculated them against smallpox and recommended the practice.

Fourcroy criticized sharply a practice of parents in certain French localities of having their sons castrated in order to get them exempt from army service. The castrations were usually on boys afflicted with hernia. Certain unscrupulous surgeons profited from the operations. He heard of one surgeon who had castrated seventeen children in a single day in a village near Clermont. The shocking practice had come to his attention while serving as a recruiting officer and found so many youths exempt from the service. In a single morning he counted forty-six castrates out of about 160 youths who reported at his recruiting station. Fourcroy denounced the practice not only in the name of humanity but for its effect on the French population. He would change the regulation granting military exemption to castrates.[5]

The antiphilosophic Bernadin de Saint-Pierre, in an essay submitted in a prize contest of the Academy of Besançon in 1771,

---

[4] *Ibid.*, 155-60, 193.

[5] *Les enfans élevés dans l'ordre de la nature* (Paris, 1775), 20-22, 27-31, 49-63, 72-82, 170, 208-11, 225-28.

argued strongly against the use of corporal punishment for children, asserting it to be contrary to nature and reason and not to be found among savage beasts or the American redskins, and rarely among the northern peoples of Europe. He called it an unfortunate practice handed down from the ancient world. He also criticized the mothers of his day for wishing only the joys of marriage and for neglecting the duties of maternity.[6] Increasingly in the last decades of the century views like these were expressed by agitators for reform, but it was more particularly in the Revolutionary period, when the question of state education was to the fore, that opposition to physical punishment was most frequently voiced.

A reviewer in the *Journal de Paris* in 1778 declared that "most of the physicians of this century have arisen against the usage of swaddling clothes for infants." The occasion was a book by Lascazes de Compayre, a physician of the Isle of Alby, who shared this view, asserting that such clothes enlarged the head, diminished the brain, and distorted other parts of the body. He also advocated the use of cow's milk for the children of city mothers, whom he thought not to have sufficient health to nurse their children, and contrariwise had too much caprice and passion. He objected to infants being sent to peasant wet nurses, whom he regarded as dirty and negligent. He encouraged the young women of the cities to enjoy their pleasures and to nurse their children on cow's milk.[7] Here was a thinker who by no means agreed with Rousseau in all respects. His reviewer, however, took issue with him, saying that "M. Lascazes will have difficulty in persuading us that these children [nursed by their mothers] are weaker and wickeder than those he would nourish with his cow milk."

Louis Sebastian Mercier pictured women of the year 2440 as breastfeeding their own children and producing strong, healthy youths. They did this "without considering it a great effort."[8] The idea that mothers should suckle their offspring he reasserted in his popular *Tableau de Paris*, published in the 1780's. He also supported Rousseau on the matter of physical punishment, saying

[6] *Oeuvres posthumes de Jacques-Henri Bernardin de Saint-Pierre*, ed. by L. Aimé-Martin (Paris, 1833), II, 450-51.
[7] *Journal de Paris*, August 17, 1778, pp. 913-14.
[8] *L'an deux mille quatre cent quarante*, 337.

the repeated use of switch and ferrule to correct the behavior of children was inhuman.[9]

A few other small points were raised by one writer or another, such as the need of the state to support poor mothers so that they might be able financially to rear their children, and the need of establishing nursing bureaux in other French cities modeled after that of Paris so that better nurses might be engaged. However, the suggestions to parents about the proper rearing of their children were not numerous, and the most forceful critic in this respect was Rousseau.

In the second field of recommendations, the care of foundlings, vastly more was written; it was not because there were more foundlings than children reared by their own parents, but because they became wards of the state and constituted a governmental problem of no small consequence. The size of the problem may be seen when it is stated than in the 1780's, on the eve of the Revolution, nearly six thousand foundlings were brought each year to the General Hospital of Paris. Of these more than two thousand were brought to Paris from the provinces. By no means, however, were all French foundlings brought to Paris. While it was the chief entrepôt, every French city and town of consequence had them and supported them usually through its general hospital. Perhaps the total number of admissions per year in France was eight or ten thousand. Of these a large percentage were children of legitimate birth. Some eighteenth-century writers alleged that the greater portion of the foundlings were of legitimate birth, being exposed by their parents because they were too poor to provide for them. That many poor parents exposed their children was true, but Léon Lallemand, leading authority on the subject, declares that the opinion that the majority of the foundlings were of legitimate birth "is absolutely false," and by way of proof he cites hospital figures for 1760 wherein out of the 5,032 admissions at Paris there were only 735 of legitimate birth, or about one-seventh of the whole.[10]

[9] *Tableau de Paris*, II, 48-49; III, 240.

[10] Léon Lallemand, *Histoire des enfants abandonnés et délaissés: études sur la protection de l'enfance aux diverses époques de la civilisation* (Paris, 1885), 162-63, 741. Here Lallemand presents a chart of annual admissions at the Hospital for Foundlings in Paris from 1640 to 1820. Elsewhere (p. 161) he gives some additions and shows that a total of 340,387 foundlings were admitted there in the years 1700-1789.

The most distressing fact about the admissions, however, was not that there were so many families too poor or too heartless to care for their children but that so many infants died before they reached the general hospitals or shortly after admission. The mortality rate was frightful, 90 percent of those brought to Paris dying within three months. Within three years 95 percent or more perished. Nor was the situation better in Great Britain or other countries. Common opinion in the eighteenth century laid the blame for this mortality upon city air, regarded as banal for children. Rural air, on the contrary, was considered healthy and desirable. Accordingly the general hospitals no sooner received the children than they farmed them out to wet nurses in the country districts, where they would be reared in peasant families for the first five years of their lives, and afterward, unless these families desired their continued stay, they were commonly returned to the general hospitals for training and work toward their maintenance. An elaborate system was worked out for their inspection and supervision, the state underwriting the expense.[11]

Ever since the days of Colbert the French government manifested solicitude in the matter of its population, and this solicitude increased greatly during the latter half of the eighteenth century. It was shared by a large portion of its writers and thinkers, and no doubt was a common topic of conversation among the cultivated classes.

The Abbé de Saint-Pierre, one of the earliest of the *philosophes*, advocated government assistance to large families, insisting that the children be reared in their own homes. He would have a special bureau set up in each parish for examination into the needs of citizens for assistance. He himself assumed the expense of rearing and educating several children.[12]

Montesquieu, another of the early *philosophes* and perhaps the most conservative, insisted that the expense of supporting unfortunate children should devolve upon their fathers whenever these were known or could be ascertained. In his *Esprit des lois* he asserted that peoples almost everywhere have placed this responsibility upon the father. In illicit cases the father generally shunned this responsibility, and in consequence the population

[11] See a chapter on the subject in my *Government Assistance in Eighteenth-Century France* (Durham, 1946).
[12] Drouet, *L'Abbé de Saint-Pierre*, 209-10.

increased very little from extramarital intercourse.[13] Montesquieu thus ranged himself on the conservative side of a question that drew increasing interest and controversy as the century proceeded, namely whether the fathers of exposed children should be compelled by the government to pay for their maintenance in the hospitals, and whether in their refusal or inability to do so they should be imprisoned as debtors. Imprisonment on this ground was called imprisonment for the "month of nursing" (*mois de nourrice*). After the midcentury it became increasingly unpopular and in the *cahiers* of 1789 it was repeatedly set forth as an injustice that should be eradicated. In consequence, the Legislative Assembly proceeded to abolish it in August, 1792.[14]

One reason for its unpopularity was the ease with which an innocent man could be victimized. The law recognized the testimony of the mother of the exposed child in regard to the identity of the father; in fact the law required that the mother must name an innocent man who was in better circumstances than the actual father. Many innocent men were thus victimized. It is reported that unscrupulous girl-mothers frequently made priests their targets, as generally they were in financial position to pay and their professional ties rendered it necessary that they pay.[15] Denial of fatherhood on the part of the man accused availed nothing; the courts accepted the word of the mother. The way was thus opened to rank injustice, and the people of France in general were bitter about it. From time to time the government, to mark some notable occasion, would free a number of these imprisoned fathers, partly as an act of generosity but more so perhaps as a means of winning popular applause. Thus in 1778, due to the generosity of Marie Antoinette, fifty-three fathers imprisoned for their failure to pay the *mois de nourrice* were released from Parisian prisons and reportedly forty-seven others were also to be released.[16]

The decision that rural life was better for the foundlings than was that of the city had already been made in the late seventeenth century, and its wisdom was never doubted in the eighteenth.

[13] *Esprit des lois,* book XXIII, ch. XI.
[14] *Réimpression de l'ancien Moniteur,* XIII, 527.
[15] Prud'homme, *Michel de Servan,* 26-27.
[16] *Journal de Paris,* May 16, 1778, cited by Prost de Royer, *Mémoire sur la conservation des enfans* (Lyon, 1778), 59-60.

Efforts, however, were made to extend the rural period, and it met with success. Prior to 1696 there had arisen the practice of sending the foundlings from the General Hospital of Paris to the homes of nurses in the provinces for a period of three years. In 1696, partly due to crowded hospital conditions and partly to the realization of the need of rural air for the children, the period was increased to five years. It continued thus until 1761, except that the crowded condition of the hospital necessitated leaving the children with their nurses beyond the five-year period. In 1761 it was ordered that thenceforth the children were to be left with the nurses and their families as long as these would keep them, the state providing for their maintenance. It was provided, moreover, that any man giving residence to a foundling might use him as a substitute in the event of draft for military service, or even might substitute him for his son, brother, or nephew. Since the foundling was paid nothing for his work even after he reached his teens, it was observed that often he was exploited in this respect, and accordingly in 1772 the government stipulated that thenceforth foundlings might not be kept without the payment of wages beyond the age of twenty. This revised system worked satisfactorily and was commended by the National Assembly's Committee of Mendicity in 1790.[17] Throughout the century there were many who commended this practice of rearing the foundlings in the country, and none apparently who criticized it.

Another feature much commended was the Bureau of Nurses at Paris created in the latter part of the century for supplying competent nurses to care for foundlings or for other children. The bureau thus was an efficiently run employment agency. The nurses for the most part were rural women, and apparently wet nurses, since the bureau operated primarily for the benefit of the General Hospital. Before one could qualify for registration, she must provide a certificate from her curé, which gave her address, her name, her husband's, the husband's occupation or trade, her reputation, the size of their family, the age and state of health of their last child, information whether she had any other nursling at the moment, and sundry other details that would indicate whether she was qualified for the charge she sought. The bureau was directed by a woman termed a *recommandaresse,* appointed

[17] Lallemand, *Histoire des enfants abandonnés,* 188-92.

by a magistrate who had it under his jurisdiction. The nurses came to Paris to register and to receive their nurslings, and carried them to their homes after receiving definite instructions about what was expected of them. Before they might depart, each nurse must be checked by a physician, and on arrival at her home she must present a certificate to her curé, who in turn would give her a certificate that she must return to Paris within a fortnight. Thenceforth she was to be under the observation of her curé, who was to keep a register for this purpose. Periodically there were to be visits from inspectors paid by the government.[18]

This institution was highly praised by Prost de Royer, lieutenant general of police at Lyons, who in a paper read before the Academy of Sciences, Belles-Lettres, and Arts of that city, recommended the establishment of such a bureau there. He termed the Paris bureau "this precious establishment" and said that it had "the greatest influence over the population, over the conservation of the citizenry, and over prosperity." Similar bureaux had already been formed at Bordeaux, Versailles, Saint-Germain-en-Laye, and other cities.[19]

Prost de Royer would guarantee prompt and regular payments to nurses and *meneurs* (agents who carried the children) by means of a Bureau of Assurance affiliated with the proposed Bureau of Nurses, in like fashion as that at Paris which had existed since 1769.[20]

Mercier in his *Tableau de Paris*, in 1782, likewise praised the Parisian Bureau of Nurses as well run and serving a useful purpose, although he deplored the failure of French mothers to nurse their own children.[21]

The *Journal de Paris* of June 27, 1778, carried a long, commendatory review of Prost de Royer's book, which served to bring the needs of child welfare before a wider circle of readers. In this review not only was the work of the Bureau of Nurses commended, but also the solicitude of the lieutenants general of police at Paris De Sartine and Le Noir.[22]

In order to encourage good care of the children by their nurses, some anonymous donor, possibly the philanthropist Montyon, set

---

[18] Prost de Royer, *Mémoire sur la conservation des enfans*, 25-30.
[19] *Ibid.*, 30-31.   [20] *Ibid.*, 48-49.
[21] *Tableau de Paris*, IV, 144-45.   [22] Pp. 709-10.

up an annual prize of three louis d'or to be awarded the nurse adjudged the best. Distribution of the prize was entrusted to Le Noir, who proceeded to triple its value. The winner was not given money but a silver goblet and a silver medal, the latter bearing on one side the queen's likeness. The author Nougaret, who aspired to imitate Mercier's popular description of Paris, reported keen competition for the prize, and briefly described two of the contestants in the year he was writing. One who lived at Marly had nursed twenty-two infants, of whom twelve still survived. The other, at Rouen, had nursed nine children of her own and fourteen others. No mention is made of the number in this case that had survived or died. Nougaret commended the idea of the prize and spoke highly of Le Noir as an official with "extreme zeal for the public good."

Nougaret also reported that in 1785, on the birth of the dauphin, an anonymous gentleman had contributed twelve thousand francs toward liberating prisoners being held for failure to pay the *mois de nourrice*.[23]

A problem that gave some trouble in the nursing of children was venereal disease. To protect the children against infection from nurses, the Bureau of Nurses at Paris required of the nurses a certificate of health from a physician attached to the bureau. Evidently the nursing bureaux of other cities had similar provisions. In addition there were the periodic visits of inspectors and the constant surveillance of the local curés. Even so, licensed nurses not infrequently became infected with venereal germs. To meet the situation, the Bureau of Nurses at Paris had an establishment where infected nurses could be treated. This later developed into the *maisons de santé,* where parents and others as well as nurses might be treated at government expense.[24] It was charged, however, that some of the children inflicted with venereal disease had acquired it from their parents rather than their nurses. To protect the nurses against such infants, precautionary measures had to be taken. Some hospitals placed children of this type on animal milk. Thus the General Hospital of Dijon confided all its children of venereal or scrofulous tendencies to a woman

[23] P. J. B. Nougaret, *Table mouvant de Paris, ou variétés amusantes, ouvrage enrichi de notes historiques et critiques, et mis au jour* (London, 1787), I, 61 n1, 66-67.

[24] Prost de Royer, *Mémoire sur la conservation des enfans,* 30.

who fed them cow's milk, to avoid contagion; and the General Hospital of Grenoble, in 1769, decided to feed its foundlings thenceforth goat milk.[25] The hospitals found it both a troublesome and a costly problem.

Children afflicted in other ways were also given special consideration. If they were invalid, cancerous, or epileptic, the General Hospital of Dijon placed them under the care of individuals and underwrote their expense throughout life. Occasionally they were admitted into the wards of the old men or the old women at the hospital, according to their sex. The government reimbursed the hospital sixty livres a year for their upkeep.[26]

Whereas the problem of mortality and health evoked much comment from the writers and philosophers of the times, little comment indeed was made on the matter of venereal or otherwise afflicted children. Among the few to comment on the latter was Madame de Genlis, who proposed a way to cure hunchbacked children by having them to draw weights attached to pulleys for exercise, like drawing water from a well. She claimed to have gotten the idea as a girl from hearing that servants were seldom hunchbacked because of being forced to draw water. During the Revolutionary period, when she was a refugee in London, she prevailed upon the Duke of Gloucester, then at the head of several hospitals, to establish a hospital there for hunchbacked and rickety children.

Destruction of the child by the mother through abortion or child murder was a problem provoking some comment. Montesquieu in his *Persian Letters* (1721) cast satire on the practice, charging that the French women did it "in order that their pregnancy might not make them disagreeable to their husbands." Then he commented that there were "dreadful laws" against abortion, for any young woman who did not declare her pregnancy before a magistrate and lost her child was put to death.[27] In his *Esprit des lois* (1748) he attributed this law to Henry II, of the mid-sixteenth century, and condemned it. In his opinion it should suffice that the pregnant woman informed one of her closest rela-

[25] Martin-Doisy, *Dictionnaire d'économie charitable, ou exposé historique, théoretique et pratique de l'assistance religieuse, publique et privée, ancienne et moderne* (Paris, 1855-1864), IV, 571; *Inventaire sommaire des archives départementales antérieures à 1790 . . . l'hôpital de Grenoble*, E 22, p. 99.

[26] Martin-Doisy, *Dictionnaire d'économie charitable*, IV, 572-73.

[27] Letter CXXI.

tives of her condition and it stopped there. It was natural that shame would prevent many girls from reporting their pregnancy to officials.[28] Beccaria in his *Essay on Crime and Punishment* likewise raised the question whether a woman who bore a bastard child and killed it could be greatly blamed, in view of the ignominy of becoming such a mother. He argued for a modification of the law.[29]

Brissot in his prize essay of 1780 commented on the prevalence of infanticide in his day, by abortion and otherwise, and described procedures adopted by Frederick II of Prussia and Gustavus III of Sweden to correct it. Like Montesquieu, whom evidently he had read, he asserted that the French law was too severe and needed modification.[30]

Under the Old Regime children born out of wedlock suffered severely from social stigma, and even in inheritance and professional opportunity. It is true that Louis XIV and Louis XV recognized as natural children certain of their bastard sons and daughters, gave them titles of nobility, married them off well, and endowed them with money. There were other natural children that formed exceptional cases. In general, however, bastards were scorned and handicapped. They "had no claim to inherit from either parent," although in actual fact there were exceptional customs in certain regions. If a bastard child died without legitimate children, his property was adjudged to the king; on the other hand, his children by marriage qualified as legitimate heirs and inherited property without difficulty.[31] It was well-nigh impossible for a bastard to be admitted as master in a guild or enter the priesthood. He faced the same problem in regard to marriage. As Captain Bousmard writing on the problem of the bastards pointed out, "Does he wish to marry? The legitimate daughter of the beggar will consider that she is marrying beneath herself in giving him her hand."[32] Professor Brinton has observed that the

[28] Book XXVI, ch. III.   [29] Pp. 131-32.

[30] *Les moyens d'adoucir la rigueur des lois pénales*, 45.

[31] Crane Brinton, *French Revolutionary Legislation on Illegitimacy, 1789-1804* (Cambridge, 1936), 7; Paul Robiquet, "Les Enfants naturels et la Révolution: deux petitions à l'Assemblée Nationale," *RF*, XXI (1891), 76.

[32] Henri Jean Baptiste de Bousmard, *Mémoire sur cette question: Quels seroient les moyens compatibles avec les bonnes moeurs, d'assurer la conservation des bâtards, et d'en tirer une plus grande utilité pour l'état? Ouvrage qui a remporté de prix de la Société Royale des Sciences et des Arts de Metz en 1787* (Metz, 1788), 46.

middle class was the most rigid in its prejudice on this matter; the aristocracy was much more tolerant. The same tendency prevailed in eighteenth-century England.[33]

This condition drew much criticism in France on the eve of the Revolution. The Société Royale des Sciences et des Arts of Metz in 1787 sponsored an essay contest on the subject "What Should Be the Means Compatible with Good Manners for Assuring the Conservation of Bastards, and of Drawing the Greatest Utility from it for the State?" The prize was won by a captain of the Royal Engineering Corps stationed at Metz, Henri-Jean-Baptiste de Bousmard (1749-1807), son of a president of the parlement of Metz and a graduate of the military engineering school at Mézières. He was greatly interested in the betterment of conditions for the poor, which he espoused both in the cahier for the nobility of Saint-Mihiel in 1789 and subsequently in the National Assembly of 1789-1791 as representative of the nobility of Barrois.[34] Second place in this contest was won by a young lawyer of Arras, later to become distinguished in the French Revolution, Maximilian Robespierre. Both essays were published by the Société.

Shortly later Boucher d'Argis, Parisian lawyer and reformer, made some references to bastard children in his *De la bienfaisance dans l'ordre judiciaire* (London, 1788).[35] It was at this same period that Malesherbes and certain other lawyers wrote in behalf of government recognition of Protestant marriages.

Robespierre deplored the stigma that society had placed on bastards, yet he would not grant them full equality with other children in the inheritance of property.[36] Mercier, too, deplored their lot and urged their adoption as a solution to the problem. He commented that every year eight thousand were brought to the Hospital of the Enfants-Trouvés in Paris and thence were farmed out to nurses in the country. They came from all classes of society—the prince, the cobbler, the lunatic—the son of Rousseau and that of Cartouche. Half of them were destined to die their first year. It was fashionable for rich women of the cities to have as pets little Negroes and dogs. Mercier would have them

[33] Brinton, *French Revolutionary Legislation*, 13-14.
[34] A biographical sketch of Bousmard is found in *NBG*, VII, 118.
[35] P. 67.   [36] *Discours couronné par le Société de Metz*, 45.

adopt the foundlings. Some adoption existed, to be sure, but very little. He complained that the French law on adoption was too severe on the father, and should be modified, permitting the father to deny responsibility in time if the child became displeasing to him. This the Romans had done, and he would follow Roman law on the subject.[37]

Bousmard, like Mercier, proposed adoption of bastard children as the solution to the problem. He would not permit celibates, whether man or woman, to adopt children; indeed he would prefer that the wife in the family making the adoption be in a state to suckle the child herself. Here one sees an expression of the idea of Rousseau that the mother should suckle her own child. He proposed that the state should pay couples adopting foundlings at the rate of a hundred livres per month until the youths were sixteen, and that the state at the same time should put in a fund twenty livres per month for the youth to establish himself in a livelihood when he should be sixteen. For the girls, the money would serve as a dowry. These children moreover should share in the inheritance of the family in like manner as the children of legitimate birth. He drew up a proposed decree that he would like to see enacted. In order to prevent professional discriminations against the adopted child he would have the adoption papers from the government recorded on the local church registers, but the public excluded from access to this register save in a lawsuit over litigation of property.[38] Clearly Captain Bousmard went farther than anyone else before the Revolution in his solution to this vexing question. It is an interesting book, opening with a historical introduction, and offering suggestions to the many facets of the problem. The *Mercure de France*, leading literary journal of the day, gave it a long and favorable review.[39]

A matter that puzzled Bousmard was how the Christian church could be indifferent to a matter so grievous. "How is it that a religion founded by a poor God, in whose eyes the sinful woman found grace, and from whom the adulterous woman obtained a generous pardon, suffers that the innocent be punished for the culpable. Why does it reject from the ministry of its altars that

[37] *Tableau de Paris*, VII, 188-96.
[38] Bousmard, *Mémoire sur cette question*, 23, 27-36, 38-41, 46-48.
[39] Issue of May 24, 1788, pp. 162-72.

one who has only God for his father?" Elsewhere Bousmard stated that the motive for his writing was not to win the prize but his love for humanity.[40]

Bousmard did not realize how quickly a law would be made in endeavor to alleviate the situation, although it differed from his proposals. He indeed might have been a deputy to the National Convention that enacted it, even as he was a member of the National Assembly, but war had called him to the colors and he was fighting the invading Austrians and Prussians when the law of November 2, 1793, was passed, whereby illegitimate children were given equal rights in ownership of property and in inheritance with those of legitimate children, provided that the father would acknowledge them. Illegitimates, on their part, might not make research into the question of their paternity. The law also had certain retroactive aspects that were revoked by the Directory on August 2, 1796. The purpose of the law of November 2, 1793, according to the late Professor Sagnac, was the desire of the Conventionals "to wipe out, as far as possible, all the social distinctions rooted in the laws and prejudices," and he asked, "what prejudices and what laws [were] more tyrannical than those which fell on natural children?" It was not that the Conventionals wished to weaken the importance of marriage; rather it was their desire to see that the illegitimate was no longer "to remain the innocent victim of an action that he had not made." Again, they wished to return to the old principle that the father, when he recognized his child, should support him and make him an heir. Sagnac suggested that the law might have given the illegitimate child rights equal in all respects to the legitimate child, which it did not, and that it might have accorded him the right of research into the question of his paternity. The law thus was a compromise with principle, but it marked a great advance over the pre-Revolutionary legislation under which illegitimates were not eligible to inheritance.[41]

This legislation, however, was criticized by the retired jurisconsult François Michel Vermeil (1732-1810) in a commentary

[40] *Mémoire sur cette question,* 3, 63.

[41] Brinton, *French Revolutionary Legislation,* 42-44; Philippe Sagnac, *La législation civile de la Révolution française (1789-1804)* (Paris, 1898), 319-24. The retroactive clause legitimated children born out of wedlock whose parents died in the period from July 14, 1789, to November 2, 1793.

published in 1798/1799 saying that it placed the illegitimate child on the same basis in inheritance as the legitimate child, which he considered a blow at the legal institution of marriage. "Healthy morality demands," he said, ". . . that marriage be honored, that one give great importance to the duties that it imposes, and that one attach some consideration to those who carry them out with exactitude." Other than this he offered no criticism, in a work that revealed him to be a learned and moderately conservative man. He did raise the question whether these laws granting legitimacy under certain conditions did not also carry by implication political rights as well. The matter was discussed wholly as a legal question, and the author did not interpose his own opinions.[42] All in all, it was an able little treatise that had much information on the status of the bastard both before the Revolution and as a result of it.

The legislative act of November 2, 1793, has been criticized more recently by Paul Viollet, who declared that it failed to attain its ends. It did not improve the lot of illegitimate children save in relatively few instances. It did not encourage paternal recognition of illegitimates, and it made more difficult than previously legal inquiry by a bastard child into his paternity, since it opened the way to blackmailing well-to-do families.[43]

The National Convention also set about to provide against the misfortunes of illegitimacy by legalizing adoption. Strange though it may seem, France since the sixteenth century had no process of legal adoption, whereby a child might become an heir to property and other rights. The Committee of Mendicity in its fourth report in 1791 recommended to the National Assembly a law to this effect. At length the Convention set it forth in its civil code of 1793, offering citizenship to all who would adopt children. It is not clear, however, whether the committee recommending it was more actuated by a desire to aid the children or to level fortunes. To prevent rich families without children from passing on to an adopted child all their wealth, it was stipulated that the maximum inheritance of an adopted child could not exceed three hundred quintals of wheat. During the years 1793-

[42] *Code des enfans naturels, ou recueil complet des lois et arrêtés qui leur sont relatifs* (Paris, 1798/1799), 7-8, 56-58.
[43] *The Cambridge Modern History*, VIII, 738-39.

1794 effort was made to encourage adoption of war orphans, with small success. It does not appear that adoption, the measure so popular in the United States during the past two or three decades, was at all popular in eighteenth-century France.[44] The foundling continued as he had been, a ward of the government, on a pitiful allowance, and without the love and attention of a home.

Professor Brinton has suggested that perhaps it is surprising that this legislation was enacted when there had been no great movement in its favor prior to the Revolution, and when in fact hardly any of the cahiers of 1789 had expressed a wish for legislation of this type. He also has ventured the opinion that whereas humanitarianism was a great movement in the late eighteenth century and influenced legislation, other factors less noble also were at work. These, however, he does not discuss. Most of the illegitimates, he reports, were born in the cities rather than in the rural districts.[45] During the Revolutionary years and the period of Napoleonic rule, when France was at war, the number of illegitimate births dropped heavily, from the annual figure of near 6,000 for the 1780's to less than 4,000 for the years in the 1790's after 1792.[46]

The third field of discussion on child welfare during the eighteenth century was education. While a few writers prior to 1700, including Montaigne and Fénelon, had discussed education of the youth, many more wrote on the subject after that date. One of the first during the eighteenth century to treat it was the Abbé de Saint-Pierre, who according to his biographer Joseph Drouet "was occupied all his life with the education of children." While the Abbé did not advocate universal education, he did want to see the children of the lower classes educated, saying that they should receive education as well as the children of the rich. Both primary and secondary education should be directed toward a utilitarian end. To the peasant children he would teach not only reading, writing, and arithmetic, but also some practical ideas of agriculture, medicine, veterinary care, morality, and religion. He

[44] Sagnac, *La législation civile*, 315-16; Camille Bloch, *L'assistance et l'état en France à la veille de la Révolution* (Paris, 1908), 440; *GE*, s.v. "Adoptionisme," I, 615; *Mercure français, historique, politique et littéraire*, Feb. 15, 1794, pp. 312-13.

[45] *French Revolutionary Legislation*, 11, 15-19.

[46] Lallemand (*Histoire des enfants abandonnés*, pp. 741-42) gives a statistical chart on French foundlings for the years 1640-1884.

was familiar with the work of the Christian Brothers of Jean Baptiste de la Salle, a lay order created in the late 1600's to bring utilitarian education to the poor. The Abbé himself founded a school for the gratuitous instruction of the children of Saint-Pierre-Eglise. He desired to make education interesting for the children and as far as possible remove constraint. Here of course he anticipated Rousseau. If education were made interesting, he was confident that the children would be eager to learn.

The Abbé suggested that there should be collaboration between the various schools so that they might discover the best methods of teaching and set forth a common policy. His biographer credits him with suggesting the ministry of public instruction "almost a century before its foundation."

In that period there was a choice between private instruction and college instruction. The Abbé preferred the latter, considering that a boy gains much from association with his comrades. He recommended in fact that the French dauphin be educated in college with the sons of the high nobility as his companions. This he set forth in his treatise *Projet pour perfectionner éducation*.

Likewise he would have girls educated in colleges, and not solely by their mothers. He considered that girls should receive education as well as boys, and that their education too should be practical. Fénelon before him, in 1687, had written a tract on girls' education, in which he advocated their instruction in religion, morality, sewing, and the household arts, to fit them to be good housewives. Saint-Pierre wanted them to study the same subjects taught the boys in college, although he did not advocate coeducation. Like Fénelon, he wished the girls to be housewives, and not to enter the professions. In fact no one in France at that time advocated the latter. Finally he advocated that the school for aristocratic girls founded at Saint-Cyr by Madame de Maintenon should be transformed into a normal school for the training of schoolmistresses. These ideas marked the Abbé as an advanced thinker for his day.[47]

Rousseau, in *Emile* (1762), likewise advocated what he termed a practical education, despite the fact that it would be the most expensive known, inasmuch as he would have a highly capable instructor for each pupil. The pupils would not be educated in

[47] Drouet, *L'Abbé de Saint-Pierre*, 247-67.

schools or even in classes, and would fail to get the democratic touch that Rousseau elsewhere so much advocated. He would not, in fact, have his pupils to begin their studies, or even to learn to read, until they were twelve years of age, insisting that childhood should be an age of enjoyment. Clearly Rousseau had the idea that study is unpleasant. And yet he recognized that education is a process that far transcends the acquisition of knowledge from books, for very aptly he stated that education begins at birth and that it consists in our acquaintance with the universe in which we live. He would have the boy learn gardening by planting seeds and cultivating the plants. He would teach him the idea of private property by letting him plant seed on a neighbor's land and thereby get in trouble with his neighbor, to his discomforture. At no time would he use corporal punishment, for that tended to crush a youth's personality. He would not even reprimand Emile or teach him to apologize to anyone; rather he would let circumstances take their course and nature alone punish him.

He criticized the use of Latin in the schools of that day as the medium of education, and injudiciously stated that before a child is twelve he should know only his native language. In line with the other *philosophes,* Rousseau deplored the use of the ancient languages. History should not be taught before the child is twelve, since before that age he cannot understand cause and effect, or its significance. Blazonry he very rightly declared had no value whatever. Geography should be taught differently from the accustomed manner, with less reliance on maps and definitions and more on practical observations by the teacher. As he would diminish the study of languages (a strange teaching for anyone in Europe where knowledge of languages is such an asset), he would give more attention to the sciences. Here too his views were in line with those of the other *philosophes.*[48]

Even in the eighteenth century the *Emile* exercised much influence. Bernardin de Saint-Pierre in a tract on the education of women in 1771 reproduced certain views expressed in it: namely

---

[48] *Oeuvres,* V, 163, 168-70, 214-25. Few books in modern times have had more influence than *Emile.* It is the chief base of the so-called "progressive" education dominant in the public-school system of the United States today, and it has both its admirers and its enemies. The late Professor Preserved Smith, who was among the latter, called it in his *History of Modern Culture* (II, 442), "the most celebrated and influential treatise on education ever written, and the worst."

that education begins at birth and that corporal punishment of children should be discarded. He commented that until his own day the European governments had "ignored that they ought to protect children."[49]

Mercier, too, criticized the physical punishment of children and the stuffing of children at school with Vergil and Livy.[50] Degrading forms of punishment must go and youth must discipline itself, were ideas expressed in a pamphlet in 1788 by Léonard-Jean-Joseph de Bourdon de la Crosnière, who planned to set up that year a boarding school for boys entitled the Royal Society of Emulation. He would institute what at some American colleges and universities today is designated the student government system, in which certain students elected by their fellows have the responsibility of sitting in judgment on cases demanding disciplinary action. Although his school was designed for the sons of well-to-do parents who could pay ample tuition fees, he planned to admit a few poor students also, at the rate of one in ten. These would wear the same uniform as the others but the quality of their cloth would be of a cheaper grade. They would work in the garden and at other tasks, though not as servants, and thus in a sense they would pay for their education.[51]

Students from six years of age to eighteen would be received. They would be divided into three groups, according to their advancement. The subjects taught would cover a wide range, including Latin (but not Greek), the modern languages (Italian, German, and English), logic, history, mathematics, several of the sciences, music, dancing, drawing and painting, fencing, swimming, military exercises, etc. Those who completed the third course or form might continue in the institution for studies that would be arranged by mutual agreement. The list of subjects carries interest in that it evidently was modeled after that of the knights academies of the century, and represented concessions to the sciences and modern languages, being definitely utilitarian in its design.[52]

[49] Oeuvres posthumes de Jacques-Henri-Bernardin de Saint-Pierre, II, 450-51.
[50] Tableau de Paris, II, 48-49.
[51] Plan d'un établissement d'éducation nationale, autorisée par arrêt du conseil du 5 octobre 1788, sous le titre de Société Royale d'Emulation (Orleans, 1788), 19, 27, 41.
[52] Ibid., 25-26.

Bourdon would have the boys eat at round tables, evidently to avoid raising the question of rank. Eleven of them and an instructor would sit at each table. Each week the group at each table would be changed by lot. He well realized the educational value of association at meals as well as in the classroom. In all these things he displayed good judgment. However he was something of a pedant or martinet, since he prescribed a rigid routine for every hour of the day, a rigid menu for meals, and a rigid code of discipline. His pedantry reached the ridiculous when he would put glass doors to the rooms of the boys in order to keep their actions under observation, and when he would attach to each bed bolster a device to ring an alarm in the guard's room when boys should attempt to slip out at night.[53]

Three subsequent brochures on education, all embodying more or less the same ideas, were published by Bourdon during the next several years. It is of passing interest that his school was adopted by the cabinet of Louis XVI in 1788 and then dropped. Later the Convention tried it for three years with war orphans. Bourdon reported that it was very successful, but from the fact that it was dropped the reader may decide otherwise. A lawyer by profession, Bourdon was elected from Loiret as deputy to the National Convention in 1792 and took an active part both in the Terror and in the Thermidorian reaction. In 1795 he was imprisoned after an abortive attempt to overthrow the government. Later he was elected to the Council of the Five Hundred, and in time reverted to a public-school director.[54]

In one of his later brochures he declared that the physical education of a child is equally as important as the mental, and thereby he was a precursor of a stand altogether too commonly taken nowadays.[55]

A scheme in many respects similar to Bourdon's was suggested in 1789 by a certain Bousquet, who planned to set up a boarding school for boys at Bordeaux. It would accommodate about forty boys between the ages of six and twelve. There would be several

[53] *Ibid.*, 30-31.
[54] *Mémoire sur l'instruction et sur l'éducation nationale* (Paris, 1793/1794), i-iii. See sketch of Bourdon in *NBG*, VII, 65-66.
[55] *La voeu de la nature et de la Convention de l'an 3, sur l'éducation générale; applicable, dans ce moment, à celle des orphelins des défenseurs, et autres enfans ou élèves de la patrie* (Paris, n.d.), p. 14.

instructors: one to teach science, a young Englishman to teach English, a zealous priest to give religious instruction, a swimming instructor, an instructor in military arms, and perhaps others. The expense for such an establishment would naturally be great, and only the sons of well-to-do families could attend. Fees would run annually from 800 to 1,200 livres, depending on the physical exercises and studies the student would pursue, and must be paid in advance by quarter or semester.[56]

The students would be dressed in uniform alike, the idea being to inculcate democracy. The greatest attention would be given to their health, for the writer was very conscious of the need of cleanliness, sanitation, and physical exercise. He stated that they would occupy "a vast house [his home], well aired, situated in a healthy quarter." Half a league from the city another house had been constructed where they would spend holidays and vacation periods. Near their school in the city a swimming hole would be provided in a canal. Like Bousmard, he was opposed to corporal punishment, and he proposed to let the students elect their own leaders who would mete out penalties to their fellows. If, however, a student was incorrigible, after attempts had been made to change him, he would be sent home. "Punishments will always be made with justice and moderation," he wrote; "we shall never forget that we are correcting some Frenchmen."[57]

The course of studies was similar but not identical to that Bourdon had suggested. Greek and Latin, French, English, geography, history, mathematics, ethics, drawing, writing were the subjects listed. Bousquet did not include German, and he revealed less interest in the sciences. Like Bourdon, he mapped out the activities of his students for each hour of the day.[58] There is no indication whether he was able to set up his school or not. The fact that he and Bourdon had similar ideas along several lines does not necessarily indicate that one was indebted to the other, but more probably that these ideas represented the common viewpoint of advanced thinkers of that period. The tendency was distinctly against the classical tradition then in vogue and in favor of the modern studies which were considered more utilita-

---

[56] *Plan d'éducation nationale, presentée à MM. les quatre-vingt-dix électeurs des communes de Bordeaux* (Bordeaux, 1789), 28-29.
[57] *Ibid.*, 8-10, 15-16, 27.   [58] *Ibid.*, 25-28.

rian in value. The schools of these two men would be of little concern were it not that certain of their ideas could be applied on a larger theater.

At this stage the Revolution occurred. While child welfare was not one of the subjects to attract major interest, many demands were made for it, chiefly in the field of education. Many cahiers from Languedoc requested a national educational system.[59] The village of Dauboeuf, in Normandy, asked for free elementary schools in the rural regions; the village of Viger, in the Hautes-Pyrénées, requested a schoolmaster in common with a neighboring parish; the third estate of Civray, in the department of Vienne, complained of the neglected condition of the public schools and the universities, and asked for correction; the third estate of the bailliage of Carenton, Normandy, asked for a national system of education to be created, under the supervision of the magistrates; the community of Freyssinet-le-Gélat, in the department of Lot, called for a tontine created by church funds and contributions from newly married couples, to provide education to children of large families through loans.[60] These by no means exhaust the list; they merely reveal the type of thinking that was going on in certain communities widely scattered over France. There were others demanding that the government provide better care of illegitimate children, that it provide dowries for foundling girls, and that it train foundling youths for life at sea or for work in the country rather than for carding wool and cotton and other unhealthy tasks. In short, there was a fair degree of solicitude in child welfare expressed in the cahiers.

The National Assembly was too occupied with other problems to give much attention to the matter of education. On September 10, 1791, it heard a report on the subject by Talleyrand but took no action. A new committee appointed by the Legislative Assem-

[59] *Histoire générale de Languedoc*, XIV.
[60] Comité de Calvados, *Cahier de doléances du bailliage de Honfleur pour les Etats Généraux de 1789*, publiés par Albert Blossier (Caen, 1913), 156; Département des Hautes-Pyrénées, *Cahier de doléances de la sénéchaussée de Bigorre*, publiés par Gaston Balencie (Tarbes, 1925), 620; Départment de la Vienne, *Cahiers de doléances de la sénéchaussée de Civray pour les Etats Généraux de 1789*, publiés par P. Boissonnade et Leonce Cathelineau (Niort, 1925), 13; *Cahiers de doléances du bailliage de Cotentin*, publiés par Emile Bridrey (Paris, 1907), I, 775; Département du Lot, *Cahiers de doléances de la sénéchaussée de Cahors pour les Etats Généraux de 1789*, publiés par Victor Fourastié (Cahors, 1908), 151-52.

bly made a lengthy report on April 21-22, 1792, through Condorcet, which was truly remarkable in its character, and which must have been largely the work of Condorcet himself, for the ideas are too profound, too well expressed, to be the work of a common political committee.[61]

He declared that education should be free, secular, available to all, and compulsory. Girls should be educated as well as boys, but taught separately from them. There should be an elementary school in every village of four hundred inhabitants and effort must be made to render schools available to the children living in rural districts. The teachers must have been trained for their task and must hold a certificate. They must teach not only reading, writing, arithmetic, and grammar, but also morality, practical ideas about agriculture, industry, and other matters, especially social and civic duties. The teachers furthermore must see to the health of the children by giving them physical exercises.[62]

For children qualified, there should be a secondary school in each district and one in each town of four thousand inhabitants. The studies should consist of mathematics, natural history, chemistry, commerce, ethics, and social science. He foresaw that the industrial processes are constantly reducing the time necessary for labor, and that man needs something to occupy and interest him during this leisure he is coming to enjoy.[63]

Above the secondary schools would exist the institute, of which there would be 110 in France. It would be roughly similar to the lycée of today. There for a period of five years the students would be introduced to professional studies. Finally, above the institute would be nine lycées, distributed over France so as to be available to the youth of every region. These were to be the universities.[64]

All four divisions or stages of the educational system would be free to the students. This, Condorcet explained, must be so since the state must use the talent of its poorer classes.

The report was not adopted by the Legislative Assembly, due

[61] The report may be found, in English translation, in *French Liberalism and Education in the Eighteenth Century: The Writings of La Chalotais, Turgot, Diderot, and Condorcet on National Education,* tr. and ed by F. de la Fontainerie (New York, 1932), 323-78, and save for some few deletions in John Hall Stewart's *A Documentary Survey of the French Revolution,* 347-70.

[62] Stewart, *A Documentary Survey,* 350-52.

[63] *Ibid.,* 351-52.   [64] *Ibid.,* 352-60.

possibly to its concern over other matters. The National Convention, which shortly came into being, appointed a new Committee of Public Instruction, which through its spokesman Lepeletier de Saint-Fargeau presented in July, 1793, a plan for an elementary-school system, wherein the state would have a monopoly. The Convention at length, on December 20, 1793, adopted a plan which was neither that of Condorcet nor that of Lepeletier de Saint-Fargeau. It concerned only elementary schools. Attendance was to be free and compulsory for children of both sexes. The children must attend for at least three years. Some option was extended the father as to where the children must go. The teachers would be paid by the state, at a rate proportional to the number of students taught. Members of religious orders might teach, but like other teachers must have a certificate of civism, which of course precluded most of them. The state would publish the textbooks, but it is not indicated that these would be free. The pupils were to be indoctrinated in the ideas of the Declaration of the Rights of Man and the Citizen. Surveillance over the schools would be exercised by the parents and by the local political authorities.[65]

Lack of funds and time were important factors in preventing this school system from reaching the ends desired during the period of the Convention. Another important factor was the lack of desire to cooperate on the part of a large segment of the population. They did not care to send their children to republican schools for indoctrination in Jacobin principles. Some kept their children at home; others had them taught secretly by nonjuring clergy. Never in the 1790's was the compulsory feature of the state schools made effective.

On October 25, 1795, the Convention in its dying moments enacted a new law regarding public education, in which the views of the more conservative wing of the middle class were expressed. The pupils henceforth were to pay for their schooling, if financially able; as many as one-fourth, however, might be exempted from this payment on account of indigence. The teachers might be appointed only after being examined by a local committee of citizens. They then were to be selected by the departmental

---

[65] *Ibid.*, 516-19; Lefebvre, *La Révolution française*, 568-69.

administration (regional political officers), and were to be subject
to it and to the local municipal administration.[66]

The same act of October 25, 1795, set up an excellent secondary-
school system, known as the central schools, from the fact that
there was to be one in each department; also some special schools,
in medicine, veterinary medicine, music, the fine arts, natural
history, and for instruction of deaf-mutes and the blind. The Convention also, in 1794-1795, created a series of other establishments
which had their part in the educational system or in serving as
auxiliaries to education, such as a normal school, a polytechnical
school, a school of mines, a military school, a school of bridges
and highways, a series of museums, the Bibliothèque Nationale,
and the national and departmental archives. [67] Save for the normal school and the central schools, they were not without their
precursors under the Old Regime, but they now were totally
renovated, subjected to the will of the people, and made available
to a broader segment of the population than hitherto.

The reform in education and the improvement in the opportunity for the pursuit of knowledge constituted quite remarkable
achievements of the revolutionaries. The government of the Old
Regime, more particularly after 1760, cannot justly be accused
of being indifferent to the extension of education among its subjects, but the Revolutionary governments, or, more properly, the
National Convention, approached the matter with zest and organ-
izational genius. Much of this last was indebted to Condorcet's
famous report. Opportunity for youth of the middle and lower
classes, never entirely absent, was made vastly greater during
the century, and for all this discussion paved the way for action.
One could not find the same concern for childhood and youth,
either in discussion or legal action, in any previous century. The
range of man's interest and concern for social problems had been
greatly extended.

[66] Stewart, A Documentary Survey, 635-36.
[67] Ibid., 636-40; Lefebvre, La Révolution française, 569-70.

CHAPTER ELEVEN

Public Health

O N DELVING into the records of the eighteenth century one is impressed not only with the almost universal disregard for public health as shown in practice, but also with a surprisingly large amount of concern for this matter expressed by thoughtful individuals of the day—pamphleteers, government and police officials—and sometimes even by the general public. The century clearly marked, in this respect, a transition between the Middle Ages and the present day. An elaborate set of regulations drawn up in 1629 by the parlement of Aix existed in southeastern France before the great outbreak of the bubonic plague occurred in that area in the years 1720-1722. These were put into effect at once in August, 1720, when the plague was recognized by physicians as present in Marseilles. Unfortunately police enforcement broke down in Marseilles and neighboring cities in 1720, even as it did subsequently over France in 1789, and what resulted was a travesty. Had the municipal regulations and those of the parlement of Aix been rigorously enforced, the great debacle might have been avoided.

The utter breakdown of police control in Marseilles was illustrated in the city's inability to dispose of the dead bodies. Hundreds of corpses lay on the streets, some reportedly for two or three weeks. The stench was awful and the menace to health alarming. This provided the Chevalier Roze with the opportunity for his great deed of heroism. Whereas the police were attempting to meet the situation by forcing all beggars and vagabonds to work at digging graves, he discovered two empty towers or dungeons that might be used for mass burials, obtained the right to employ galley slaves from nearby Toulon, and from horseback himself directed the removal of the corpses to these towers, where they were covered with quicklime. The giant dungeons were filled, but the streets were freed of the dead bodies. From that time onward it appears that galley slaves were employed at the task of body disposals, and they did their job efficiently, being promised their freedom if they survived. Alas, out of six hundred so employed, few survived. As a preservative they were bidden to carry a handkerchief over their nose and mouth dipped in vinegar or some other supposed disinfecting fluid.

The multitude of quarantine regulations interest us. A cordon of soldiers was drawn around the stricken area, and no one was allowed to enter or to leave it except under the strictest government regulation. This action no doubt saved the rest of France from the malady. Rigid harbor regulations likewise made it impossible for ships to stop at Marseilles, or for those caught there to move elsewhere. The physicians and nurses attending the sick wore a waxed robe over their clothes, a waxed head covering, gloves, and in their hands they carried a cane for prevention of bodily contact. Despite this, many died. Some of the physicians, however, notably those from the medical faculty of Montpellier who were sent by the government, scorned this aloofness and hesitated not to sit on the beds beside their patients, felt the swellings of buboes, and in some instances lanced them.

Houses in which the plague had occurred were disinfected. This was carried out with surprising thoroughness. The bedding and clothing of the sick were burned; furniture and other contents of the homes were aired, washed, and sometimes subjected to chemicals; the windows, floors, and walls were scoured or whitewashed; and then with the windows and doors closed, sulphur was burned or disinfectants were emptied in containers throughout the house. Physicians and surgeons from Paris, Montpellier, and elsewhere who served on government orders and at government expense in the area were subjected to forty days of quarantine at the end, to baths and changes of clothes, even as other citizens.

This was the last outbreak of bubonic plague in France, thanks possibly to strict enforcement of port rules. Outbreaks did occur elsewhere in Europe during the century, as at Messina, Sicily, in 1734, where reportedly forty-three thousand persons died within three months. All the European countries had rigid port regulations against it, save Turkey, where it existed endemic throughout the century, and it will be recalled that Napoleon's army was to suffer from it at Acre in 1799. France did experience a number of epidemics of other types during the century, but all were localized and in none were new features in regard to public health exhibited.

France actually experienced more trouble from epizootics during the eighteenth century than from epidemics. It was found that some owners tried to sell sick animals to butchers and that meat of suspect nature was placed on sale. Throughout the century government regulation forbade this and imposed heavy fines for its violation, but after 1763 increasing attention was given it. The government had progressively become interested in the effect of the epizootics upon human health. Severe penalties were placed upon the sale of meat of a suspect animal and on the sale of animals in the epizootic area which did not receive a bill of health from the owners and local inspecting officials. Even then, animals sold for butchering purposes had to be slaughtered within twenty-four hours.[1]

Animals as well as humans were protected against unwholesome food. In the early eighteenth century a law existed against the feeding of dead animals to dogs or hogs. There was also a law with a rather heavy fine forbidding brewers to sell soured malt to keepers of animals for feeding purposes. In 1743 court action was brought against a party for having fed sour malt to his own cattle. This revealed some popular concern in the welfare of animals.[2]

As the century advanced, the concern increased. In late 1775 when concessionnaires for the navy set up a meat-salting plant at Grenade, in Languedoc, the government ordered that a

[1] J. B. J. Paillot, *Manuel complémentaire des codes françaises et toutes collections des lois* (Paris, 1845), I, 127-28; Isambert, *Recueil général des anciennes lois françaises*, XXII, 178-79, 186-91; XXIII, 107-109, 136-37; XXVII, 444-48; Freminville, *Dictionnaire*, 88-89, 92, 212-19; Eugène Maury, *L'hygiène et l'assistance publique à Bar-sur-Aube (Aube) au XVIIIe siècle* (Paris, 1903), 7-8; *Histoire générale de Languedoc*, XIII, 1260.

[2] Freminville, *Dictionnaire*, 64-65; Nicolas Delamare, *Traité de la police* (2d ed. enl., Paris, 1719-1738), IV, 286.

physician or a veterinarian should be stationed there to inspect the viscera of all animals slaughtered, ere their meat might be salted.[3] This was followed in June, 1782, by some elaborate regulations regarding the sale of meat by butchers. All unauthorized persons were forbidden to butcher animals or to sell their meat in any form. Restaurant and hotel proprietors moreover were prohibited to use meat that had not been slaughtered by master butchers and bought from them. Even master butchers might sell meat only in their licensed shops. This prohibited the peddling of meat at Paris in carts. The decree also forbade the slaughter of sick animals or the sale of any meat not in perfect condition.

Meat was not the only food on which health regulations existed prior to the Revolution. Mercier in his *Tableau de Paris* told of police regulations at Paris in the 1780's against the delivery of milk by dealers in copper vessels. He doubted the effectiveness of the ordinance, however, saying that the peasants who did the milking continued their time-honored practice of drawing the milk in copper vessels, and only transferred it later to tin containers. He charged, too, that the milk was adulterated with water, and that sometimes milk was sold from a cow that had just calved.[4]

It was forbidden to put drugs in wines, even though most wine merchants were accused of having done so. In 1745-1746 a certain wine merchant and a vinegar merchant were brought into court on this charge and fined heavily. Their wine was poured into a stream.[5] The government also prescribed that wine merchants were not to pour wine into lead-covered containers or to put "ashes of lead" in wine, since poisoning resulted. It likewise forbade the sale of liquors in tin cups. It even forbade the use of copper balances in weighing quantities of salt, tobacco, and fruits.[6]

In the latter half of the century much attention was given to the drinking water of Paris. This of course came from the Seine, and was in no way filtered or treated with chemicals. Twenty thousand men transported water in buckets over the city, taking

[3] *Histoire générale de Languedoc*, XIII, 1260.
[4] VII, 269.   [5] Freminville, *Dictionnaire*, 124.
[6] Count Maxime de Sars, *Le Noir, lieutenant de police, 1732-1807* (Paris, n.d.), 107-108; Freminville, *Dictionnaire*, 144.

it into homes and apartments, for everyone was dependent upon this form of supply. Water pipes and hydrants had not yet been established. The first person to give attention to the need of something better apparently was the philanthropist Chamousset, who in August, 1768, published at Paris a several-page *Prospectus* in which he proposed a plan for providing the city with pure drinking water. Commenting that it was difficult to keep the water of streams fit for drinking when they flowed by cities where filth of all sorts was thrown into them, and that even filters did not remove the contamination apt to lead to sickness, he proposed the establishment of some gigantic cisterns in which would be placed "pure" water taken from the Seine in boats above the sewer entrances from the Hôtel-Dieu and the Gobelins manufactory. He considered that water taken from the middle of the river above these two prominent sources of contamination would be pure. From the great reservoirs delivery wagons would be dispatched in all directions carrying the precious fluid to the homes of the people. The medical profession of Paris approved the scheme, and Chamousset began the construction of one reservoir, but the contributing public was apathetic and the scheme died abortively, the people being unwilling to pay extra for the water so furnished.[7]

Another solution proposed was the diversion to Paris of the waters of the Yvette, a small stream flowing into the Orge. This was suggested for some years by an engineer named De Parcieux. When he died in 1768, Antoine Lavoisier, the chemist, championed it in a paper read before the Académie des Sciences and enlisted the interest of city authorities. But money necessary for the task was not available and this proposal failed of achievement.[8]

In 1781 Périer Frères set up at Chaillot some steam pumps that forced filtered water from the Seine into some enormous reservoirs high above the river. This became a curiosity at Paris rivaling the gigantic wheel set up by Louis XIV at Marly; and like the machine at Marly, drew large numbers of spectators and

[7] Abbé Cotton Des-Houssayes, *Oeuvres complètes de M. de Chamousset* (Paris, 1783), I, xcii; II, 65-73.

[8] Sidney J. French, *Torch & Crucible: The Life and Death of Antoine Lavoisier* (Princeton, 1941), 38.

provided a topic of general conversation. Other hydraulic devices came to be proposed during the next two decades.[9]

Among those concerned about the matter was the radical propagandist Louis Sebastien Mercier. He predicted in his *L'an deux mille quatre cent quarante* that in the year 2440 man will have devised artificial torrents and cataracts much more powerful than the wheel at Marly, which might be used for manufacturing purposes as well as others.[10] Some years later in his *Tableau de Paris* he told of foreigners in Paris commonly getting diarrhea from drinking water taken from the Seine, and commented that it could be prevented by their putting a spoonful of white vinegar in each pint of the water.[11]

This perhaps explains practices in vogue in the early 1790's at Paris. Among items of expense in connection with the charity workshops for the poor in that city in 1790 was one for 660 livres designated for vinegar which had been put in the water of the workers.[12]

Mercier in his *Tableau de Paris* expressed a humanitarian interest in the poor men who cleaned the latrines and kept the sewers in order. The work paid poorly and the conditions under which they worked were well-nigh unbearable. It undermined their health, and Mercier asserted that it was necessary for them to drink brandy and other liquors to acquire the necessary stupefaction to endure the task.

Cemeteries and churches having tombs frequently were centers of foul odor and insanitation. It is surprising that so much disregard of the matter prevailed when the government from time to time had shown much concern in it. It is curious that the government ignored the usage of quicklime in private burials, whether in cemeteries or in churches. After 1760, however, much protest was made against these conditions in Paris and other cities, as French public opinion came slowly but increasingly to be stirred on the matter.[13]

[9] Shelby T. McCloy, *French Inventions of the Eighteenth Century* (Lexington, 1952), 116-17.

[10] P. 259 and n.   [11] I, 154-55.

[12] Alexandre Tuetey, *L'administration des ateliers de charité, 1789-90. Rapport de J. B. Plaisant* (Paris, 1906), 66.

[13] Auguste Prudhomme, in his *Histoire de Grenoble* (Grenoble, 1888), 571-72, tells of a cemetery in that city being closed by the bishop because it had become a menace to public health, and of an annex being opened on other grounds.

In 1758 and 1776 the parlement of Rennes ordered the removal of all bodies from churches and their transfer to cemeteries, with little effect. The condition of the churches, as foyers of insanitation, was very bad. In 1777 and 1779, respectively, it became necessary for the cities Lesneven and Brest to choose new cemeteries, due to overcrowding and the resulting foul conditions. The Parlement of Paris, on May 21, 1765, ordered the removal of bodies from the existing cemeteries, but the order long remained a dead letter.[14]

In 1776 the clergy, in their convocation, called the government's attention to the fact that for several years complaints had been made of the "frequent burials in churches" and of burials in cemeteries adjacent to churches as being insanitary. Police and the magistrates, they added, had long been concerned over the matter. They recognized the need of changed ecclesiastical rules. These the king set forth in a declaration of March 10, 1777. Thenceforth the right to interment in churches was restricted to archbishops, bishops, curés, patrons, and high functionaries (haut-justiciers), and even these must be buried in earth to a depth of six feet. All burials thus must be made in the floor of the church, none in the walls. Monks, nuns, and members of the Knights of Malta might be buried in the cloisters of their monasteries or convents, but not in their chapels; and they, too, must be buried to a depth of six feet. Evidently the measure was enforced, as no further complaints were made in regard to church burials.

Complaints continued, and increased, however, in regard to the cemeteries. Though the king in 1776 issued an ordinance directing cities and towns to move their cemeteries outside the corporate limits, it met little or no compliance.[15] As complaints continued in Paris, more particularly by residents living in the neighborhood of the ancient Cemetery of the Innocents, where it was estimated that more than a million bodies had been buried since the Middle Ages, the police appointed a physician, Cadet

14 Mercier, Tableau de Paris, I, 130; Alfred Franklin, La vie privée d'autrefois (1st. ser., Paris, 1887-1901), VII, 205-13; Michel Möring and Charles Quentin, Collection des documents pour servir à l'histoire des hôpitaux de Paris (Paris, 1883-1887), II, 78 et passim.
15 A. Dupuy, "Les épidémies en Bretagne au XVIIIe siècle," Annales de Bretagne, I (1886), 121-22.

de Vaux, to investigate the matter. His long and detailed report, read before the Académie des Sciences in 1781 and published in the *Journal de physique* for 1783, had the result of bringing an end to burials in that cemetery. That very year excavations were begun and the bones were transported outside the city to the Catacombs. Over the next two or more decades other cemeteries were treated in like fashion. The close of the eighteenth century thus saw something tangible resulting from the complaint about cemeteries.

Among the matters of public health that engrossed the attention of the French in the last decades of the eighteenth century was improvement in hospital sanitation, and more particularly at Paris in the removal of the giant hospital of the poor, the Hôtel-Dieu, to a place, or rather to four places, on the outskirts of the city, where it was considered that purer air might be found. Most of the French hospitals of that day were overcrowded, insanitary, and marked with heavy mortality rates. The Hôtel-Dieu of Paris was notorious in all these respects. Something like 25 percent of its patients died. Its frightful mortality at length awakened public criticism. Its critics maintained that its insanitary conditions were incurable, since it was situated on a bank of the Seine in the heart of the city, where it was screened from the air currents needed to cleanse it.

It is not clear who first called attention to the situation. Perhaps it was Chamousset, who in 1756 published a pamphlet advocating reform of the Hôtel-Dieu. Under the title *Vues d'un citoyen* it was republished in 1757. In 1773 and again later, he published more on the subject. In all four brochures he pointed to the severe mortality rate of the Hôtel-Dieu and proposed the sending of at least a portion of its patients to other city hospitals. From June, 1761, to April, 1762, Chamousset had served under the Choiseul ministry as intendant general of sedentary hospitals of the royal army, having supervision of sixty-eight military hospitals. His eighteenth-century biographer, Cotton Des-Houssayes, credits him with the introduction of some drastic reforms that considerably reduced the mortality rates of these hospitals.[16]

16 Cotton Des-Houssayes, *Oeuvres de Chamousset*, I, xxxi-xli, lxv-lxx with notes. Tenon and other writers of the period, however, made no mention of his reforms.

In 1773 the scientist Jean Baptiste Leroy, member of the Académie des Sciences, proposed to read a speech on hospital construction on the occasion of the reopening of St. Martin's, but was forbidden by one of the king's ministers to whom the speech had to be referred. The remarks on hospital construction were ordered excised, on the grounds that they were designed to create alarm in regard to the rebuilding of the Hôtel-Dieu, which had suffered a severe fire the year previously.[17] This silenced Leroy, but only temporarily.

In the early 1780's Mercier severely attacked conditions at the Hôtel-Dieu, in his *Tableau de Paris,* calling the hospital a death-trap and sneering at the very term "Hôtel-Dieu."[18] By this time the subject had become so warm that in 1786 the Académie des Sciences was directed by the government to study the situation. It appointed a committee, with Leroy, Bailly, and Tenon among its members, to study the situation. After a careful investigation of approximately two years, in which conditions in England too were studied for comparison, the committee through its chairman Tenon published its report, recommending the abandonment of the Hôtel-Dieu, since conditions there were regarded as irremediable, and the transference of its patients to four other hospitals in the suburbs. The government at once adopted the report and made ready to carry out the proposed changes. Then came the Revolution, with the government's shortage of funds and the people's interest in other affairs. The matter was passed by, and to this day the Hôtel-Dieu continues in its time-honored buildings along the Seine.[19]

For a time in the early period of the Revolution, discussion continued on the matter. For example, the *Révolutions de Paris* in September, 1790, carried "An Address to the Friends of Humanity," urging the need of building more sanitary hospitals and discussing the features they should have.[20] An elaborate report by the Committee of Mendicity on the hospitals and

[17] Jean Baptiste Leroy, *Précis d'un ouvrage sur les hôpitaux* (n.p., n.d.), 1-3. From a reference to the date 1788 on p. 16, the brochure must have been published in the period 1789-1790.

[18] III, 226-32.

[19] Jacques Tenon, *Mémoires sur les hôpitaux de Paris* (Paris, 1788), 472. This book affords excellent insight into ideas of the time on public health.

[20] Issue no. 65 of 1790, pp. 609-13.

asylums of France was made to the National Assembly in 1791. On the committee's recommendation the government confiscated all hospital property in France and assumed responsibility for its maintenance. However, it let the hospitals sink into worse neglect than before. In 1793 Hébert called for more asylums to care for the blind and other unfortunates. And in October, 1794, Paganel, speaking before the National Convention for the Committee of Public Aid, criticized the conditions prevailing in the various types of asylum.[21] In general, however, political reform and war were transcendent in French minds in the 1790's and little building resulted.

These things reveal but do not exhaust the degree of interest in public health in eighteenth-century France. Much might be added on the concern for infant mortality, for the mortality of mothers in childbirth, for the prevention of smallpox by inoculation, and on other matters. Enough has been presented nevertheless to make it clear that there definitely was increasing interest in the matter of public health as the century advanced, and indeed that there was no void of interest when the century opened. The movement developed *pari passu* with other matters of humanitarian concern, and its most rapid progress was after 1760. It developed in parallel with the influence of the *philosophes,* although these latter had comparatively little to do with it. Its promoters were above all physicians and surgeons, police officials, cabinet members, and intendants of the Old Regime. The conservative Chamousset wrote as much on the subject as did the radical Mercier. The police lieutenants of Paris, De Sartine, Le Noir, and De Crosne perhaps each had a more important role in furthering the public health movement than any single *philosophe.*[22] The chief contributions of the *philosophes* to the humanitarian movement lay in other fields. It is impossible to trace the interest in the development of public health and sanitation to any single group, and it is possible that the names of some who were most original in their contributions are totally unknown to us. The public health movement was, to be sure, one of the minor aspects of the era of humanitarianism.

[21] *Réimpression de l'ancien Moniteur,* XVII, 754; XX, 396-97.
[22] Maxime de Sars, *Le Noir,* chs. VI-VII; Hugues de Montbas, *La police parisienne sous Louis XVI* (Paris, 1949?), 110-19.

It never absorbed the attention of more than a limited circle of writers, readers, and officials. The Revolution brought no great transformation of conditions, as in other fields. Even in the mid-nineteenth century, sanitary conditions in France were still very bad.[23] In her progress in sanitation France moved even more slowly than in other matters.

[23] David H. Pinkney, "Napoleon III's Transformation of Paris: the Origins and Development of the Idea," *The Journal of Modern History*, XXVII (1955), 129-30.

CHAPTER TWELVE

Pacifism
and Peace Schemes

EIGHTEENTH-CENTURY France gave birth to several remarkable peace schemes. Such schemes were not entirely new, but their multiplicity in the eighteenth century and the elaborate detail in which most of them were worked out is indeed surprising and leads to wonderment as to the cause. It might be observed that those who express themselves in print are perhaps always few in proportion to the silent advocates of a cause. The literature of the eighteenth century abounds in expression of pacifism, and the latent, unexpressed pacifism must have been vastly greater.

What explains this great pacifist movement? On the one hand, the growing specter of war, which was becoming increasingly expansive. Already before the end of the seventeenth century it was transcending the European continent and including that of North America as well. With the early eighteenth century it drew within its orbit virtually every European state. North America also was included. With the advent of the two great world wars of the mid-eighteenth century, India in addition to North America was sucked into the vortex of battle. And so it continued into the War of the American Revolution and into the wars of the French Revolutionary period, when South Africa too came to be affected by the tides of battle.

The decision for war was made not so much in the forum of public opinion as by the rulers of states and their cabinets. This is not to say that these last lacked weighty reasons for their actions. Nevertheless their actions were no doubt altogether too often realized but faintly by a populace largely illiterate and little informed of the issues. It was still the day of mercenary armies, and the number of participants was very small in proportion to those of our times. Not until the French Revolution was any thoroughgoing attempt made toward drafting a national army, and then it produced insurrection throughout the larger portion of France. One of the widespread complaints in the cahiers of 1789 had been against the drafting of men for the militia and the seizure of men for the navy. In England during the period of the American Revolution, it will be recalled, so unpopular was the war that it was difficult to enlist men and it was necessary to resort to Scots and Germans. Armies of the century, save in the last decade, were far from being what today we would call national, and the methods of recruiting were very different from ours.

European politics were oriented around the delicate system called the balance of power. This system had operated since the sixteenth century, and many have been the wars fought over its preservation; but at no time was it guarded more jealously than in the 1700's. The dominance of the Continent by a single power would imperil the institutions, the culture, and the commerce of the lesser countries.

The men who devised the peace schemes were not ignorant of the issues at stake, for most of them were highly cultured and well informed on the political affairs of their day, and perhaps none at heart would have desired to see the institutions we associate with freedom overthrown. Most of them were not advocates of "peace at any price," but desired that every attempt be made to solve the issues of dispute by arbitration if possible, rather than by war. In fact they advocated the use of war to force an unyielding member state of their European or World Confederation into submission. Thus they were willing to fight for peace in order to obtain it. The advantages they painted in rosy hues, little aware that by "freezing" the map of Europe or of the world at its current stage they were putting a padlock on the doors of opportunity to future political and social change.

The first from the standpoint of time if not also of importance among the eighteenth-century proponents of world peace was the Abbé de Saint-Pierre (1658-1743), member of the French

Academy and one of the earliest of that literary circle in Paris that came to be called the *philosophes*. During the winter of 1707-1708, while on a visit to the little town of Saint-Pierre-Eglise in Lower Normandy to attend to some family matters, he first gave attention to the problem. While there, he composed a preliminary sketch of his famous book, *Mémoire pour rendre la paix perpétuelle en Europe*, not published until several years later. This was in the midst of the War of the Spanish Succession (1702-1713), when already France was feeling the severe effects of the struggle, as described in Vauban's celebrated *Dixme Royale*. Eventually in 1712 the war approached its end, and by accident the Abbé was chosen to accompany the Cardinal de Polignac to Utrecht as secretary for discussion of the terms of peace. It has been traditional for writers to state that this set the occasion for the origin of the Abbé's peace scheme; but his biographer, Joseph Drouet, points out that actually the Abbé had given thought to the matter for several years and had drawn up two sketches before this time.[1] The third was sent to press in 1711 and was published at Cologne in 1712. In support of his position, Drouet cites a manuscript of the Abbé in the Bibliothèque de Rouen and two letters of June and July, 1711, from the Duchess of Orléans to Princess Sophia of Hanover. At the outset of his book, in fact, the Abbé himself remarked that he had been four years at work on the project.[2]

Its 348 pages are wearisome reading. The Abbé would have done well to reduce the contents to one-half or one-third the space. The paper on which the book is printed is of poor quality, the spelling is often faulty, and there is recurring repetition. Nevertheless, because of its ideas it is one of the great books of the eighteenth century.

He discussed at some length the many advantages that would come to states from their adoption of such a union as he proposed. It would insure each state against loss from war or insurrection, it would protect from loss of commerce, and it would do all this at a minimum of expense.[3]

Nations might well fear to submit matters for arbitration lest

---

[1] *L'Abbé de Saint-Pierre*, 107-108, 110-11.
[2] *Mémoire pour rendre la paix perpétuelle en Europe* (Cologne, 1712), 3.
[3] *Ibid.*, 21ff.

they lose the decision, but he insisted that in the long run they would not lose so much either in value or in pride as in an unfortunate war—since each sovereign would sit on cases affecting other states than his own. He pointed out that wars had cost both countries and individuals up to a hundred times what the object sought was worth. The best favor toward them actually would have been a decision whereby they lost it at the outset.[4]

As for the mode of international union he would set up, he advocated a European diet similar to those of Germany, Switzerland, and Holland. He declared that there was nothing new about his scheme, for in fact the Greeks in their Amphictyonic League two thousand years previously and the Germans in their Empire of his own day (the Holy Roman Empire) employed it. He discussed the German Union whereby some two hundred states had been able to avoid wars among themselves and to present a united front to other states that might transgress against them.

His plan of organization for the international union was set forth in seven articles. It is of interest that he suggested a form of organization strikingly similar in certain respects to that of the United Nations today. There would be a deliberative body composed of delegates from the various member states termed a Senate that would convene from time to time in some central and acceptable city to attend tó matters coming before it, while a small Council of Five Senators would sit more or less in permanent fashion and act on all matters of a pressing nature. The deliberations of the Senate would be published, and there would be a secretary general who would keep the minutes, distribute published matter, and tend to other particulars.

He considered twenty-seven member states, drawn from Europe, North Africa and the Near East, as composing the Union, and each was to send a single delegate to the Senate. He was opposed to giving a delegate to states like Russia and Turkey for each territory governed lest they come to dominate the Union.

Each member state would pay the Union an annual subsidy of three hundred thousand livres (French) or the equivalent in some other coin for each two million subjects. Thus a populous state would pay much more than a small one. These sums would

4 *Ibid.*, 13-14, 35-36.

come in monthly payments to the treasurer general of the Union, to defray expenses of the organization.[5]

In wars that the Union might wage, each state, on the other hand, would furnish the same number of troops. He apparently failed to see that this would work greater hardship on the smaller states. He assured rulers that internal affairs would not be tampered with by the Union. By way of assuring the rulers of large states that the smaller ones might not "gang up" on them to divide their territory, he specified that a unanimous vote of the Senate would be necessary to take away territory or any right (*droit*) from a state. Here, therefore, we have an anticipation of the veto power of the Council of the present United Nations.[6]

The Abbé was very enthusiastic about his plan. In 1713 he published a second and much expanded edition of his book. In 1717 he added a third volume. In 1729 he brought out a single-volume abridgement of the whole. This volume, somewhat expanded, he reproduced in 1738. It obsessed his thoughts, and he is said to refer to the scheme in various other writings during the later years of his life. The book was widely read, notably in the period following the Peace of Utrecht. We are told that most readers did not take the Abbé seriously and that he came to be regarded as a visionary.

But there were some who did take him seriously, and who were greatly influenced by his *Memoir for Universal Peace*. One of them was no less a person than René Louis de Palmy, Marquis d'Argenson (1694-1757), the minister of foreign affairs for a period under Louis XV. He and the Abbé were both members of the Club de l'Entresol and apparently good friends. Moreover he believed in a league of nations for the purpose of keeping the peace, but he considered that one nation should assume its leadership, and that nation must be France. She would employ her might and influence to force the other states to arbitration.

Of more significance was the Abbé's influence on Jean Jacques Rousseau. The Abbé at his death had left a weltering mass of writings—seventeen volumes in print and six cartons of manuscript material. Rousseau was persuaded to undertake the editing of some of these works, and he made an offer to this end to the Comte de Saint-Pierre, nephew of the Abbé, which was readily

[5] *Ibid.*, 77, 101-105.   [6] *Ibid.*, 77-79, 89-90.

accepted. Late in 1754, accordingly, the materials were turned over to Rousseau at the Hermitage, and there he worked on them until 1756. Actually Rousseau edited only some four or five items in the collection, the most important being the *Projet de paix perpétuelle* and *Polysynodie*. The *Paix perpétuelle* he rewrote and condensed into an essay of some twenty or thirty pages, with his own reflections infused. The outcome was as much the creative work of Rousseau as of the Abbé de Saint-Pierre. Rousseau found the *Paix perpétuelle* a labyrinth of repetition, for the Abbé was devoid of literary artistry, and transmuted the significant parts into a very readable essay.

Rousseau warmly supported the Abbé's peace scheme. He commented that it had brought the Abbé ridicule, but this ridicule resulted only from the fact that the scheme had never been applied; had it been applied, it would have proven one of the greatest blessings to mankind. The countries of Europe were constantly at war with one another, Rousseau said, despite the many reasons why they should have been at peace. This led him, as the Abbé de Saint-Pierre and earlier devisers of peace schemes had done, to discuss the causes of war in the belief that knowledge of them ought to lead to their solution.

Like the Abbé de Saint-Pierre, he would guarantee to each member state the continued possession of its territories. Future contentious successions to thrones would be settled by decisions of the Diet of the Confederation. This, of course, would be intervention in a state's internal affairs, but since it could be a cause of war or rebellion, Rousseau no doubt felt justified in taking his stand. Any state violating decisions of the Diet "would be placed under the ban of Europe and treated as a public enemy." The other states would contribute men and money to force the violator to lay down his arms and to make such reparation as the Diet should judge proper.

Like the Abbé de Saint-Pierre, Rousseau claimed that all the member states of the Confederation would benefit from the union. None of the nineteen sovereigns to whom he would give seats in the Diet would be powerful enough to lead an insurrection or to place himself at the head of a faction likely to gain control. Likewise no wars of conquest would be possible. Small states might therefore rest in security, since their territories would be respected. A great saving of money would be effected, and this could be turned over to useful purposes, such as the development of agriculture, commerce, and the arts.[7]

Not only Rousseau and the Abbé de Saint-Pierre but the *philosophes* rather generally were hostile toward war. Only Rousseau and the Abbé de Saint-Pierre, however, drew up a scheme to prevent it by international organization. Certain of the *philosophes* thought that wars of self-defense were justifiable. In this class came Montesquieu and the Abbé Raynal. Voltaire and Condorcet, it would appear, were scornful of all war. Condorcet, too, scoffed at mechanical devices like leagues of nations as projects of universal peace. To him it was important, rather, to create international public sentiment against resort to war. When peoples of the earth are thoroughly awakened to the stupidity of wars, and are convinced that their best interest dictates a policy of peace, war will disappear.

Other *philosophes,* like Diderot and D'Holbach, shared this hostility to war, and so did friends of the *philosophes* like Turgot and Necker. Turgot, on the occasion of Louis XVI's accession to the throne in 1774, proposed to him the adoption of a revised oath in the coronation ceremony by which, among other items, the king would swear "never to make war except for just and indispensable cause." In a letter to his warm friend Du Pont de Nemours, August 9, 1771, he expressed his opposition to war rather piquantly saying that "a good book" on the grain supply, or taxes, or war "would be worth more than what I shall ever do as intendant." He added that men had lived in blindness for ten thousand years, and that what they needed everywhere was the light.[8] Necker, in his *Administration des finances,* bitterly condemned war as one of the chief sources of human ills. He considered it obsolete so far as bringing good to the human race or even a nation was concerned, and pointed out several ways in which the money needed for prosecuting a war could otherwise benefit a nation.[9] Pacifism in the eighteenth century was not however by any means limited to the *philosophes* and their friends, nor did it originate with them. It was shared by men of

[7] Vaughan, *The Political Writings of Rousseau,* I, 376-78, 383-84.
[8] *Oeuvres de Turgot,* ed. Daire, II, 501n; *Oeuvres de Turgot et documents le concernant,* III, 493.
[9] III, 283-307.

culture rather generally throughout Europe. As Professor A. Salwyn Schapiro in his biography of Condorcet says, "Anti-war sentiment was widespread in Europe, especially among the educated classes who were cosmopolitan in spirit."[10]

Among those outside the philosophic circle attacking war and setting forth peace schemes was Ange Goudar (1720-1790), a French economist born at Montpellier. His treatise on the subject was published anonymously at Amsterdam in 1757.[11] The book grew out of a discussion between Goudar and some politicians. They had challenged his remarks on one occasion and asked him for a longer discussion of his views; the book resulted.

Citing Voltaire for authority, he estimated that during the past 160 years Europe had experienced at least forty general wars, besides some private ones, and in them had lost a total of twenty million young men. Not only did their removal from the economic scene constitute an immense loss, but their leaving few or no families constituted a tremendous loss in population to the Continent. Agriculture, commerce, manufacture, mining, all had suffered in consequence. Europe would be richer and more independent of the rest of the world were it not for her wars.[12]

He anticipated Malthus in saying that men multiply at a geometrical progression, but he did not anticipate the rest of Malthus' theory, viz., that the food supply increases only in arithmetical progression. He commented that wars are often said to have a beneficial value in curbing the human population, but he did not agree that this was needed.

The way to end wars, he declared, was for the nations of Europe to make an agreement whereby wars would be renounced for a period of twenty years, and if during that time any state for whatever reason made war on another state, the other nations, which would be organized in a general union, should defeat it and impose on it a fine to cover all their expenses incurred by the war. He was confident that the experiment of twenty years would be so beneficial to all the participating states that there would be little likelihood thereafter of a return to wars. Inci-

10 Pp. 143-44.
11 *La paix de l'Europe ne peut s'établir qu'à la suite d'une longue trêve ou projet de pacification générale combiné par une suspension d'armes de vingt ans, entre toutes les puissances politiques.*
12 *Ibid.*, 164-66.

dentally, while he made room for a diet of the nations, he said little or nothing about the part that it might have in arbitrating disputes.

In Louis Sébastien Mercier, France had a militant pacifist during the last four decades of the century. Aspiring to literary fame, he repeatedly entered essays in the prize contests of the Académie Francaise in the 1760's. He had no success, but he afterwards published these papers in part or in modified form. One such essay was his pamphlet *Des malheurs de la guerre et des avantages de la paix. Discours proposé par l'Académie Française en 1766*, published at the Hague. Writing with strong emotion, he damned war as banal, a curse to mankind, and something to be found more among civilized nations than primitive peoples. He charged that Europeans had introduced it to the New World, not knowing that the redskins of America had wars of their own. All the blame for wars he laid on kings, who were motivated by ambition and greed.[13]

Was it possible to change the situation? Yes, by kings' changing their attitude, and he had confidence this would happen, even during his own century. Strangely enough he praised Louis XV, then reigning, as a peace-loving king.

This was but the beginning of Mercier's attacks on the institution of warfare. In his *L'an deux mille quatre cent quarante* (1771), his *Mon bonnet de nuit* (1784), his *Tableau de Paris* (1782-1783), and perhaps elsewhere Mercier resumed the attack, always with passion, always with vitriol. Mercier not only was bitter toward war and kings but also toward patriotism. Patriotism was a despicable word in his vocabulary, employed, if not created, by kings for use in the subjugation and destruction of the human race. He asked why he should regard an Englishman as his enemy.

The 1780's and 1790's brought forth another advocate of peace in the strange person of a former galley slave, Pierre André Gargaz, who had served a twenty-year sentence at Toulon in connection with a homicide. He had returned to his natal town of Thèze in the Pyrenees, and was engaged as schoolmaster in 1782. His first pamphlet was published that year through the assistance of Benjamin Franklin, then resident at Paris as repre-

[13] Pp. 9, 15, 17, 19, 47.

sentative of the Thirteen Colonies at the French court. Earlier, in 1776, Gargaz had written Voltaire, trying to elicit interest in his peace scheme; but he had no success.[14] Then in 1779 he wrote to Franklin and sent him a copy of his manuscript, asking that Franklin assist him in getting it published. Other letters followed in late 1779 and in 1781; but it was not until Gargaz tramped by foot from Thèze to Paris and presented himself in his rags that Franklin became seriously interested. Franklin then had the brochure published and gave him fifty copies to send to such personages as he wished—persons whom Gargaz thought might assist in setting up the International Union he wished to create. Six of these copies were returned to Gargaz. The others gathered dust for nearly a century and a half, until one came to the attention of George Simpson Eddy, an American, who in 1922 republished it with information on its author, under the caption *A Project of Universal and Perpetual Peace*. This in turn came to the attention of the historian Aulard, who after some research published a chapter on Gargaz in one of his studies on the French Revolution.

Gargaz in his brochure revealed familiarity with the peace projects of Henry IV (or Sully) and the Abbé de Saint-Pierre. Like them he advocated an International Confederation and parliament in which each member nation would be represented by a delegate appointed by its sovereign. Since the design of the body is peace, he considered that the sovereigns would appoint as delegates only men of the highest culture and ideals. The body would thus consist of the élite of Europe. He suggested as its meeting place the city of Lyons or any other city that members of the organization might choose. Its president would be the oldest reigning member.

Like Sully and the Abbé de Saint-Pierre, he would "freeze" the map of Europe as it existed at the moment of beginning the union. He suggested that the Diet at its first meeting might make decisions concerning any territories under dispute. After that, however, no territorial changes might be permitted. If a throne fell vacant without a clear successor or if a state made war without permission of the Diet, the Diet would be empowered to

[14] Voltaire replied with a few lines of bantering verse, which were of no aid to Gargaz. They are reproduced by F. A. Aulard, *Etudes et leçons sur la Révolution française* (9th ser., Paris, 1924), 30-31.

put on the throne of that state a member of its choice from some other royal house of Europe. In case of a war declared by the Diet, each member state must "furnish all the aid" demanded of it. And to be in a position to do this, each member state would be free to maintain its own army and navy without limitations as to size and to have such fortresses as it wished, provided that they were "two thousand five hundred geographical paces from the border" (slightly more than a mile). Moreover, freedom of the seas would prevail. He considered that many advantages would result to Europe from such a Union. With the monetary gains that would come, he suggested that canals might be constructed through the isthmuses of Suez and Panama.[15]

The little work read well, possibly due to some literary revision by Franklin, and it showed much common sense. Franklin, in fact, was much impressed by it, as he reported by conversation and letter to certain English friends.[16]

Several times during the 1780's Gargaz petitioned the French government, without success, for rehabilitation as a citizen. This would largely have removed the stigma of his service in the galleys. It appears that perhaps Franklin tried to be of assistance in one or more of these attempts. When Franklin was relieved by Jefferson, Gargaz addressed two letters to him, but evidently they went unanswered.

This, however, was not the last of Gargaz, who in the Year V of the French Republic (1796-1797) was living at Toulon, a citizen and the author of another brochure on world union.[17] Written in the simplified spelling that Gargaz by an earlier pamphlet of the 1770's had advocated (the spelling of words according to their pronunciation), it was far from easy to read.

Gargaz now was not only a citizen but also, it would seem, a Freemason, and the world union that he envisaged was to be one of Freemasons, with Toulon as its capitol. The nations uniting would each send to the congress five citizens, all above forty years of age, and to them the world problems demanding arbitration would be brought. He referred variously to the

---

[15] Pp. 11-22.   [16] *Ibid.*, pp. 1-12.

[17] Entitled *Contrat social, surnommé Union Francmaçone, entre tous les bons citoyens de la république françoise, e[t] entre la même république e[t] toutes les nations de la terre. Ou Projet de decret, par le citoyen Pierre André Gargas.* According to Aulard (*Etudes et leçons,* p. 41), it went into a second edition that same year.

countries so united as "the United Nations" and "the Freemasonic Union." In this Union each nation would stand on armed guard against attack. In this general defense it would employ not only the young and old men but also the women, on the evident model of the *levée en masse* that had served France so well during the period of the National Convention.

A new feature in this peace scheme was the use of economic blockade at sea and the boycott of any nation which might not obey the rules of the Union on the size of naval forces or on other matters. The ports of all member nations would be closed to the offending country, but open to others. This, in his opinion, would force the troublesome state to its knees.

Gargaz distinctly was a creature of his own day, and so, too, was another French Revolutionary exponent of world peace through international union. This last visionary was not a native Frenchman but a Prussian named Jean Baptiste Cloots (1755-1794), who was living in Paris at the outbreak of the Revolution and immediately became enthusiastic over it, writing much and participating in French political clubs. In 1790 he assumed the name of "Anacharsis," and sometime later (1791) "the designation of Orator of the Human Race," believing that he spoke on behalf of all mankind. He was among the fifteen foreigners of distinction that the Legislative Assembly in August, 1792, made honorary French citizens, and in the National Convention he sat as a Jacobin member. Unfortunately he became associated with the Hébertists, and with them he was guillotined in 1794. The peace scheme that he had set forth in several writings did not entirely collapse with him, for later Napoleon reportedly nursed in secret a somewhat similar plan.[18]

In 1792 he denounced war as an agency of oppression, the means by which the first slaves had been made. He deplored the current war in which the French were engaged as one forced upon them by "tyrants" of other countries.[19] It was clear that he approved of the French defense.

Even then he advocated a world state, with the capital at

---

[18] *Anacharsis à Paris, ou letter de Jean-Baptiste Cloots, à un prince d'Allemagne* (Paris, 1790), 28; *Bases constitutionnelles de la république du genre humain* (Paris, 1793), 44; and *Etrennes de l'orateur du genre-humain aux cosmopolites* (Chef-lieu du globe [Paris], 1793), 66.

[19] *Etrennes de l'orateur du genre-humain*, 19.

Paris. In a speech delivered before the Legislative Assembly September 9, later published as *Etrennes de l'orateur du genre-humain aux cosmopolites,* he visualized the day when the entire universe, "broken into a thousand departments," after the manner of the eighty-three comprising France, would be united into "a single state." The terms "England" and "France" would be dropped from use, inasmuch as they would excite international bitterness. The term "German" would be chosen for the new empire, since it did not arouse bitterness.[20]

His idea of the Universal Republic was simply that of Republican France of 1792-1793 expanded to embrace all nations. Like Lenin and Trotsky of the twentieth century, he declared that the whole world must enter the Union, for no one nation nor even several nations could live free in a world where opposing nations might fetter trade and national security.[21] Persuasion to enter the Union would be made through "the art of Gutenburg" —printing. He was so naive as not to see that propaganda through printing can be a two-edged sword cutting both ways. The propaganda of Cloots' Union would penetrate everywhere, even to the capital of the Dalai Lama, commonly regarded as impenetrable.[22] To become members of his Universal Republic, nations would only have to declare themselves in favor of uniting. This, he realized, would perhaps make the more distant states slower in joining than those near at hand.

In Cloots' World State, the French Declaration of the Rights of Man would serve as the basis of all conduct. No other laws would be needed. This World State would be atheistic, and the youth would be educated to extirpate religion.[23]

After his World State would be set up, Cloots declared that national governments would gradually disappear as unnecessary, and laws would be few. The word *étranger* would disappear as a barbarism, as a relic of days when men were ferocious. All persons would come to pride themselves as members of a world state and not as members of a nationality. Ambassadors no longer would be needed and would be discarded, along with the tares they sowed.[24]

[20] *Ibid.,* 32-33; *Bases constitutionnelles,* 29-30; Williams, *Letters containing a Sketch of the Politics of France,* 141.

[21] *Bases constitutionnelles,* 3.

[22] *Etrennes,* 19, 32.

[23] *Bases constitutionnelles,* 19, 21, 31.

[24] *Ibid.,* 23-25, 34.

Great would be the economic advantages resulting to mankind. Acts of navigation would no longer be needed. "The pretended national barriers" would disappear, and free trade would come about. Smuggling would dry up. Wars would cease and the enormous expenses of maintaining armaments—absorbing three-fourths of French expenses—would be saved. The cost of living would come down and abundance would exist for all. The *sans-culottes* of the world would be united and happy.[25]

It would be easy to extend this chapter with the details of the schemes described above and with the views and proposals of many other pacifists who lived in France during the 1700's, for pacificism was very widespread. Aspersions on warfare, for instance, may be found in Bernadin de Saint-Pierre's *Etudes de la nature,* Lacretelle's treatise of reforming the criminal laws, the Abbé Maury's address before the Académie Française, in the cahiers of 1789, and in other places. The historian Albert Mathiez, in an able article on "Pacificisme et nationalisme au XVIIIe siècle," has declared that never in any century, unless perhaps our own, has there existed so much cosmopolitan, so much pacifist spirit, desirous of eliminating from Europe and the whole world future wars.[26] These war haters embraced all classes of society, the Vendeans of 1793 who rose in revolt against the military draft laws, the French Anabaptists who that same year petitioned the government for the privilege of transmuting their service to something else than bearing arms, the *philosophes,* the anti-*philosophes* Maury and Bernardin de Saint-Pierre, the minister of war D'Argenson, the ex-galley-slave Gargaz, and the ranting, atheistic Cloots. All saw with dimness but enthusiasm the means of attaining and maintaining their hope of universal peace. All thought and wrote in terms of the political and economic institutions of their own day. The world subsequently has widened and changed enormously, and yet still we think along lines plotted by thinkers like the interesting Abbé de Saint-Pierre. Eighteenth-century French thought has been a leavening force in the world ever since that day; and there are few places where its influence has not been felt, even the land of the Dalai Lama.

[25] *Ibid.,* 16, 20-22, 25.   [26] P. 1.

Conclusion

IT SEEMS incongruous that tragic consequences should befall so many who worked for reform. Two leaders in obtaining toleration and civil rights for the Protestants, Malesherbes and Rabaut Saint-Etienne, were executed during the Terror, though not for espousing this cause, and a third—Lafayette—was imprisoned for several years. Of those who worked for abolition of the slave trade and slavery, Brissot, Clavière, Condorcet, and Olympe de Gougas met death during the Terror, either from execution or suicide. Other outspoken reformers as Mercier and Grégoire were able to escape. Many suffered imprisonment or exile or execution, like Lavoisier, Cloots, Danton, Robespierre, and the Duc de La Rochefoucauld-Liancourt. By 1795 a large proportion of those who had taken a prominent part in the movement for reform either on the eve of the Revolution or during the Revolution had passed away, and in some cases their property had been confiscated by governments representing the classes they were solicitous to aid. It may be asked, Was France a madhouse? Does suffering humanity really want saviors? Through all history men like Socrates and Jesus who wished to aid mankind have been put to death. Later generations have written their history in admiration. One is equally justified in being cynical or appreciative.

Probably the reforms came too fast. Men are fundamentally conservative by nature, adopting in most instances the ideas of their fathers, save for slight modifications. In religion and politics, in prejudices and tastes, they tend to follow those of the milieu in which they have been reared. The home is thus the greatest school on earth. Small changes men often welcome, but when the changes come fast they generally hold back and rebel. Some are swept along with the tide and lose stability altogether. The Revolutionists of 1789-1795 were not different. There were some like the Abbé Sieyès who negotiated all the rapids and saved their heads from the guillotine, but before 1795 most of the French population was suffering from surfeit and yearning for repose and a return to mother church. As for politics and other matters, they were moving toward conservatism too.

In part the Revolution came as the culmination of the Humanitarian Movement, and the two were dextrously interwoven. The objectives of the humanitarians might have been achieved even had there been no Revolution; at least this can be argued. But it would have been a long, slow process. The Revolution brought rapid action, and the humanitarian causes became intermixed with politics. Politicians needed the support of the humanitarians, and the latter saw the expediency of aid from the politicians. Sometimes the humanitarian advocate was also political deputy, sitting in the National Assembly or in the National Convention. It was logical to get the reforms enacted into law, and yet sometimes, as under the Convention, the law did not necessarily represent the attitude of the majority of the French people. That the minority often took their defeats with bitterness is attested by the large-scale emigration and the bitter internal struggles of the Reign of Terror. To the advocates of reform the Revolution was a boon, for their ends were achieved, and the two movements had a certain identity. And yet there were differences. The Revolution was much more than the last phase of the Humanitarian Movement, and its meaning to nations subsequently has been more than that. It was a political, class, economic, and religious upheaval that transcended the objectives of the humanitarians. The influence of the Revolution, still felt in the world today, does imply the continuation of humanitarian objectives, but more.

The influence of the Humanitarian Movement also outlived the eighteenth century. Most of the reforms enacted remained as permanent enactments. Perhaps the most notable exception was that of slavery, reinstituted by Napoleon and permitted in the French colonies until 1848. Nevertheless the pamphlets of various eighteenth-century antislavery writers continued to be read in the nineteenth century and to have their influence in France,

Britain, and the United States. Indeed the writings of the major *philosophes* urging various reforms have never ceased to be read down to the present. After the first quarter of the nineteenth century prison and penitentiary reform renewed its interest for the French, as well as for the British and Americans, and much attention was given to it. The Industrial Revolution which made great development in France during the reign of Louis Philippe brought its attendant evils of inadequate housing, insanitation, child labor, and exploitation of workmen, and it was not until the Second Empire of Louis Napoleon that steps were taken to ameliorate them. Child welfare attracted further attention in the 1880's, when education was made free and compulsory for all children throughout France. The economic depression of the 1890's and early 1900's focused the need of social insurance of various types, for the aged, the unemployed, the sick. From time to time reforms of humanitarian character continue to be made in France, yet never have they been so numerous or widespread as to rival the humanitarianism of the 1700's.

Certain of the measures of reform that demanded the attention of eighteenth-century writers and legislators continue among the burning issues of the present. The race issue was incandescent in the 1930's and 1940's as Hitler attempted to exterminate the Jews, and since the war the Negro problem in South Africa, the desegregation problem in the United States, and the Jewish-Arab problem in the Near East have made racism one of the acute problems of our time. There are today, moreover, as in the late eighteenth century, those who think that the problem can be resolved once and for all by some quick solution, such as by passing a law. There is also the acute issue of avoidance of war through a concert of nations to outlaw it. War has become startlingly more terrible that ever before with the development of modern science, and the waste in manpower, intelligence, culture, and economic resources has become such that it is imperative to find some other solution to international disputes. Almost any diplomatic defeat is preferable to the chaos and legacy of war. In the United States this is less realized than elsewhere, except possibly in the South, as this country was a winner in the last two wars and never in the arena of these wars. The United Nations today is the world's chief avenue to peace, an instrument dreamed of by the Abbé de Saint-Pierre and others of the eighteenth-century peace prophets. Of lesser importance, but issues far from small in our world of today, are those of child welfare, education, and public health. In all three matters vast improvement has taken place since the 1700's, but they are yet in their infancy if viewed from the world standpoint. There is vast inequality in them between peoples, and there can be no real contentment until relatively equal opportunities prevail for all. The world cannot and will not be "frozen" at its status quo of today. These issues of the past still continue, and the spirit of reform continues also.

It may not be inapropos to compare the humanitarian movement in Britain with that in France. England, too, in the eighteenth century had numerous agitators who called for reform in various matters, but met little success until after the Napoleonic wars. It is customary to say that the Revolution in France frightened the British into postponing the solution of their problems. The real humanitarian, or reform, movement in Britain therefore was not until the nineteenth century, and it has continued into the twentieth. The British muddled along, in reform as in so many other things, achieved much, and suffered no bloodshed aside from that resulting from a few riots. The French, on the other hand, rushed into reform, in various ways anticipating the British (whom they originally set out to emulate), accomplished almost a miracle, but at the cost of sharp division, great bloodshed, and bitter memories. While there has been occasional reform and much government paternalism to develop in the nineteenth and twentieth centuries, the true humanitarian movement in France was in the eighteenth century, more particularly in the period 1760-1795.

The French in their movement revealed themselves to be a much more intense people than the British, less willing to compromise, less willing to concede defeat when it came, and less willing to cooperate with their recent opponents. This is not to disparage in any way the fighting qualities of the British who have shown over and over in history that they have what it takes to stick in a combat, but the British also realize that they cannot always win or have their way. The Frenchman is more individualistic than the Britisher and less averse to bloodshed. He is also more willing to fight for ideological concepts. It was France that furnished the bulk of the Crusaders of the Middle Ages. It was France, and not Britain, that experienced decades of civil war over the issue of the Protestant Reformation. It was France that from 1792 on became enthused with a world mission to disseminate the fruits of the Revolution. The French are commonly regarded as very realistic, interested only in the mundane and practical. That conclusion is not borne out by history, which reveals that no people has been more animated by ideas or more willing to charge into battle for them.

One can hardly exaggerate the debt that the world of today owes to the men of eighteenth-century France treated in this study. Their achievements were not restricted to France, but their blessings have been disseminated throughout the world. If the French showed themselves rash in rushing headlong into their Revolution and performing a miracle in short order, they thereby electrified the world to the extent that it has been animated ever since with the spirit of the Revolution. Not only have the words Liberty, Equality, and Fraternity been carried over the world, but everywhere too those of Reason, Humanity, and Justice.

BIBLIOGRAPHICAL COMMENT

THIS BOOK has been chiefly based on the books, brochures, speeches, letters, and memoirs of participants for reform during the eighteenth century. A vast literature exists on the matter. The writings of many of the more eminent participants have been republished in the collected works of these men. Much of the literature on the subject can be found in any of the larger American libraries, while almost the whole of it is in the Bibliothèque Nationale. Even the pamphlet literature on the Jewish question is almost intact. Rumor ran in Paris that during the German occupation of the last war Hitler ordered the director of the Bibliothèque, Dr. Bernard Fay, to destroy all its material treating of the Jews, but that the latter avoided this by the ruse that he must first compile a list of this material. Happily it is still there, and indeed it is rare that a book or brochure on any matter in this entire field is missing.

Other basal sources have been the collections of laws and certain contemporary periodicals. For the laws of the Old Regime, the *Recueil des anciennes lois françaises* of Isambert and others has been thoroughly studied, and for those of the Revolutionary era the *Réimpression de l'ancien Moniteur*, supplemented by Duvergier's *Collection complète des lois*. Study of the laws is important, not because they were always enforced but because they represented the crystallization of public opinion and so delineated important stages in the development of thought. Among the large number of journals available for the period, minute study was made of the *Réimpression de l'ancien Moniteur* and the *Mercure de France*, the latter from 1765 to 1795, and examination was made of certain other journals for brief periods. The journals were of value for the editorial opinion and for an account of the parliamentary discussion on the matters in the Revolutionary legislative bodies.

The cahiers of 1789, found in the *Archives parlementaires de*

1787 à 1860, in Miss Hyslop's *Guide to the General Cahiers,* and in the many volumes of regional and local cahiers edited by local archivists, offer valuable material on public opinion on the eve of the Revolution. Very much more use of them has been made than the few references herein would indicate. Similarly the collection of *Inventaires sommaires des archives départementales,* both for the period before the Revolution and during it, has been important for reflection of regional and local opinion. Various collections of documentary material, some regional like the *Histoire générale de Languedoc,* and others topical, like Stewart's *Documentary Survey of the French Revolution* and Hildenfinger's *Documents sur les Juifs à Paris au XVIIIe siècle,* have rendered service. Akin to the documents, Tuetey's *Répertoire générale des sources manuscrites de l'histoire de Paris pendant la Révolution française* has provided material not found elsewhere.

The secondary literature on the subject embraces special studies on various aspects of it in learned journals, monographs, biographies, and encyclopaedias. Among the learned journals, heavy dependence has been placed on *La Révolution française,* the *Annales historiques de la Révolution française,* the *Bulletin de la Société d'Histoire du Protestantisme Française,* the *Revue des Etudes juives,* and lesser use has been made of the *Revue historique, Revue des deux mondes,* and several others. Many phases of the subject have been treated in monographs, of which these may be singled out for particular mention: Souleyman's, *The Vision of World Peace in Seventeenth and Eighteenth-Century France;* Seeber's *Anti-Slavery Opinion in France During the Eighteenth Century;* Lokke's *France and the Colonial Question, 1763-1801;* Funck-Brentano's *Prisons d'autrefois;* Dauban's *Les prisons de Paris sous la Révolution;* Brinton's *French Revolutionary Legislation on Illegitimacy, 1789-1804;* Chassaigne's *L'affaire Calas;* and Dedieu's *Histoire politique des Protestants français (1715-94).*

Special studies of a broader nature, like Esmein's *Histoire de la procédure criminelle en France,* Seligman's *La justice en France pendant la Révolution,* and Sagnac's *La législation civile de la Révolution française (1789-1804),* likewise have been of great service. The field of legal reform in fact has been carefully studied by these three eminent authorities. Among the many biographies that have been useful, Drouet's on the Abbé de Saint-Pierre, Prudhomme's on Servan, and Allison's on Malesherbes may be named. The *Encyclopedia of the Social Sciences* has been of some help for perspective, while Hoefer's *Nouvelle biographie générale, La grande encyclopédie,* and the historical dictionaries by Chéruel and Marion have been able to clear up many points of uncertainty. Other encyclopedias, too, have been consulted.

By no means is this a recapitulation of all the sources used, nor have all been cited in references, for citation soon becomes wearisome to the reader. The sources for this study, both primary and secondary, are enormous in number, as the subjects of reform here studied attracted great attention both during the eighteenth century and subsequently. They concern some of the most tangible results of the French Revolution. A broader reading in the periodical literature of the century might have been valuable for the editorial opinion. Likewise study in the archives might have revealed interesting views on reform as held by French officialdom, more particularly before the Revolution. The reading for this book, however, has been extensive and I have reason to believe that I have not omitted many important facets.

INDEX

Almanac des prisons, 5.

Amis des Noirs. *See* Société des Amis des Noirs.

Argenson, Marquis d', 173-74, 251.

Aubert du Bayet, J. H. B., 73.

Aulard, F., 81.

Bailly, J. S., 159, 160.

Barère, 48, 154, 204, 205, 209.

Basnage, Jacques, 8.

Bâville, 10, 16, 17.

Bayet, Aubert de, 73.

Bayle, Pierre, 24, 58.

Beccaria, Marquis de, on prisons, 146; on legal reform, 180-84, 189, 190, 195-96, 200, 204, 221.

Bégouen, 104.

Bellon de Saint-Quentin, J., 105.

Bentham, Jeremy, 158, 168-69.

Bergasse, Nicolas, 101, 102, 103, 188, 195, 208.

Bernadin de Saint-Pierre, J. H., opponent of slavery, 95-97, 103; 125; on corporal punishment, 212-13; on education for girls, 228-29; pacifist, 260.

Berr, Cerf, 54, 71-72, 75, 76.

Bosc, Paul, 22.

Boucher d'Argis, 187, 192, 195, 198-99, 200, 208, 222.

Bourdon de la Crosnière, L. J. J., 229, 230, 231-32.

Bourge, J. C. A. de, 76-77, 111.

Bousmard, H. J. B. de, 222, 223-24.

Bousquet, 230-31.

Brancas, Duc de, 53, 57, 78.

Branding, 173, 192.

Brinton, Crane, 221, 226, 268.

Brisson, Pierre Raymond de, 100.

Brissot, J. P., on Louis XVI, 5; visits Frossard, 22; Jewish sympathy, 57; on slavery, 88, 93, 94, 99, 102-103; founded Société des Amis des Noirs, 94, 102-103; on imprisonment, 119, 121, 123-24, 146, 166, 170; on legal reform, 187-88, 190, 194, 196-97, 208, 209; on infanticide, 221; fate, 261.

Broglie, Prince de, 16, 77.

Brunet de la Tuque, 47.

Calas case, 18-22, 28-30, 31, 32, 39, 172, 185, 198, 201, 268.

Camisard insurrection, 15-17.

Capital punishment, condemned, 179, 181, 189-90, 191, 204-205, 206; abolished in Russia, 181, 183, 190, 205; reform in 1788, 201; reduced, 205, 207; grounds extended, 208.

Cavalier, 15, 16.

Chamousset, C. H. P. de, 2, 3, 210-11, 240, 243.

Chastellux, Marquis de, 94-95.

Chayla, Abbé, 15.

Clairon, Mlle., 136.

Clavière, 99, 102, 125, 185, 261.

Cloots, "Anacharsis," 62, 258-60, 261.

Code Noir, the, 83, 84-86, 94, 96.

Colbert, J. B., 138, 215.

Condorcet, on Voltaire's letters, 3; on Protestant toleration, 33-34; condemnation of slavery, 88, 90-92, 96, 102, 103, 108, 110-11, 113, 121, 124; on capital punishment, 191; report on education, 233-35; fate, 261.

Court, Antoine, 7, 8, 26-27.

Court de Gebelin, 22, 26, 42, 62.

Cugoana, Ottobah, 101.

Damiens, 173, 190, 191.

Dedieu, Abbé Joseph, 17, 49, 50, 268.

Désubas, 9.

Diderot, Denis, his *Encyclopédie*, 3, 32; interest in Calas case, 32-33; Jewish sympathy, 57-58; hostility to slavery, 88; prison treatment, 136; pacifism, 253.

Dohm, C. W. von, 62-63.

ABOUT THE AUTHOR

The Humanitarian Movement in Eighteenth-Century France is Shelby T. McCloy's third major book in the social history of this important nation and era. Professor of history at the University of Kentucky, Mr. McCloy recently has returned from a year's study in Paris. He holds degrees from Davidson College and Oxford University, the latter institution twice having named him a Rhodes scholar. The Ph.D. degree was awarded him by Columbia University. Before coming to the University of Kentucky in 1944, Mr. McCloy taught at Roberts College in Istanbul and at Duke University. In 1952 his *French Inventions of the Eighteenth Century* was published by the University of Kentucky Press.

ABOUT THE BOOK

The Humanitarian Movement in Eighteenth-Century France was
composed and printed at the University of Kentucky. It is set in
Linotype Caledonia, with headings in ATF Garamond. The book
is printed on Warren's Olde Style antique wove paper and bound
by the C. J. Krehbiel Company in Columbia's Riverside vellum
cloth.